Teach® Yourself

Beginners' British English

Cindy Cheetham

First published in Great Britain in 2016 as *Get Started in Beginner's British English* by Hodder Education. An Hachette UK company.

This edition published by Teach Yourself in 2026

An imprint of John Murray Press

1

Copyright © Cindy Cheetham 2016, 2026

The right of Cindy Cheetham to be identified as the Author of the Work has been asserted by them in accordance with the Copyright, Designs and Patents Act 1988.

All rights reserved. No part of this publication may be reproduced, stored in a retrieval system, or transmitted, in any form or by any means without the prior written permission of the publisher, nor be otherwise circulated in any form of binding or cover other than that in which it is published and without a similar condition being imposed on the subsequent purchaser.

A CIP catalogue record for this title is available from the British Library

Paperback ISBN 9781399824880
ebook ISBN 9781399824903

Printed and bound in Great Britain by Clays Ltd, Elcograf S.p.A.

John Murray Press policy is to use papers that are natural, renewable and recyclable products and made from wood grown in sustainable forests. The logging and manufacturing processes are expected to conform to the environmental regulations of the country of origin.

John Murray Press	Teach Yourself
Carmelite House	Hachette Book Group
50 Victoria Embankment	123 South Broad Street
London EC4Y 0DZ	Ste 2750
	Philadelphia, PA 19109, USA

www.teachyourself.com.

John Murray Press, part of Hodder & Stoughton Limited
An Hachette UK company

The authorised representative in the EEA is Hachette Ireland, 8 Castlecourt Centre, Dublin 15, D15 XTP3, Ireland (email: info@hbgi.ie)

Contents

About the author		v
How the book works		vi
How to be a good language learner		xvi
Key points about British English pronunciation		xix
1	**Hello! Where are you from?** Greeting people • Giving and finding out personal information • Using polite and friendly phrases • Filling in a simple form • Saying the letters of the alphabet • Reading email and web addresses	**2**
2	**Family and friends, jobs and home** Talking about your family • Talking about jobs and workplaces • Talking about where you live • Describing people and places	**22**
3	**Numbers, times and dates** Saying numbers • Talking about the date and the time • Asking and answering questions about dates and times	**48**
4	**Everyday life, sports and free time** Talking about everyday routines and free time activities • Talking about likes and dislikes • Talking about ability using *can*	**77**
5	**Going out** Asking how people feel • Saying how you are • Talking about plans and preferences • Making and responding to suggestions and invitations	**102**

	Review 1	126
6	**Transport and directions**	
	Talking about travel and transport • Buying tickets and asking about journey times and distance • Understanding simple instructions and announcements • Asking for and giving directions	132
7	**Hotels and accommodation**	
	Managing simple business in hotels • Complaining about problems politely • Making requests	152
8	**Sightseeing and the weather**	
	Making recommendations • Talking about the weather • Talking about the past • Comparing things	170
9	**Restaurants and food**	
	Talking about food and drink • Describing food and restaurants • Conversations in cafés and restaurants	190
10	**Shopping and money**	
	Managing simple business in shops • Shopping online • Returning products to shops	210
	Review 2	232
	Answer key	238

About the author

I have worked in English as a foreign language teaching for over 40 years, as a teacher, trainer, trainer of trainers, examiner, assessor and materials writer.

My first teaching job was in Spain and I have since worked in Portugal, Brazil and the UK. I have taught all levels, from complete beginners to advanced, and to a very wide range of students. I have taught ten-year-old children, teenagers, university students, factory workers, company directors, retired bankers and senior politicians. One of my favourite levels is beginners. For a teacher, it is very rewarding to see the dramatic progress that beginners can make.

I studied French and Spanish at school and learnt Portuguese while I was living in Portugal and Brazil, so I understand the difficulties of learning a new language. I believe that learning vocabulary, and not just individual words but whole phrases, is just as important as learning grammar rules. I hope the emphasis on vocabulary in this book helps you make progress more quickly. I also think it is really important to keep things as simple as possible, particularly if you are learning without a teacher. English, like many languages, can be complicated but if things get too complicated, people often give up and I don't want you to give up!

I really hope this book helps you learn English and you find it simple and easy to use. There are so many things you can read and listen to when you understand some English. It is all very exciting!

Good luck!

Cindy Cheetham

How the book works

Who is *Beginners' British English* for?

I can't speak English very well	beginners	Don't worry! The book is very simple. Use a translation app if you need help.
?	people who studied English at school but have forgotten their English	The book is a good way to remember and study again.
	business people	You have help with reading and writing emails, meeting people and introducing yourself, travelling, socializing and making arrangements.
	tourists and people going to the UK on holiday	You learn phrases to use in hotels, restaurants, tourist information centres, when travelling, sightseeing or shopping.
	studying alone	All the information is in the book. The explanations, the exercises and the answers. You are the student **and** the teacher!
	studying with a tutor	All the information you need is in the book, but it's great if you have someone to help you when you have a question and correct you when you make a mistake.
	studying in a class	The book can give you extra help and practice with vocabulary, grammar, listening, speaking, reading and writing.

	people who like English	There are a lot of words for you to learn and activities for you to do.
	teachers of English	There are a lot of resources you can use in class or as homework to supplement your course book (topic-based vocabulary exercises, activities and exercises to focus on and practise specific grammar and language points, reading, listening and writing practice, speaking tasks, tests and information about life in the UK). You can also use it as a course book – everything you need is included.

Why choose *Beginners' British English*?

▶ It has everything you need – vocabulary, grammar, pronunciation, listening, speaking, reading, writing and review units for revision.
▶ The material is simple to use so you can find what you want easily.
▶ You can use the different sections separately: for example, you can use just the listening and speaking material, or just the vocabulary material.
▶ You can use the culture sections to learn about life, customs and traditions in the UK and compare it with life, customs and traditions in your country.
▶ You can decide how often to study (every day? once a week?) and how long to study for (ten minutes every morning? half an hour after work? two hours in the morning at the weekend?). The course can fit in to your life.
▶ The material is in short sections, so you can make good use of whatever time you have, even if it is just ten minutes.
▶ The audio gives you pronunciation practice, conversations and other things to listen to.
▶ Full listening audioscripts and a language summary list for each unit can be downloaded for free from the Teach Yourself Library app (for Android and iOS) or www.library.teachyourself.com.

How to use this book

This book consists of an introduction to key practical expressions you'll need **Before you start** to help you understand the instructions and exercises and some **Key points about English pronunciation** to familiarize you with the basic sounds of English. The core of the book are ten units which will help you learn basic language function and introduce key topics for everyday communication.

A little goes a long way! Try to use the book little and often, rather than for long stretches at a time. This will help you to create a study habit, much in the same way you would a sport or music. Leave the book somewhere handy so that you can pick it up for just a few minutes.

Before you start, make a plan! Setting goals affects the programming of your brain, strengthening neural pathways and ultimately making it more likely that you will achieve those goals. Before you begin, think about how much time you want to devote to learning, which skills or areas you want to focus on, and identify specific ideas you want to be able to communicate or activities you want to engage in.

Track your progress! Start a notebook to use for study, where you can create vocabulary lists, a grammar summary, questions you'd like answered, etc. Keep track of your resources – films, podcasts, songs or blogs you like, and jot down a few words or expressions you may have recognized or learned. The more you can reflect on your learning process, the deeper your connection with the language will be. For guidance in this process, we recommend Teach Yourself's *Fluentish: Language Learning Planner & Journal* by Jo Franco.

Use the tools at the beginning of each unit to help you set goals, plan your time, and keep track of the work you do.

IN THIS UNIT, YOU WILL LEARN HOW TO:

Each unit begins with an overview of the language you will be learning and skills you will be acquiring.

MY PROGRESS TRACKER

Use the progress tracker to plan your study time and to keep a record of what you've accomplished. The first column tracks time, and the remaining 5 columns represent the skills you'll be working on: listening, pronunciation, reading, writing and spoken interaction.

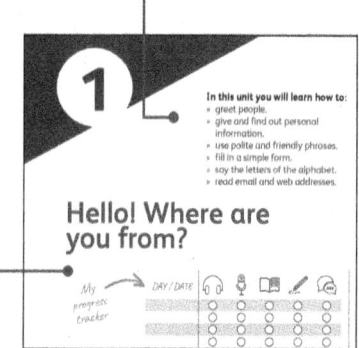

Personalize the tracker: Instead of the date or day, you can enter an increment of time. Add columns for culture, vocabulary, grammar or any other area you wish to focus on. Make it your own! Review your tracker regularly and see which areas could use more practice.

Use the **Self check** at the end of each unit to evaluate your progress.

Try to practice each skill every day

The icons in the progress tracker are used throughout the book to help you easily identify and locate the skills you want to practice:

Listening skills

Reading skills

Speaking – pronunciation skills

Writing skills

Speaking – conversation skills

Remember: there are many ways to build your skills in addition to those provided in this book: use a language-learning app, listen to music or podcasts, watch TV shows or movies, go to a restaurant, follow social media accounts in English, read blogs, newspapers or magazines, switch the language settings in your apps to English, or sign up for a language exchange or a tutor. You can also use AI tools to practice conversation, get explanations, or improve your writing—but remember that responses may not always be accurate, so double-check important information with reliable sources.

How to use this book

UNITS 1–10

There are ten units in this book, and each unit has these sections:

Culture

Each unit has a topic (for example, Unit 4 is about sport and free time; Unit 10 is about shopping). At the start of the unit there is a short text about the topic.

Vocabulary

In each unit there are vocabulary exercises to help you learn the key words and expressions for that topic. There is an audio for you to learn how to pronounce all the words and usually an exercise to practise using the words.

Language discovery

This is where you learn the grammar or phrases. First you hear a conversation and answer some questions to check you understand it. Then you have some 'discovery' questions. These questions help you look at the grammar or phrases and understand when and how you can use them. You also learn the pronunciation and then practise using the language.

Listening practice

You practise listening in each unit and listen to typical things for the topic, for example, listening to airport announcements or understanding tourist recommendations. The listening also gives you more practice with the vocabulary and grammar.

The audio for this course can be downloaded to the Teach Yourself Library app or streamed at library.teachyourself.com/all/Beginners/19021.

Speaking practice

You practise speaking in each unit with typical and useful tasks, for example, ordering food in a restaurant, enrolling on a language course or complaining in a hotel.

Pronunciation practice

You hear the vocabulary and grammar and then practise saying the words and phrases. There is a lot of work on pronunciation to help you have a good British English accent. There is a guide to British English pronunciation at the start of the book. It's a good idea to look at this after one or two units when you have a little more English.

Reading practice

You practise reading in each unit and read typical things for the topic, for example, reading a social media post, reading tourist information leaflets or reading a hotel review.

Writing practice

You practise writing in each unit with typical and useful tasks, for example, writing an email, writing a review of a restaurant, booking a room or filling in a form.

Test yourself

These exercises at the end of each unit help you check how much you know and understand.

There are two review units. **Review** unit 1 checks you understand the grammar and vocabulary from Units 1–5. Review Unit 2 checks you understand the grammar and vocabulary from Units 6–10. At the end of the course, there is an **Answer key**, with all the answers to all the exercises. Finally, you can download a **language summary** from the Teach Yourself Library app or www.library.teachyourself.com. The language summary lists all the grammar, phrases and vocabulary from each unit. There is also a list of UK/US vocabulary. Most words in British English and American English are the same, but there are some differences, for example, in the UK we say *taxi*, but in the US they say *cab*.

HELPING YOU LEARN – A FEW SUGGESTIONS AND IDEAS

- ▶ Start with Unit 1 and do the units in the book in order (Unit 1, Unit 2, Unit 3, …).
- ▶ Make sure you are confident with the language in one unit before you start the next.
- ▶ Don't do all the vocabulary or all the grammar exercises together. Do a different vocabulary or grammar exercise each day.
- ▶ Do the exercises again and again. It helps you remember.
- ▶ Test yourself on the vocabulary and grammar and see how much you can remember.

- ▶ Repeat the conversations as many times as you can ... try to memorize them and say them quietly to yourself.
- ▶ Listen to the conversations as many times as you can ... and listen when you are doing something else (when you are walking home, waiting for a bus ...).
- ▶ Find a study friend. You can test each other and help each other and it is great to have someone to practise with.
- ▶ Read the section 'How to be a good language learner'.
- ▶ Use an online translator if you have trouble understanding any explanations and instructions for exercises throughout the units.
- ▶ Don't forget:

  Learning = understanding + remembering

Before you start

Learn the vocabulary you need for the book

For the answers to these exercises, see the end of this section.

1 **Complete the table. Put the word in the correct (✓) place, a–i.**

> word   phrase   sentence
> conversation   picture   question
> answer   table   text

a phrase	No problem!
b _____	My name is Ana.
c _____	What's your name?
d _____	
e _____	
f _____	
g _____	
h _____	I live in London.
i _____	English

2 Put the words in the correct (✓) place, a–l.

> fill in   check   practise saying
> read   listen to   write   look at
> choose   match   repeat   find   put

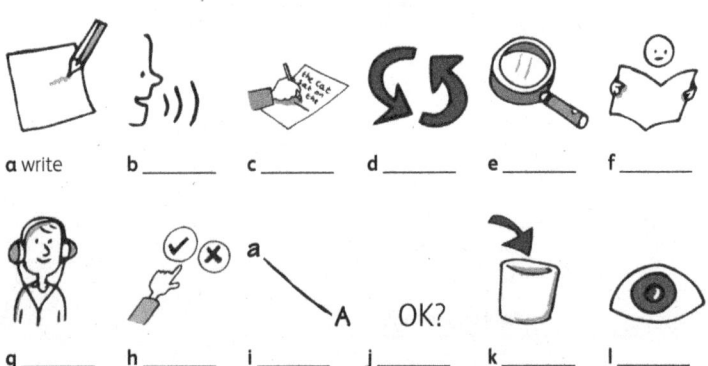

a write   b _____   c _____   d _____   e _____   f _____

g _____   h _____   i _____   j _____   k _____   l _____

3 Use the words to complete the tables. Put one word in each space a–h.

> questions   gaps   true   no
> words   read   correct   order

🗣️	Practise saying	the words.
📖	a _____	the phrases.
🎧	Listen to	the sentences.

	Write	the conversation.
	Look at	the text. the answers.

Choose	a	word. phrase. picture.
	the **b** _____ (✓)	word. phrase. picture. answer.
	a, b or c. yes or **c** _____. **d** _____ (✓) or false (X).	

Match	the **e** _____ and the answers. the words and the pictures.	

Put	the pictures the words the phrases	in the correct (✓) **f** _____ (3, 1, 2 → 1, 2, 3).
		in the correct (✓) part of the table.

Fill in	the **g** _____ (the g_____ps)	in the sentences. in the table. in the examples. in the rules.
Use the **h** _____ to complete		the sentences. the table. the examples. the rules. the missing information.

Before you start: Answers to exercises

1 b answer c question d conversation e text f table g picture h sentence i word

2 b practise saying c fill in d repeat e find f read g listen to h choose i match j check k put l look at

3 a read b correct c no d true e questions f order g gaps h words

How to use this book

How to be a good language learner

The Discovery method

Everyone can learn another language but it is sometimes difficult and there are a lot of different ways to learn. This course uses the 'Discovery method'. The 'Discovery method' helps people learn and remember languages better and more easily. If you are active in learning and do things for yourself, you remember things more easily so in this book, we don't **tell** you the grammar rules. You look at examples in a conversation, answer questions and find out (or **'discover'**) the grammar rules for yourself. With this book, you are the student and the teacher!

Learn to learn

There are many strategies that can help you become a successful language learner. Different people have different learning styles and some of these approaches will be more effective for you than others. Use this list as a point of inspiration when you want to find the most effective ways to advance your skills and begin your journey to fluency.

VOCABULARY

- Have a vocabulary notebook with a page for each topic.
- Read, listen, say and write the words again and again.
- Keep lists on your phone and look at them – often!
- Make a word cloud for each topic (type 'word + cloud + free + English' in a search engine on the internet) and put it on a wall at home.

- Make a mind map and use it to remember words.

- Make flash cards and look at them every time you have five minutes free.
- Keep the flash cards in different boxes: Box 1 – 'words I know'; Box 2 – 'words I nearly know'; Box 3 – 'words I don't know'. Try to move some cards from Box 3 to Box 2 and Box 2 to Box 1 every day!
- Try to find more words to add to the topics in the book.

GRAMMAR
- Compare English and your language – how different is it?
- For each pattern you learn (for example, *love* + verb + *ing*: *I love reading*), make a list of examples, as many as possible with different words.
- When you read, look for more grammar patterns or examples of patterns you know.

PRONUNCIATION
- Do the pronunciation exercises more than once.
- Record yourself and compare to the original.
- Write a list of words or sounds you find difficult.
- Use the internet to hear how to make the sounds or words you find difficult.
- Practise those sounds or words more.
- Repeat the conversations in the book line by line and copy the pronunciation.
- Try to remember the whole conversation.
- Remember about word stress, sentence stress, weak forms, linking and intonation.

LISTENING AND READING
- When listening or reading, try to concentrate on the main idea. Understanding every word is sometimes difficult but you can get a lot of information from the main idea.
- You can also imagine the situation and guess what people are going to say (for example, in a café, people talk about food).

- Don't panic if you don't understand and don't stop listening – try to guess what they are saying and keep following the conversation.
- Don't worry about individual words and try to guess key words. Check in a dictionary later.

SPEAKING

- Try to change a few words in the dialogues in the book (for example, the phrase *I love swimming* can change to *I like swimming, I like running, I quite like cycling*).
- Have conversations using an artificial intelligence (AI) platform. You can either have conversations and just focus on speaking or you can ask it to correct what you say.
- Take every chance to speak English – the best way to improve your speaking is to speak.
- If you don't know a word, describe it or use gesture or mime – but don't stop the conversation.
- If you are learning English in your country, imagine doing everyday things in English (for example, going to a shop or asking for directions).

LEARN FROM YOUR MISTAKES

- Some people get very worried about mistakes and only say something if they are sure it is correct. This stops you learning and making progress and makes it difficult to have a conversation.
- Don't worry about making mistakes (it's normal)!
- Most mistakes aren't important – people can usually still understood you (for example, if you say 'my sister live in London' or 'I don't like go to the cinema', these sentences are not correct but everyone can understand them).
- If possible, remember your mistakes and later, try to learn the correct version.

DON'T WORRY IF YOU ARE NOT SURE OR DON'T UNDERSTAND

- If you are reading or listening and don't understand, don't worry. Keep reading and listening, you might understand more later.
- Don't use your dictionary for every new word. Try to guess the meaning. If you can, read or listen to it again.
- If you still don't understand and it is an important word, check it in a dictionary.
- You can also just ask someone! ('Sorry, excuse me ... What does X mean?')

Key points about British English pronunciation

SOUNDS

It is sometimes difficult to know how to pronounce an English word. English spelling and English pronunciation are not always the same.

1 00.01 **Look at the highlighted letters. Is it the same sound in both examples? Choose Yes or No.**

Example sentence 1	Example sentence 2	Same sound?
a Ch**oo**se the correct answer.	It's T**ue**sday today.	Yes/No
b N**o**, I don't.	I don't kn**ow**.	Yes/No
c That's r**igh**t.	Wr**i**te the answer.	Yes/No
d I've got s**o**me money.	Have you got any h**o**mework?	Yes/No
e I h**a**te swimming.	Yes, I h**a**ve.	Yes/No
f I g**o** to work at nine o'clock.	I d**o** my homework after dinner.	Yes/No

Some words have a similar spelling but a different pronunciation. Some words have a different spelling but the same pronunciation. Because of this, phonetic symbols are a useful way to show how to pronounce a word and we sometimes use them in the book.

2 00.02 **There are 26 letters in the alphabet but 44 sounds. Listen to the sounds (vowel sounds, diphthongs and consonant sounds) and note the symbols we use to represent them. Listen again and repeat the sounds and examples.**

Vowel sounds

ʊ	æ	ɪ	ə	ʌ	ɒ
p**u**t, l**oo**k	b**a**nk, m**a**n	**i**t, b**i**g	**a**bove, cin**e**m**a**	c**u**p, **u**p	h**o**t, st**o**p
uː	ɑː	iː	ɜː	ɔː	e
bl**ue**, tw**o**	c**ar**, f**a**ther	m**e**, **ea**t	h**er**, l**ear**n	m**ore**, f**our**	t**e**n, m**e**n

Diphthongs

ɪə	eɪ	aɪ	əʊ
n<u>ear</u>, h<u>ere</u>	s<u>ay</u>, <u>eight</u>	f<u>i</u>ve, m<u>y</u>	g<u>o</u>, h<u>o</u>me
ʊə	eə	aʊ	ɔɪ
<u>Eu</u>rope, t<u>ou</u>rist	wh<u>ere</u>, th<u>eir</u>	n<u>ow</u>, <u>out</u>	b<u>oy</u>, n<u>oi</u>sy

Consonant sounds

p	b	t	d
<u>p</u>en, <u>p</u>ut	<u>b</u>ig, <u>b</u>ook	<u>t</u>ea, ge<u>t</u>	<u>d</u>o, goo<u>d</u>
f	v	θ	ð
<u>f</u>ive, i<u>f</u>	<u>v</u>ery, fi<u>ve</u>	<u>th</u>ink, <u>th</u>ank	<u>th</u>is, <u>th</u>e
k	g	s	z
<u>c</u>an, loo<u>k</u>	<u>g</u>o, <u>g</u>et	<u>s</u>peak, thi<u>s</u>	<u>z</u>oo, plea<u>s</u>e
tʃ	dʒ	ʃ	ʒ
<u>ch</u>oose, <u>ch</u>eck	<u>J</u>uly, <u>j</u>uice	<u>sh</u>e, wa<u>sh</u>	A<u>s</u>ia, televi<u>s</u>ion
m	n	ŋ	h
<u>m</u>an, <u>m</u>ake	<u>n</u>o, te<u>n</u>	morni<u>ng</u>, thi<u>ng</u>	<u>h</u>ow, <u>h</u>ello
l	r	w	j
<u>l</u>ook, <u>l</u>ove	<u>r</u>ed, <u>r</u>ight	<u>wh</u>at, <u>wh</u>ere	<u>y</u>es, <u>y</u>ou

Don't worry if it is difficult to remember the symbols. When we use the symbols in this course, we give you a lot of examples and there are usually some symbols that are easy to read because they look similar to letters in the alphabet. This can help you.

3 00.03 **Can you read these words?**

 a /wʌt/
 b /neɪm/
 c /gɪv/
 d /frɛndli/
 e /hɒspɪtl/

Listen and check.

If you want more practice, look in a good dictionary, and you can see words in phonetics.

STRESS

The word *France* has one syllable. The word *London* has two syllables. The word *America* has four syllables. A syllable is part of a word with a vowel sound.

4 00.04 **How many syllables are in these words? Listen and answer.**
  a English
  b bye
  c understand

When a word has two or more syllables, one of the syllables has more emphasis than the others. It is **stressed**.

5 00.05 **Look at the words. Listen and note the stressed syllable. Which syllable is stressed?**
  a London
  b Australia

This is word stress. You can check word stress in a dictionary. It doesn't change.

In phrases and sentences, one or more of the words (or syllables) has more emphasis than the others. It is **stressed**.

6 00.06 **Look at the phrases. Listen and note the stressed words (or syllables). Which word (or syllable) is stressed?**
  a Good morning.
  b How are you?
  c My name's Cindy.

This is sentence stress. You can't check sentence stress in a dictionary. It changes depending on the situation. We usually stress the important or information words.

7 00.07 **What are the information words in these sentences?**
  a I live in Rome.
  b I come from Spain.
  c I don't know.

Listen and note the stressed words. They are the information words.

Key points about British English pronunciation

CONNECTED SPEECH

When we say two or more words together, the way we say some words sometimes changes, and the beginning and endings of words sometimes change.

The way we say some words – weak forms

8 00.08 **Look at the highlighted words. Is it the same pronunciation in both examples? Choose Yes or No.**

Example sentence 1	Example sentence 2	Same sound?
a Does she speak English?	Yes, she does.	Yes/No
b Can you swim?	I can speak French.	Yes/No
c Yes I can.	She can speak Arabic.	Yes/No
d I'd love to.	I'm going to France.	Yes/No
e There are two chairs.	How are you?	Yes/No
f Are there any more?	Yes, there are.	Yes/No

9 00.08 **Listen again and note the stressed words (or syllables). Which word (or syllable) is stressed? What do you notice?**

Some words in English have two different pronunciations. All the words in the box have two different pronunciations, a strong pronunciation (when the word is stressed) and a weak pronunciation (when the word isn't stressed). We often say the weak form. The weak form of these words has the sound /ə/.

> a, an, of, at, from, for, to, and, does, was, were, can, am, are, have, has, there

The beginning and endings of words – linking

10 00.09 **Listen to this sentence. What happens between the words where you see ‿ ?**

My name‿is Marta.

When one word ends in a consonant sound (in this sentence, /m/) and the next word starts with a vowel sound (in this sentence, /i/) we link the words together. It sounds like one word: My /neimiz/ Marta.

11 00.10 **Look at these sentences. Note where one word links to the next word.**
   a I live in China.
   b Get started in English!

INTONATION

12 00.11 **Listen to two people saying *hello*. Which person sounds friendly? Choose Person A or Person B.**

Our voice can go up and down or stay flat. This is intonation (or the music of our voice). Intonation is very important in English because it shows how we feel. We use intonation to be friendly and polite and to show if we are interested or not. If our voice doesn't go up and down but stays flat, we sound unfriendly or rude or not interested. Is intonation important in your language?

13 00.12 **Listen to more sentences. Are the people friendly, polite and interested – or not?**

	Friendly, polite, interested 😊 〰️	Not friendly, rude, not interested ☹️
a Hello		
b Good morning		
c How are you?		
d Thank you		
e Sorry		
f Excuse me		
g OK		

14 00.12 **Listen again and copy the pronunciation of the friendly people.**

In this course there are exercises to help you with pronunciation. There are exercises on sounds, word stress, sentence stress, weak forms, linking and intonation.

Key points about British English pronunciation

1

In this unit you will learn how to:
» greet people.
» give and find out personal information.
» use polite and friendly phrases.
» fill in a simple form.
» say the letters of the alphabet.
» read email and web addresses.

Hello! Where are you from?

My progress tracker

US and UK cities

1 Match the cities to the letters on the maps.

London, Washington D.C., San Francisco, Manchester, Glasgow, New Orleans, Los Angeles, Birmingham, New York, Belfast

2 01.01 **Listen and repeat. Note the stressed syllable, for example, _Lon_don, New _York_. Practise saying the words.**

Vocabulary builder

VOCABULARY 1: GREETINGS

1 Complete the table. Put the greetings in the correct part of the table.

Hi	Good afternoon	Good bye
Hi there	Good evening	See you later
Hello	Bye	See you tomorrow
Good morning	Bye bye	Good night

	INFORMAL	FORMAL
HELLO		Good morning
GOODBYE	Bye bye	

2 01.02 **Listen and repeat. Note the stressed syllable, for example, Good _morn_ing, Hel_lo_. Practise saying the words.**

VOCABULARY 2: COUNTRIES

1 Match the countries to the letters on the map.

Japan	France	Korea	Spain
Canada	Indonesia	Germany	India
Russia	Australia	Portugal	South Africa
Brazil	The United States	Egypt	China
England	Scotland	Wales	Northern Ireland
The United Kingdom			

1 Hello! Where are you from?

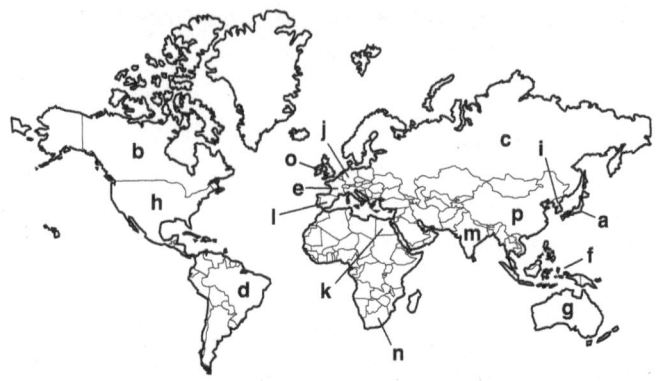

2 Label the map of the United Kingdom a–e.

United Kingdom   England
Scotland   Wales   Northern Ireland

3 01.03 Listen and repeat. Note the stressed syllable, for example, *Indon<u>e</u>sia*, *Austr<u>a</u>lia*. Practise saying the words.

Conversation 1: *What's your name? Where are you from?*

1 01.04 Tom and Anita meet for the first time. Read and listen to the conversation. Choose the correct name, *Tom* or *Anita* and put it next to the flag.

4

> **Tom:** Hello.
> **Anita:** Hi.
> **Tom:** My name's Tom. What's your name?
> **Anita:** My name's Anita. Where are you from?
> **Tom:** I'm from England. And you?
> **Anita:** I'm from India.

2 What do they say? Fill in the gaps.

My _____ Tom. I'm _____ England.

_____ name's Anita. _____ from India.

3 01.05 **Listen and repeat. Note the stressed words, for example, *My name's Tom*. Practise saying the sentences.**

4 Complete sentences for three other people. You choose the names. Use the countries in Vocabulary 2. Then write about you.

My _____ (Name). I'm _____ (Country).

_____ _____ _____

5 What's the question? Fill in the gaps.

Question:	Answer:
A: What's _____ _____?	B: My name's Paulo.
A: Where _____ _____ _____?	B: I'm from Brazil.

6 01.06 **Listen and repeat. Note the stressed words, for example, *What's your name?* Practise saying the questions.**

VOCABULARY 3: NATIONALITIES

1 Complete the missing countries and nationalities.

COUNTRY	NATIONALITY
India	Indian
	German
	French
The United States	
	Spanish
	Brazilian
	Egyptian

1 Hello! Where are you from?

COUNTRY	NATIONALITY
	Indonesian
	English
	Welsh
Russia	
	South African
	Canadian
	Japanese
	Korean
Australia	
	Chinese
	Portuguese
	Irish
	Scottish
	British

2 01.07 **Listen and repeat. Note the stressed syllable, for example, *Chinese, American*. Practise saying the words.**

Conversation 2: *I'm* + nationality

1 01.08 **Read and listen to the conversation. What extra words do Tom and Anita say? Fill in the gaps.**

Tom:	Hello!
Anita:	Hi.
Tom:	My name's Tom. What's your name?
Anita:	My name's Anita. Where are you from?
Tom:	I'm from England. I'm _____. And you?
Anita:	I'm from India. I'm _____.

2 01.09 **Listen and repeat. Note the stressed words, for example, *My name's Tom*. Practise saying the sentences. Say sentences about you.**

3 **Complete the table. Make sentences for the people.**

Example: a *My name's Ali. I'm from France. I'm French.*

	COUNTRY	NATIONALITY
Ali	France	French
Nelson	Brazil	Brazilian
Sarah	South Africa	
Yuki		Japanese
Natasha	Russia	

4 01.10 **Listen and check your answers to Exercise 3. Write sentences about you.**

5 **Complete the conversations. Use the information from Exercise 3.**

Ali:	Hello!
Anita:	Hi.
Ali:	My name's Ali. _____ _____ _____?
Anita:	My name's Anita. Where are you from?
Ali:	_____ _____ _____. I'm _____. And you?
Anita:	I'm _____ _____. I'm Indian.
Nelson:	Hello!
Sarah:	Hi.
Nelson:	_____ _____ _____. What's _____ _____?
Sarah:	_____ _____ _____. Where _____ _____ _____?
Nelson:	_____ from _____. I'm _____. And you?
Sarah:	_____ _____ South Africa. _____ _____ _____.

6 **Write a conversation for Yuki and Natasha.**

7 **Write a conversation for you and a friend.**

1 Hello! Where are you from?

Vocabulary builder

VOCABULARY 4: LANGUAGES

> **LANGUAGE TIP**
> We often use the same word for language and nationality, but not always.

1 Complete the table.

COUNTRY	LANGUAGE	NATIONALITY
Spain	Spanish	Spanish
Germany	German	
	Portuguese	Brazilian
England		English
The United States		American
China	Chinese	
France		French
Egypt	Arabic	
		Russian
		Japanese
		Korean
	Hindi, Bengali	Indian

2 01.11 Listen and repeat. Note the stressed syllable, for example, *Portu<u>guese</u>*, *<u>A</u>rabic*. Practise saying the words.

3 What are the two usual endings for language and nationality words?

4 What languages do people speak? Here are the top ten, but they are not in order. What do you think? Put them in order. Then check the Answer key.

French   Portuguese
Urdu   Bengali
Russian   Mandarin Chinese
English   Spanish
Arabic   Hindi

5 What are the top ten languages on the internet? What do you think? Write your top ten. Then check the Answer key.

Conversation 3: *Where do you live? Do you speak English?*

1 01.12 **Read and listen to Mike and Sally. Fill in gaps a–f in the table. Use one word in each gap.**

Mike:	Hello.
Sally:	Hi!
Mike:	My name's Mike. What's your name?
Sally:	My name's Sally. Where are you from?
Mike:	I'm from the UK. I'm British. And you?
Sally:	I'm from the UK too. I'm British but I live in Canada.
Mike:	Do you speak French?
Sally:	No, I don't. I speak English but I don't speak French. And you? Where do you live?
Mike:	I live in France.
Sally:	Oh! Do you speak French, Mike?
Mike:	Yes, I speak a little French.

SALLY	MIKE
I live in **a** _____	I live in **b** _____
✓ **c** _____	✓ **d** _____
✗ **e** _____	✓ **f** *English*

1 Hello! Where are you from?

2 What do they say? Fill in the gaps.

Sally: I _____ _____ Canada. I _____ English. I _____ _____ French.

Mike: I _____ _____ France. I _____ _____ _____ French.

3 Look at the table and fill in the missing words.

Canada	English	French	Chinese
a I _____ _____ Canada.	b I _____ English.	c I speak a little French.	d I _____ _____ Chinese.

4 01.13 **Listen to the sentences in Exercise 3 and repeat. Note the stressed words, for example, *I live in Canada*. Practise saying the sentences.**

5 Make more sentences.

Example: *I live in Brazil. I speak Portuguese.*

Example: Brazil	Portuguese
a India	Bengali
b Egypt	Arabic
c Hong Kong	Chinese

 Write a sentence about you.

6 Make more sentences.

Example: *I speak English. I speak a little French. I don't speak Chinese.*

✓	✓	✗
Example: English	French	Chinese
a Spanish	Arabic	English
b Russian	Portuguese	Bengali
c German	English	Korean

Write a sentence about you.

7 What's the question? Fill in the gaps.

Where _____ _____ _____? I live in England.

_____ you _____ French?   No, I don't/Yes, a little.

8 01.14 Listen and repeat. Note the stressed words, for example, <u>*Where*</u> *do you <u>live</u>?* Practise saying the sentences.

Conversation 4: Polite phrases

1 01.15 Look at the pictures. Read and listen to Conversations 1 and 2. Choose 1 or 2 for each picture.

> **Conversation 1**
> **A:** Excuse me ... excuse me ... excuse me?
> **B:** Yes?
> **Conversation 2**
> **A:** Ow!
> **B:** Oh I'm sorry! Are you OK?

1 Hello! Where are you from?

2 Look at the pictures a–d. Choose *Excuse me!* or *Sorry!* for each picture.

a   b

c   d

3 01.16 **Read and listen to a conversation at passport control. Put the pictures a–e in the correct order.**

Immigration officer:	Good morning.
Traveller:	Good morning.
Immigration officer:	Can I see your passport, please?
Traveller:	I'm sorry, I don't understand. Can you speak more slowly, please?
Immigration officer:	Can I see your passport, please?
Traveller:	Here you are.
Immigration officer:	Thank you. Enjoy your stay.

a   b   c

d   e

4 Look at the sentences. What is the difference? What word do we use to be polite and friendly?

Can I see your passport?   Can I see your passport, please? 😊

What name is it?   What name is it, please? 😊

Can you speak more slowly?   Can you speak more slowly, please? 😊

5 When do we say *please*? When do we say *thank you*? Complete the conversations.

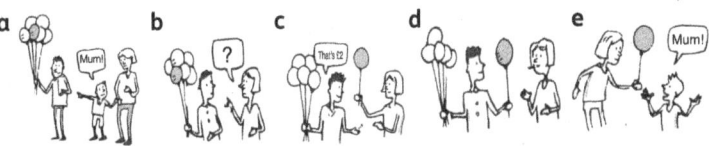

6 01.17 **Listen and repeat. Note the stressed syllable, for example, *thank you*. Practise saying the words and phrases.**

Listening, speaking and pronunciation

LISTENING: MEETING PEOPLE

1 01.18 **Listen to the conversation. Which picture shows the conversation?**

2 01.18 **Listen to the conversation again. Complete the table.**

	NATIONALITY	🏠	🗣️
Claudia	German		
Rama			

1 Hello! Where are you from?

3 01.19 **Listen to the conversation with Fatima and Sofia. Read the sentences. Choose Fatima or Sofia.**

	FATIMA	SOFIA
I'm from Russia.		
I'm from Pakistan.		
I live in Dubai.		
I live in London.		
I speak Russian.		
I speak English.		
I speak Arabic.		

PRONUNCIATION 1: GREETING PEOPLE AND SOUNDING FRIENDLY

1 01.20 **Listen to the people saying *hello* and *good morning*. Are they friendly ☺ or not friendly ☹?**

a _____   d _____
b _____   e _____
c _____

Listen again and copy the pronunciation of the friendly people.

SPEAKING: MEETING PEOPLE

1 Look at the conversation. Fill in the gaps about you.

Dieter:	Good morning. Welcome to Business Solutions. My name's Dieter.
You:	Good morning. My name's _____
Dieter:	Pleased to meet you. Where are you from?
You:	I'm from _____ I live in _____.
Dieter:	You speak English very well.
You:	Thank you. _____ _____ _____ from?
Dieter:	I'm from Berlin, Germany.
You:	Where _____ _____ _____?
Dieter:	I live in Dubai. And you?
You:	Oh I live in _____.

2 01.21 **Listen to the conversation with Dieter. Say your answers in the gaps.**

PRONUNCIATION 2: LETTERS OF THE ALPHABET, SPELLING

1 01.22 **Listen to these sounds.**

/eɪ/   /iː/   /e/   /aɪ/   /eu/   /uː/   /ɑː/

2 01.23 **Now listen to the letters of the alphabet. Put the letters in the correct part of the table.**

/eɪ/	/iː/	/e/	/aɪ/	/eu/	/uː/	/ɑː/
A, H	B, C	F, L				

3 01.24 **Listen to the spelling and complete the words.**

Names, countries, nationalities and languages all start with a CAPITAL LETTER.

Example: the United Kingdom, French, Hindi.

a _ mer _ ca
b Ne_ _ ork
c Un _ ted _ _ ngd _ m
d Q _ _ b _ c
e E _ rop _ _ _
f Ital _ _ _
g _ _ _ tral _ _
h N _ w _ _ _ land
i _ _ _ _ _ _ _
j _ _ _ _ _ _

4 01.25 **Practise spelling these city names, then listen and check your answers.**

New Orleans   Manchester   San Francisco   Birmingham

PRONUNCIATION 3: SAYING EMAIL AND WEB ADDRESSES

1 01.26 **Look at and listen to these website and email addresses.**

www.bbc.co.uk
www.tourist-information-uk.com
www.discoverlosangeles.com
www.learnenglish.britishcouncil.org/en/
attractions@visitengland.org

2 01.27 **Look at the parts of email addresses. What do we say? Listen and match a–h with the parts of email addresses in the box.**

> .   @   .com   /   .org   .co.uk   -   www

a double u double u double u
b dot
c at
d dot com
e slash
f dot org
g dot co dot uk
h dash

3 01.26 **Practise saying the web addresses in Exercise 1. Then listen again and check your answers.**

4 01.28 **Listen to four addresses and write them down.**

Reading and writing: Personal forms

1 Choose the correct word for each picture.

> married single
> children date of birth address

a _____

b _____

c *married*

d _____

e _____

16

2 Put the words in the correct part of the table.

~~male~~ female Mr ~~Mrs~~ Miss Ms

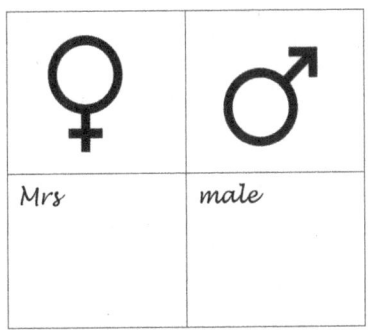

Mrs	male

LANGUAGE TIP
Some people don't identify as male or female. When you are completing a form, there are often three or four options: a) male b) female c) other d) prefer not to say.

 3 01.29 **Look at how we write titles and then listen to how we say them.**

Mr   Mrs
Miss Ms

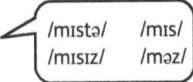
/mɪstə/   /mɪs/
/mɪsɪz/   /məz/

Are the sentences correct (✓) or not correct (×)?
  a Mrs Jones is married.
  b Miss Jones is not married.
  c We don't know if Ms Jones is married or not.

 4 01.30 **Listen to the titles. Practise saying the words.**

LANGUAGE TIP
A lot of people don't use a title. Some people use the neutral title Mx which doesn't indicate male or female.

1 Hello! Where are you from?

READING: A VISA APPLICATION FORM

1 Read Tom's visa application form. Which picture shows Tom and his family?

a

b

c

d

Given name(s) as shown in your passport	Tom
Family name	Mitcham
Gender	male/~~female~~/~~prefer not to say~~
Date of birth	07/11/1978
Place of birth	San Francisco
Country of birth	The United States
Nationality	American
Marital status	~~single~~/married
Full name of spouse/partner	Amélie Lafayette
Spouse/partner's date of birth	03/09/1981
Spouse/partner's nationality	French
Do you have any children?	yes/~~no~~
Details of children (name and date of birth)	Marie Lafayette 28/04/2011
Your full residential address and postcode	8924, Boulevard Lazare, Montreal, QC H2A, Canada
Email address	tom.mitcham@canadamail.com
Home telephone number	+1 438 0956054
Mobile telephone number	07896 1293455

WRITING 1: COMPLETING A VISA APPLICATION FORM

Complete the visa application about you. Use Tom's form to help you.

Given name(s) as shown in your passport	
Family name	
Gender	male/female/prefer not to say
Date of birth	
Place of birth	
Country of birth	
Nationality	
Marital status	single/married
Full name of spouse/partner	
Spouse/partner's date of birth	
Spouse/partner's nationality	
Do you have any children?	yes/no
Details of children (name and date of birth)	
Your full residential address and postcode	
Email address	
Home telephone number	
Mobile telephone number	

WRITING 2: COMPLETING A WEBSITE REGISTRATION FORM

Look at Tom's registration forms. Add your details to the forms.

Registering with AmazingIdeas.com

	YOU	TOM
My name is		Tom Mitcham
My email address is		tom.mitcham@canadamail.com
Confirm email address		tom.mitcham@canadamail.com
My mobile phone number is		07896 1293455
Choose a password		passwordtom0711
Confirm password		passwordtom0711

1 Hello! Where are you from?

Test yourself

1 How many greetings can you remember? Fill in the table.

	INFORMAL	FORMAL
HELLO		Good morning
BYE	Bye bye	

2 Complete the table.

		NATIONALITY
	English	English
France		
The United States		
Saudi Arabia		Saudi (Arabian)
Germany		
China		
Spain		

3 Fill in the questions and complete the answers for you.

a What's _your_ name?	My _____ _____
b Where _____ _____ from?	I'm _____ _____ (country). I'm _____ (nationality).
c Where _____ _____ live?	I _____ in _____ (city/country).
d _____ you _____ English?	No, I _____ _____ I do./a little. I speak _____ (language). I speak a little _____ (language). I _____ speak _____ (language).

4 01.31 **Can you spell out these words? Practise, then listen and check.**

language speak listen read write

5 01.32 **How do you say these web and email addresses? Practise, then listen and check.**
a www.learnenglishteens.britishcouncil.org
b www.bbclearningenglish.com
c anna.brown51@btinternet.co.uk

SELF CHECK

I CAN . . .
... greet people.
... give and find out personal information.
... use polite and friendly phrases.
... fill in a simple form.
... say the letters of the alphabet.
... read email and web addresses.

2

In this unit you will learn how to:
» talk about your family.
» talk about jobs and workplaces.
» talk about where you live.
» describe people and places.

Family and friends, jobs and home

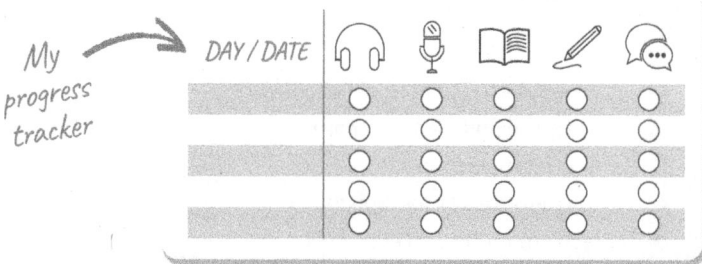

Family life and homes in the UK

Look at the questions. Do you know the answers? Choose a, b or c.

1 **How many people live in the UK?**
   a 54,000,000 (54 million)
   b 68 million
   c 74 million

2 **How many people live in London?**
   a 9 million
   b 10 million
   c 4 million

3 **What kind of home do most people in the UK live in?**

a   b   c

4 What kind of home is most popular in London?

a   b   c

5 How many people are there in most families in the UK?
   a 2
   b 3
   c 4

Read the text on family life and homes, and check the answers.
Use your dictionary for any words you are not sure of.

FAMILY LIFE

There are about 68 million people in the UK and most live in England (58 million). Five million people live in Scotland, three million people live in Wales and two million people live in Northern Ireland.

36% of the 19.5 million families in the UK are traditional families with two parents who are married or co-habiting but there are now more single (or lone) parent and blended families than traditional families. Three million adults are bringing up children on their own (single or lone parenting) and about one in three families are blended families. A blended family is two adults with children from a previous relationship. 44% of families have one child and 41% of families have two children. About eight million people in the UK live on their own.

HOMES

Most people in the UK live in towns and cities. Nine million people live in London. The other big cities are Birmingham, Leeds, Glasgow, Sheffield, Bradford, Edinburgh, Liverpool, Manchester and Bristol. The most popular type of house is a semi-detached house, but people also live in flats, terraced houses and detached houses. 31% of people live in semi-detached houses. In London, 55% of people live in flats.

Vocabulary builder

VOCABULARY 1: FAMILY, PLURAL NOUNS

1 Fill in the gaps in the table. Use the family words in the box.

> grandmother sister son husband
> children grandparents father

👨	👩	👨+👩
grandfather		
	mother	parents
son	daughter	
brother		
____/partner	wife/partner	

> **LANGUAGE TIP**
>
> When there are children in a family from a previous marriage, we add the word 'step' to some of the words in the box:
> stepmother, stepfather, stepbrother, stepsister, stepchildren, stepson, stepdaughter

2 Complete the family tree. Use the 👨 and 👩 family words.

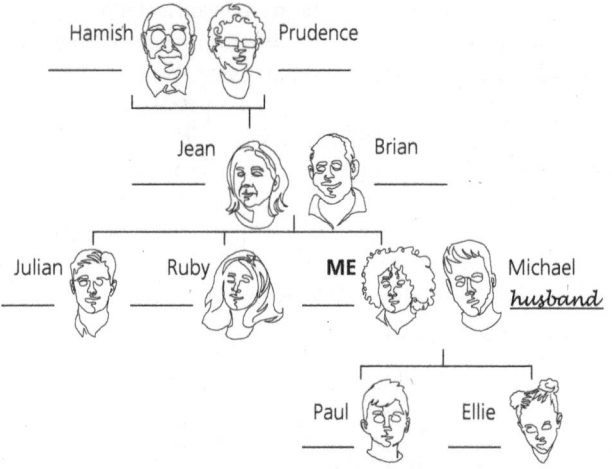

✏️ **Draw your family tree. Write sentences about your family.**

3 Look at the informal words in the table. What do the words mean? Put the correct words from Exercise 1 in the table.

	INFORMAL WORDS
a *mother*	mum
b	dad
c	kids
d	granny
e	grandpa

LANGUAGE TIP
People (and children) sometimes use informal words to talk about people in their family.

LANGUAGE TIP
When we talk about more than one, we usually add -s to the noun, for example, *one girl, two girls*. We make most plurals like this. If the noun ends in a consonant + *y* or -*fe* the spelling rules are different.

4 Look at the three rules. Put them in the correct part of the table, 1, 2 or 3.

fe → v + es

y → i + es

+ s

1	2	3	IRREGULAR PLURALS
girl – **girls** son – _____ daughter – _____ brother – _____ sister – _____ boy – _____	family – **families** baby – _____	wife – **wives** life – _____	child – **children** _____ – **men** _____ – **women** person – _____

LANGUAGE TIP
Some nouns have an irregular plural.

5 Fill in the missing irregular plural nouns in the table in Exercise 5.

6 02.01 **Listen and repeat. Note the stressed syllable, for example, *grand*mother, *par*ents. Practise saying the words.**

VOCABULARY 2: JOBS AND WORKPLACES

1 Match the places to the pictures.

I work ...
- **a** ... in a factory   <u>4</u>
- **b** ... in an office
- **c** ... in a school
- **d** ... in a shop
- **e** ... in a hospital (two pictures)
- **f** ... at home

Look up more workplaces in a dictionary and add them to your list.

2 Match the jobs to the pictures in Exercise 1.
- **a** I'm a nurse. I work in a hospital.
- **b** I'm a businesswoman. I work in an office.
- **c** I'm a factory worker. I work in a factory.
- **d** I'm a teacher. I work in a school.
- **e** I'm a doctor. I work in a hospital.
- **f** I'm a computer programmer. I work at home.
- **g** I'm a shop assistant. I work in a shop.

 3 02.02 **Listen and repeat. Note the stressed syllable, for example, *I'm a <u>nurse</u>. I <u>work</u> in a <u>hospital</u>.* Practise saying the sentences.**

 4 Talk about what you do. Use the words from Vocabulary 2 to make sentences.

Conversation 1: *Have got; a, an* and *any*

 1 02.03 **Listen to Steve and Bob talking about their families. Which picture is Bob and his family? Which picture is David (Bob's brother) and his family?**

a   b   c

Steve: Tell me about your family. Have you got any children?
Bob: Well, I'm married and we've got three children, two boys and a girl.
Steve: That's great. And have you got any brothers and sisters?
Bob: I've got a sister and a brother. My sister is married but she hasn't got any children.
Steve: What about your brother?
Bob: His name's David. He lives in Berlin with his family. He isn't married but he lives with his partner and they've got two little boys. His partner is German. David speaks a little German but their children speak English and German very well. David's got a very good job. He is a computer programmer.

2 02.03 **Listen again and fill in the gaps.**

Have you got *any* children?
We've _____ three children.
I'_____ _____ a sister and a brother.
My sister hasn't got _____ _____.
They'_____ _____ two children.
David'_____ _____ a very good job.

3 Look at the conversation. How do we use *have got*? Fill in the gaps in the table.

+	−	?
I/you/we/they *have* got	I/you/we/they _____ got	**Have** I/you/we/they _____ ?
He/she/it _____ got	He/she/it hasn't _____	_____ he/she/it _____ ?

2 Family and friends, jobs and home

> **LANGUAGE TIP**
> When we speak, we often say *'ve got* instead of *have got*, and we say *'s got* instead of *has got*.
> I/you/we/they**'ve got** ...   he/she/it**'s got** ...

4 When do we say *a*, *an* and *any*? Look at these sentences:

My sister hasn't got **any** children.

I've got **a** sister.

Put the rules in the correct part of the table.
- with singular nouns
- with singular nouns that begin with a, e, i, o, u
- with plural or uncountable nouns in a question or a negative sentence

A	AN	ANY
	with singular nouns that begin with a, e, i, o, u	
window job car *garden*	iPhone	brothers or sisters children free time

> **LANGUAGE TIP**
> Uncountable nouns are nouns which have no plural and we can't count them.
>
> | **Countable nouns** | **Uncountable nouns** |
> |---|---|
> | plural form
you can count them | no plural form
you can't count them |
> | house – houses
child – children
two houses
two children | free time – ~~free times~~
money – ~~moneys~~
~~two free times~~
~~two moneys~~ |

5 Look at the nouns. Choose 'countable' or 'uncountable' for each noun. Put them in the correct part of the table in Exercise 4.

> umbrella questions iPhone house
> garden job friends grandparents

6 02.04 Read the conversation and fill in the gaps. Then listen and check your answers.

Mary:	Tell me about your family.
Joanna:	Well, I am married and we _'ve got_ three children, two girls and _____ boy. I'_____ _____ two sisters and _____ brother. My brother is married but he _____ n't _____ _____ children.
Mary:	What about your sisters?
Joanna:	My older sister _____ n't _____ _____ children. She isn't married. She'_____ _____ a very good job. She's _____ engineer. My other sister is married and they'_____ _____ two children, _____ boy and _____ girl.

7 What about you? Have you got ...

a car?

a job?

an iPhone?

any brothers or sisters?

any children?

any grandparents?

any free time?

MY, HIS, HER, ETC.

Look at these sentences.

Tell me about **your** family.

My brother is married.

Now look at more words like *your* and *my* in the table.

my		Joe
your		?
his	name is	Paul
her		Susan
our		Stevens
their		Johnson
our	names are	Ravi and Nina
their		Anna and Bob

> **LANGUAGE TIP**
> Some people prefer to use the neutral word 'their' and so don't indicate if they are male or female.

1 You meet Joe Stevens. Use the words from the table to fill in the gaps in the conversation.

Hello! What's your name?

Hello! **a** <u>My</u> name is Joe. This is my brother. **b** _____ name is Paul.

This is my sister. **c** _____ name is Susan. This is my mother and this is my father. **d** _____ names are Anna and Bob. **e** _____ family name is Stevens.

2 02.05 **Listen and repeat.**

3 Write about your family. Use Bob's sentences in Conversation 1 and Joanna's sentences in Exercise 6 to help you.

Conversation 2: Questions and answers about *he* or *she*

1 02.06 **Tom shows Peter some photos. Who is in the photos? Listen and choose the two correct answers.**
   a his sister
   b his wife
   c his daughter

2 02.06 **Listen again and complete the table.**

		Nationality	Lives in	
Amélie	*wife*		Canada	
Louise		American		

3 Read the conversation. Fill in the gaps in the table.

Peter: Who's this?
Tom: This is my wife. Her name's Amélie.
Peter: Where is she from?
Tom: She's from France, she's French.
Peter: Does she speak English?
Tom: Yes, she does. She speaks English very well. And this is my sister.
Peter: What's her name?
Tom: Her name's Louise. She's an English teacher.
Peter: Where does she live?
Tom: She lives in Brazil.
Peter: Does she speak Portuguese?
Tom: No, she doesn't. She speaks Spanish but she doesn't speak Portuguese.

QUESTIONS	ANSWERS
What's _her_ name?	Her ____'____ Amélie. (name)
Where ____ ____ from?	____'____ ____ France. (country) ____'____ ____ French. (nationality)
Where ____ ____ live?	____ ____ in Brazil. (city/country)
____ ____ speak English? (language)	No, ____ ____. Yes, ____ ____.
What about Spanish and Portuguese?	____ ____ Spanish but ____ doesn't ____ Portuguese.

2 Family and friends, jobs and home

4 Look at these sentences from Vocabulary 2.

I work in an office. I am a businesswoman.

Change *I* to *she*. How do the verbs change?

She _____ in an office. She _____ a businesswoman.

 5 Write about two people in your family. Talk about languages, work and where they live.

VOCABULARY 3: DESCRIBING YOUR HOME

1 Match the words and the pictures.
  a a terraced house   _3_
  b a town
  c a detached house
  d a semi-detached house
  e a city
  f a flat (apartment)
  g a village

 2 02.07 Listen and repeat. Note the stressed syllable, for example, *a de<u>tach</u>ed <u>house</u>*. Practise saying the words.

3 02.08 **Here are some sentences to say where you live.**

				England
	in			France
	in the	North / West / East / South	of	Japan
I	live			Germany
	in a	(town/village)	near / 10 miles from	London / Manchester

Listen and repeat. Note the stressed syllable, for example, I _live_ in _France_. Practise saying the sentences.

Conversation 3: *Where do you live? What's it like?*

1 02.09 **Steve and Bob talk about their homes. Listen to and read their conversation. Where does Bob live? Choose the correct picture.**

a   b   c

Steve:	…. and where do you live, Bob?
Bob:	We live in a new terraced house in a very small village in the north of England. It is about 10 miles from Manchester.
Steve:	What's it like?
Bob:	Well, Steve, it's a very typical English village. There are a lot of beautiful, old houses and there is a lovely pub but there aren't any shops and there isn't a bank. The young people think it is quite boring but I think it is nice and quiet! The people are very friendly. It's a really great place to live.

2 Family and friends, jobs and home

VOCABULARY 4: DESCRIBING PEOPLE AND PLACES

 Read Conversation 3 again. The highlighted words are all adjectives.

> **LANGUAGE TIP**
>
> Some adjectives describe places; some describe people; some describe people and places. Look at the table.
>
> | PLACES | PLACES AND PEOPLE | PEOPLE |
> |---|---|---|
> | small, big, typical, new | lovely, nice, friendly, boring, old, quiet, great | serious, kind |

1 **Add the adjectives to the table. Check any new words in the dictionary.**

beautiful	hard-working
noisy	funny
important	young
modern	interesting

2 **Look at the words in Exercise 1. Fill in the missing opposites in the table.**

OPPOSITES	
small	*big*
new (places) young (people)	
	noisy
funny	
	interesting

3 Look at the words. One is negative 😞. Which one?

> lovely kind funny nice
> friendly boring great
> beautiful hard-working

4 Look at all the words in Exercises 1–3. Which words describe the place where you live? Which words describe people in your family? Write the names next to the words, for example:

hard-working	My sister, Sarah
young	My daughter, Jane
serious	My friend, Tom
beautiful	My village, Hampton

> **LANGUAGE TIP**
> We can change the meaning of adjectives with the words *really*, *very* or *quite*.

5 Use the words and phrases to complete the table.

> ~~very small/really small~~
> very big/really big
> quite small   quite big

My car is	**a** very small/really small	
	b	
	c	
	d	

2 Family and friends, jobs and home

6 02.10 **Listen and repeat. Mark the stressed syllable, for example, _typ*i*cal_. Practise saying the adjectives.**

ADJECTIVES WITH *TO BE*

1 Look at Bob's sentences from Conversation 3. What are the missing words?

It _____ nice and quiet! The people _____ very friendly.

2 With adjectives, we use the verb *to be*. Fill in the gaps in the table with the correct form of the verb *to be*.

	✓	✗	?
I	I _am_ (I'm)	I'm not	_____ I?
you we they	you _____ (you're) we _____ (we're) they _____ (they're)	you aren't we aren't they aren't	_____ you? _____ we? _____ they?
he she it	he _____ (he's) she _____ (she's) it _____ (it's)	he isn't she isn't it isn't	_____ he? _____ she? _____ it?

3 Look at the sentences. Correct the mistakes.
   a London very beautiful.   _London is very beautiful._
   b It is very big?
   c She is funny?
   d They nice and friendly.
   e I hard-working.

4 Steve asks two questions about where Bob lives. Look at Conversation 3 again and complete the questions.

Where _____ _____ live?   _____ _____ like?

Answer his questions about where you live.

I live in _____.   It's _____.

USING *THERE IS, THERE ARE*; ARTICLES

1 Anna is on holiday. Read her postcard to James. Is her holiday good?

Dear James,
I am on holiday in a very small village, five miles from a town called Buxton in the north of England. Buxton is lovely. There are a lot of shops and places to visit and there's a really good market. There aren't any nightclubs but the pubs are great. At the house there isn't any Wi-Fi or mobile reception but it's beautiful here and I am having a lovely time!
See you soon.
Love Anna
xx

James Smith
4563 Pillsbury Avenue
Minneapolis
MN 53120-4193
United States

2 What does Anna say? Complete the sentences.

There are a lot of shops in Buxton ✓✓✓

_____ a lot of places to visit. ✓✓✓

_____ a really good market in the town. ✓

_____ any nightclubs ✗✗✗

_____ any Wi-Fi or mobile reception at the house. ✗

3 How do we use *there is* and *there are* to describe the things in a place? Look again at Exercises 1 and 2. Put the examples in the correct place a–c in the table.

mobile reception

banks, people

a gym, a nightclub, a post office

	✓	✗	?
singular nouns for example: a _____ uncountable nouns for example: b _____	There is **a** hotel Wi-Fi 5G coverage	There isn't **a** cinema **any** Wi-Fi	Is there **a** dentist? **any** Wi-Fi?
plural nouns for example: c _____	There are **two** cinemas **some** restaurants **a lot of** shops	There aren't **any** cafés **any** tourists	Are there **any** restaurants? **any** pubs?

4 Look at the sentences. Find the mistakes and write the sentences correctly.

  a There is hotel.   *There is a hotel.*
  b There is a mobile reception.
  c There is some pub.
  d There isn't any cinema.
  e There are 5G coverage.
  f There are banks.
  g There are some hotel.
  h There are a lot of supermarket.
  i There are mobile reception.
  j There aren't some post office.
  k There aren't shops.

5 Look at the table. Read the sentences about the village. Choose T (true) or F (false).

	VILLAGE	TOWN	CITY
a hotel	no	yes	yes, a lot
a pub	yes	yes, some	yes, a lot
a cinema	no	no	yes, some
a café	no	yes, a lot	yes, a lot

a bank	no	yes, some	yes, a lot
a post office	yes	yes	yes, some
a supermarket	no	yes, some	yes, a lot
a market	no	yes	yes, some
a shop	yes	yes	yes, a lot
mobile reception	yes	yes	yes
5G coverage	no	yes	yes
Wi-Fi	yes	yes	yes

  a In the village there's a pub.   T/F
  b In the village there's a post office and a cinema.   T/F
  c In the village there is mobile reception.   T/F

6 02.11 **Use the information in the table in Exercise 5, and complete the text about the town.**

In the town, *there is* a hotel and _____ _____ some pubs. _____ _____ a cinema but _____ _____ a lot of internet cafés. _____ _____ a market and _____ _____ some supermarkets.

7 Write about what there is in the city.

In the city, there is _____

8 Write about your village, town or city.

I live in _____. It's _____.
There's a _____. There isn't a _____. There are _____.

Listening, pronunciation and speaking

LISTENING: DESCRIBING FAMILY AND WHERE YOU LIVE

1 02.12 **Listen to the conversation. Put a, b or c in the gap.**

Michael and his family live here. _____

Christina and her family live here. _____

a b c

2 02.12 **Listen again. Look at the pictures a–d. For each picture, choose M (Michael's family), C (Christina's family) or L (Louise's family).**

a _C_   b _____

c _____   d _____

PRONUNCIATION: WEAK FORMS AND LINKING – PREPOSITIONS AND ARTICLES

 1 02.13 **Listen to these sentences. Note the stressed syllables.**

How do we pronounce the words *a* and *an*?

What happens between the words where it is highlighted?

There's a café.	I've got a cat.
There isn't a shop.	He's got a car.
There isn't any Wi-Fi.	She hasn't got an umbrella.
There aren't any tourists.	We haven't got a garden.
Is there a hotel?	Have you got an iPhone?
Are there any shops?	

> **LANGUAGE TIP**
>
> We usually pronounce *a* and *an* as /ə/ and /ən/ and stress the noun.
>
> When one word ends with a consonant sound (for example /s/ or /t/ or /r/) and the next word begins with a vowel sound (for example /ə/ or /iː/), we usually say them together and it sounds like one word, for example *gotanumbrella* and *gotanIphone*.

 2 Listen again and practise saying the sentences.

SPEAKING: DESCRIBING FAMILY AND WHERE YOU LIVE

1 02.14 **Listen to the first part of Christina and Michael's conversation again. Fill in the gaps.**

Christina:	Is this your family, Michael?
Michael:	Yes. It's not a very good photo but this _is my wife_, Helen, and _____ _____, Harry. _____'_____ _____ three children. This is a good photo, my wife with Harry and next to Harry is _____ _____, Paul and _____ _____, Anna.
Christina:	Is this where you live?
Michael:	Yes. It's a small _____ _____ in a very beautiful _____ _____ the south _____ England. It's about 50 miles _____ London. It's very quiet and _____ _____n't a lot to do, but we like it. _____ _____ a shop and a pub but _____ _____n't _____ restaurants or cafés and _____ _____n't a bank or a post office. What about you, Christina? Where do you live?

2 02.15 **You are Michael. Listen to the conversation and answer Christina's questions.**

3 02.14 **Listen to Michael and Christina again and check your answers to Exercise 2.**

4 **Michael asks you about where you live and your family. Complete the conversation for you.**

Michael:	Tell me about your family. Do you have any brothers and sisters? Where do they live and work?
You:	_____
Michael:	Do you have any children?
You:	_____
Michael:	Where do you live? What's it like?
You:	_____

2 Family and friends, jobs and home

Reading and writing

READING 1: PERSONAL DETAILS

1 Read Tom's visa application form again, in Unit 1, Reading 1. Answer the questions.

a Where is Tom from?   *He's from the United States.*
b What's his wife's name?
c Where is his wife from?
d Have they got any children?
e Where does Tom live?

READING 2: DESCRIBING YOUR HOME

1 Read the description. Choose the correct picture.

This is a big, modern flat in Notting Hill. It's very near Ladbroke Grove tube station and quite near a very big shopping centre. There are also a lot of lovely restaurants and cafés and the great Portobello Market is near the flat.

There is a big living room with two windows and a really big sofa. There is one big and one small bedroom and a bathroom with a bath and a shower. There is a new kitchen with an oven, a microwave, a fridge-freezer and a washing machine but there isn't a dishwasher. There is a dining table with chairs in the living room. There is Wi-Fi but there isn't a phone or a TV. There isn't a garden and there isn't a lift.

2 Read the description again. What is there in the flat? Note the correct pictures.

a   b   c   d

Look at a house rental website for more words to describe homes.

WRITING 1: A DESCRIPTION OF WHERE YOU LIVE

1 Look at the pictures. Complete the description of the flat for the house rental website.

There is a big living room with a _____ and a _____. There _____ _____ bedrooms, one with a single bed and one with a double bed. There _____ a bathroom with a _____ but there isn't a _____. In the kitchen, there is an _____ and a _____ but _____ _____ a microwave. There is _____ in the flat but there isn't a _____. _____ _____ _____ garden.

 Write the description again. Choose positive words from the box and put them in your description.

> beautiful lovely noisy nice modern
> boring great new old really very

 2 Now write a description of your home for the house rental website website.

WRITING 2: INTRODUCING YOURSELF AND YOUR FAMILY

 You ask a new friend to your house for a few days. Choose some photos and write to them. Introduce your family and describe where you live.

Dear Sarah

I am very happy that you can stay with us for the weekend. Let me tell you a little about my family and where we live. Here are some photos.

- Say who is in the photo (your wife/husband or your children or your brothers and sisters or your parents).

- Say their names.

- Say what they do or where they work.

- Say what kind of house you live in (flat/house …).

- Say if you live in a village/town/city and in the north/south/east/west and say which country.

- Say how far it is from a big city (and which city).

- Say what it is like (quiet/modern/big …).

- Say what there is/isn't and what there are/aren't.

Have a good journey and see you in two weeks.
Best wishes

Test yourself

1 Fill in the gaps.

a Tom is my father. I am his _daughter_.

b Gemma is my wife. I am her _____

c Mary is my mother. I am her _____

d Peter is my brother. I am his _____

2 Correct the spelling mistakes in these plurals.

a mens   _men_
b womans _____
c childs _____
d brotheres _____
e lifes   _____
f babys   _____
g persons _____
h familys _____

3 Fill in the gaps.

a I am _a_ nurse. I work in a _____.
b I am a t_____ I work in _____ school.
c I am _____ computer programmer. I work at _____.
d My sister is a businesswoman. She _____ in _____ office.
e My grandmother hasn't got a job. She _____ work.

4 Correct the mistakes.

a This ~~are~~ _is_ my sister.
b She name Susana.
c She live in Spain.
d She speak Spanish.
e She not speak French.
f She from Australia.
g She Australian.
h She work in hospital.
i She a nurse.
j She very kind.
k She got two children.
l She not got a car.

5 Look at these sentences. Write the questions.

a _Where does he live?_ He lives in France.
b _____ He is from Germany. He is German.
c _____ His name's Johan.
d _____ English? No, he speaks French and German.
e _____ city? No, he lives in a town.
f _____ It's a very modern town.
g _____ Yes, he's got two sons.
h _____ in his town? Yes, there are three hotels.

6 Look at the words. Make sentences about the village.

a The village/very old — _The village is very old._
b It/quite small — _____
c It/very boring — _____
d The people/really friendly — _____
e ✓ ✓ beautiful old houses — _____
f ✓ lovely pub — _____
g ✗ shops — _____
h ✗ café — _____
i ✗ Wi-Fi in the pub. — _____

7 Look at the adjectives. Choose three adjectives for each part of the table. Note the positive adjectives ☺.

> beautiful lovely serious kind
> noisy nice modern boring great
> new old funny interesting young

PLACES	PEOPLE AND PLACES	PEOPLE
	beautiful	

SELF CHECK

I CAN . . .
... talk about my family.
... talk about jobs and workplaces.
... talk about where I live.
... describe people and places.

2 Family and friends, jobs and home

3

In this unit you will learn how to:
» say numbers.
» talk about the date and the time.
» ask and answer questions about dates and times.

Numbers, times and dates

Festivals, celebrations and important dates

1 Match the festivals with the 2026 dates. Put the festivals in part A of the table.

~~Jewish New Year (Rosh Hashana)~~   Jewish Feast of Passover
Muslim Festival of Eid al-Adha   Christian festival of Christmas
Chinese New Year   Muslim Ramadan
Diwali, Hindu Festival of Lights   Christian festival of Easter

A	B	C
Festival	**2026**	**2027**
	17 February	
	17 February–18 March	
	1–9 April	
	5 April	
	26 May	

Jewish New Year (Rosh Hashana)	11–13 September	
	8 November	
	25 December	

2 **What are the festival dates in 2027? Look online and complete part C of the table.**

3 **Look at the inventions (new ideas) a–h. Match the inventions to the dates.**

Example: a *1876*

> 1817 1876 1885 1901
> 1903 1927 1943 1973

Vocabulary builder

VOCABULARY 1: NUMBERS

1 Complete the table with the words in the box.

> three eighteen one six
> thirteen four seven
> nineteen nine sixteen
> eleven five twelve
> fifteen seventeen ten

3 Numbers, times and dates

1		6		11		16	
2	two	7		12		17	
3		8	eight	13		18	
4		9		14	fourteen	19	
5		10	*ten*	15		20	twenty

2 Choose the correct numbers.

89   100   64   23   48   75   97   32   56

- **a** twenty-three — _23_
- **b** thirty-two — ___
- **c** forty-eight — ___
- **d** fifty-six — ___
- **e** sixty-four — ___
- **f** seventy-five — ___
- **g** eighty-nine — ___
- **h** ninety-seven — ___
- **i** a hundred — ___

3 Match the numbers and the words.

200 202 220 2,000 ~~2,002~~ 2,200 2,022

- **a** Two thousand and two — _2,002_
- **b** Two hundred — ___
- **c** Two thousand two hundred — ___
- **d** Two hundred and twenty — ___
- **e** Two thousand — ___
- **f** Two hundred and two — ___
- **g** Two thousand and twenty-two — ___

4 When do we use the word *and* in numbers?

a Find three more that are NOT correct.

Twenty and two   X

One hundred and two

One thousand and two

One thousand and twenty

One thousand and twenty and two

One thousand and twenty two

One thousand and two hundred

One thousand two hundred

> **LANGUAGE TIP**
> We use *and* after 100: *One hundred **and** four, one hundred **and** sixty-nine*.
> After 1,000, we use *and* only before numbers 1–99: *One thousand **and** three; one thousand **and** thirty-one; one thousand four hundred*.

b 03.01 Now listen to the correct numbers. How do we pronounce the word *and*?

5 03.02 **Listen and repeat.**

6 03.03 **Listen to the numbers and write them down.**

5, 11, _____

VOCABULARY 2: DAYS, MONTHS, SEASONS

1 Complete the list. Put the days of the week in the correct order.

> Tuesday Friday Monday Wednesday
> Sunday Saturday Thursday

Sunday
Tuesday

2 Look at the first letter of the months of the year. Put the months in the correct order.

> December June March
> October April February
> May January August
> September November July

January	July
F	A
M	S
A	O
M	N
J	D

3 Numbers, times and dates

> **LANGUAGE TIP**
> In the UK, there are four seasons.
>
> Months are sometimes abbreviated (we just write the first part). For example, *Jan* instead of *January*.
>
> Days of the week are sometimes abbreviated too. For example, *Mon*, *Weds* instead of *Monday*, *Wednesday*.

3 Match the seasons with the pictures.

autumn spring
winter summer

a *spring*

b _____

c _____

d _____

4 Look at the abbreviated months in the table. Complete the seasons.

a	spring	b	c
Dec	Mar	June	Sep
Jan	Apr	July	Oct
Feb	May	Aug	Nov

5 03.04 **Listen and repeat. Note the stressed syllable, for example, _Monday_. Practise saying the words.**

6 **Answer these questions.**
   a What month is it now? For example, May
   b What month is your birthday? For example, July
   c What season is your birthday in? For example, winter
   d What day is it today? For example, Tuesday

VOCABULARY 3: DATES

1 **Look at the dates (A) and notice how we say them (B). Four of the dates in B are NOT correct. Write the correct date.**

A	B
7/11	the seventh of November
12/4	the twelfth of April
3/1	the third of September
5/6	the fifth of June
25/11	the twenty-fifth of December
1/1	the first of January
3/5	the third of May
31/7	the thirty-first of July
4/4	the fourth of August
21/4	the twenty-first of April
30/3	the thirtieth of March
22/9	the twenty-second of September
8/10	the eighth of December
2/10	the second of October
20/3	the twentieth of March

> **LANGUAGE TIP**
> When we say the date we use ordinals, not numbers. We say the *first* of January NOT the *one* of January 😞.

3 Numbers, times and dates

2 Complete the table with the correct ordinal words. Look at Exercise 1 to help you.

1st		11th	eleventh	21st	twenty-first
2nd	second	12th		22nd	
3rd		13th	thirteenth	23rd	twenty-third
4th		14th	fourteenth	24th	twenty-fourth
5th		15th	fifteenth	25th	
6th	sixth	16th	sixteenth	26th	twenty-sixth
7th		17th	seventeenth	27th	twenty-seventh
8th		18th	eighteenth	28th	twenty-eighth
9th	ninth	19th	nineteenth	29th	twenty-ninth
10th	tenth	20th		30th	thirtieth
				31st	

Most ordinals are the number + *th* (*4th*, *15th*, *28th*). Some are different. Look at the table again. Which ordinals have a different ending?

3 03.05 **Listen and repeat. Note the stressed syllable, for example, *twenty-second*. Practise saying the words.**

4 03.06 **What else do you notice about how we say the date? Listen to the examples.**

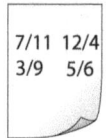

7/11 12/4
3/9   5/6

> The seventh of November   The twelfth of April
> The third of September   The fifth of June

> **LANGUAGE TIP**
> To say the date, use the pattern:
> *The* + *ordinal* + *of* + *month*.

 Listen again and repeat. Stress the ordinal and the month.

5 03.07 **Listen and repeat. Then listen again and write the dates in numbers, for example 7/11.**

6 **How do you say these dates?**
   a 1/1
   b 23/11
   c 4/10
   d 15/4
   e 22/3
   f 31/7

03.08 **Listen and check your answers.**

> **LANGUAGE TIP**
> We can write dates with numbers only (*22/03*) or we can write numbers and words (*2 April*). Sometimes people write *th*, *rd*, *nd* or *st* after the date number (*2nd April*). Look again at Exercise 2.

7 **Match these dates to the dates in Exercise 6. Then add *th*, *rd*, *nd* or *st* after the numbers.**
   a 15 April
   b 23 November
   c 1 January
   d 31 July
   e 4 October
   f 22 March

   d <u>*15th April*</u>

What's the date today?

When is your birthday?

> **LANGUAGE TIP**
>
> To say years, we usually separate them into two numbers.
> For 1819 we say *eighteen nineteen* (think 18, 19).
> For 1963 we say *nineteen sixty-three* (think 19, 63).
> For 2010 we say *twenty ten* (think 20, 10) or *two thousand and ten* (think 2,010).
> For 2011 we say *twenty eleven* or *two thousand and eleven*.
> BUT for 2001–9 we always say *two thousand and one* (think 2,001), *two thousand and two*, etc.

8 03.09 **Listen and complete the years.**

a _1591_
b _____
c _____
d _____
e _____
f _____
g _____
h _____

9 03.10 **Some years are different. Listen and read. Complete the years in numbers next to the words.**

a Nineteen oh one   _1901_
b Nineteen hundred   _____
c Seventeen oh two   _____
d Two thousand   _____
e Two thousand and one   _____
f Two thousand and nine _____

What year is it now?

Conversation 1: Using numbers in questions and answers

1 03.11 **Telma is in a language school, talking to the receptionist. Listen to the conversation. What kind of English course does Telma want?**

a a course of 15 hours a week
b a conversation course of ten hours a week for four weeks
c a conversation course of ten hours a week for one week

Receptionist:	Good morning.
Telma:	Good morning. I am looking for an English course.
Receptionist:	We've got a lot of courses. There are courses for 15 hours a week or 20 hours a week. And we've got a conversation class which is ten hours a week, that's two hours each day.
Telma:	Great. The conversation class sounds good. How much is it?
Receptionist:	There are different prices. You can do a course for one week, or for four weeks. Here is some information.
Telma:	Thank you. Yes, four weeks looks good, I'll do the four-week conversation course, please. Can I start next week?
Receptionist:	Yes, of course. You just need to complete this form. We can do that now if you like?
Telma:	Great.
Receptionist:	So, what's your name?
Telma:	Telma Silva – that's T-E-L-M-A S-I-L-V-A.
Receptionist:	Thanks. And your date of birth? What's your date of birth?
Telma:	Sorry, I don't understand.
Receptionist:	Oh, um, when were you born?
Telma:	Oh, I was born on 5 April 1993.
Receptionist:	And what's your address?
Telma:	My address is 19, Scott Street, Wellbridge.
Receptionist:	And what's your postcode?
Telma:	WB14 7JR.
Receptionist:	Lovely. And what's your home phone number?
Telma:	01723 453123.
Receptionist:	And have you got a mobile number?
Telma:	Yes, the number is 07396 213431.
Receptionist:	Just one more thing – have you got an email address?
Telma:	Yes, it's telmasilva@gnet.com.
Receptionist:	Lovely. Thank you. See you Monday.
Telma:	Yes, see you Monday!

2 03.11 Look at the language school enrolment form. Listen again and read the conversation. Complete the form with information about Telma.

3 Numbers, times and dates

Family name	Silva
Given names	**a** *Telma*
Date of Birth (DD/MM/YYYY)	**b**
Address	**c** , *Scott Street, Wellbridge*
Postcode	**d**
Home phone	**e**
Mobile phone	**f**
Email	*telmasilva@gnet.com*

3 Look at the information in the table and complete the questions.

a What's *your* date of birth? **b** When _____ you _____?	Date of birth (DD/MM/YYYY)	05/04/1993
c What'_____ _____ address?	Address	19, Scott Street, Wellbridge
d What'_____ _____ postcode?	Postcode	WB14 7JR
e What'_____ _____ phone number?	Home phone	01723 453123
f What'_____ _____ mobile number?	Mobile phone	07396 213431

Answer the questions about you.

> **LANGUAGE TIP**
> We use *were* or *was* with *born* to talk about our date of birth.

4 The receptionist asks Telma *When were you born?* What does she answer?

Can you complete the table?

Question ?	Answer .
a When were you _____?	**c** I was _____ in 1989.
When was he born?	**d** He _____ _____ _____ 1972.
b When was your daughter _____?	**e** She _____ _____ in the first year of the 21st century, in 2000!

5 When was he born? Choose 1, 2 or 3.
  a Taylor Swift was born ...
   1 in 1985   **2** in 1979   **3** in 1989 ✓
  b Pablo Picasso was born ...
   1 in 1881   **2** in 1901   **3** in 1891
  c Greta Thunberg was born ...
   1 in 2000   **2** in 2003   **3** in 1999
  d Albert Einstein was born ...
   1 in the eighteenth century   **2** in the nineteenth century
   3 in the twentieth century
  e William Shakespeare was born ...
   1 in the fifteenth century   **2** in the sixteenth century
   3 in the seventeenth century
  f Frida Kahlo was born ...
   1 in the eighteenth century   **2** in the nineteenth century
   3 in the twentieth century

Make sentences for you.

I was born on _____ (date).

I was born in _____ (month).

I was born in _____ (year).

I was born in _____ (century).

I was born in _____ (season).

PHONE NUMBERS

1 03.12 **Listen to the phone numbers. Then complete the missing numbers in the Language Tip box.**
  a 01725 839721
  b 0161 455 6792
  c 0113 601 9765
  d 0223 538021
  e 0845 349 2341
  f 01349 563341

> **LANGUAGE TIP**
>
> For telephone numbers we say single numbers (so for example, *four five three one two three* not *forty-five twelve twenty-three*)
>
> For _____ we usually say *oh* not *zero*.
>
> For _____ we say *double five*.

2 03.12 **Read aloud the phone numbers in Exercise 1. Then listen again to check your answers.**

3 Complete the table with the correct numbers.

453123	four five three one two three
	oh one nine two five
	two one three four three one
	oh seven three double two
	double six four oh double one

THE TIME

1 Look at the questions. Which is the most polite?

Excuse me. Could you tell me what time it is, please?

Excuse me. What time is it, please?

What time is it?

2 Match the times with the clocks.

a   It's one o'clock

b   It's six o'clock

c   It's midnight

d   It's eleven o'clock

e   It's midday

f   It's four o'clock

3 Complete the table with the times indicated.

(MINUTES) PAST (THE HOUR)		(MINUTES) TO (THE HOUR)	
6.05	It's five past six	6.35	It's twenty-five to seven
6.10	a	6.40	d
6.20	b	6.50	It's ten to seven
6.25	c	6.55	e

4 There are two ways of saying times. Put the sentences in the correct part of the table.

It's quarter to seven.

It's six fifteen.

It's half past six.

a It's quarter past six	6.15	
b	6.30	It's six thirty
c	6.45	It's six forty-five

5 03.13 **Listen to the times. Note the stressed syllable, for example, *It's <u>one</u> o'<u>clock</u>, It's <u>ten</u> to <u>seven</u>*. Practise saying the times.**

> **LANGUAGE TIP**
>
> People say the time both ways ...
>
> It's ten to seven.
>
> It's 6.50 (six fifty).

6 03.14 **Listen to the conversations a–h. Draw the time on the clocks.**

a   b   c

d   e   f

 g   h

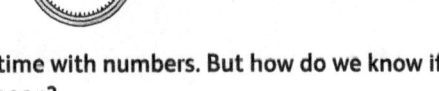

7 We usually write the time with numbers. But how do we know if it is morning or afternoon?

▶ We use *a.m.* (= morning) or *p.m.* (= afternoon or evening): *6.20 a.m., 6.20 p.m., 8.15 a.m., 8.15 p.m.*

▶ We use the 24-hour clock (*06:20* = morning, *18:20* = afternoon). We often see these 24-hour clock times on digital clocks, on computers and in travel information.

Complete the table with the missing 24-hour times.

MORNING		AFTERNOON		EVENING		NIGHT	
6 a.m.	9 a.m.	2 p.m.	4.30 p.m.	7.45 p.m.	9 p.m.	11 p.m.	2 a.m.
06.00					21.00		

What time is it now?

Say and write the time – can you do it in two different ways?

Conversation 2: What time ...?

 1 03.15 **Listen to the conversation in a tourist information office. What does the tourist want information about? Choose the three correct pictures.**

a

b

c

d

 2 Listen again and fill in gaps a–e.

3 Numbers, times and dates

Tourist:	Hello
Advisor:	Good morning. Can I help you?
Tourist:	Yes, please. Can you give me some information about the City Museum? What time does it open?
Advisor:	**a** It _____ at _____.
Tourist:	And what time does it close?
Advisor:	**b** It _____ _____ _____.
Tourist:	Thank you. And I think there's a tour of the city. What time does it start?
Advisor:	Yes, the tour is very interesting. **c** _____ _____ at _____.
Tourist:	And what time does it finish?
Advisor:	**d** _____ _____ _____ _____.
Tourist:	And can I do a tour of the castle?
Advisor:	Yes, there is a tour at 10 o'clock and a tour at 2.30.
Tourist:	And how long does it last?
Advisor:	It lasts **e** _____ hours.
Tourist:	Thank you. That's very helpful.

3 Look at the four highlighted questions in the conversation. Complete the questions in the correct part of the table.

the museum	What time does it open?	**a** What...?
the tour of the city	**b** What...?	What time does it finish?

4 Which things start and finish? Which things open and close? Use your dictionary to find any new words. Add them to the correct part of the table in Exercise 3.

> the museum the football match the bank
> the tour of Boston the TV show the park
> the movie the post office the art gallery
> the English class the concert the store

Ask questions about:
- **a** the post office
- **b** the English class
- **c** the tour of London
- **d** the bank
- **e** the film
- **f** the art gallery

5 The advisor says *It lasts two hours.* What question does the tourist ask?

Tourist _____ _____ _____ _____ _____ ?

Ask and answer the same question for the things in the table.

	Start time	Finish time	
film	7 p.m.	9 p.m.	**a** *How long does it last? It lasts two hours.*
TV programme	6 p.m.	7 p.m.	**b**
concert	8 p.m.	11 p.m.	**c**
tour of London	0900	1400	**d**

PREPOSITIONS OF TIME

1 Look at the information about Tom and his family. Read sentences a–f.

Four sentences are NOT correct. Find and correct these four sentences.

Given name(s) as shown in your passport	Tom
Family name	Mitcham
Gender	male/~~female/prefer not to say~~
Date of birth	07/11/1978
Place of birth	San Francisco
Country of birth	The United States
Nationality	American
Marital status	~~single~~/married
Full name of spouse/partner	Amélie Lafayette
Spouse/partner's date of birth	03/09/1981
Spouse/partner's nationality	French
Do you have any children?	yes/~~no~~
Details of children (name and date of birth)	Marie Lafayette 28/04/2011
Your full residential address and postcode	8924, Boulevard Lazare, Montreal, QC H2A, Canada

Email address	tom.mitcham@canadamail.com
Home phone	+1 438 0956054
Mobile	07896 1293455

   a He was born on the seventh of November nineteen seventy-six.
   b He was born in the nineteenth century.
   c His wife was born in nineteen eighty-one.
   d His wife was born in September.
   e His daughter was born in May.
   f His daughter was born in winter.

2 Read these sentences about shops and banks in the UK. Choose T (true) or F (false).

   a Shops in the UK open at ten o'clock in the morning. T/F
   b Some shops in the UK close on Sunday. T/F
   c Post offices in the UK close at Christmas. T/F
   d Some banks in the UK close at lunchtime. T/F
   e All shops in the UK close at night. T/F
   f Banks in the UK close in the evening. T/F
   g Tourist offices in the UK close at the weekend. T/F

3 Look again at sentences a–f in Exercise 1 and a–g in Exercise 2. Find the prepositions *in*, *on* and *at*.

Now look at the words in the box. Put the words in the correct part of the table.

> night dates festivals
> the weekend months
> the evening years days
> centuries time seasons

IN	ON	AT
the morning the afternoon *months*		*festivals*

4 Now look at the examples in the box. Put them in the correct part of the table.

> January dinnertime
> autumn 2012 Monday Christmas
> 8 o'clock 21 July Friday 1999
> March Easter
> spring 7.30 10/11/14
> the 20th century lunchtime

IN	ON	AT
January		

5 Complete the sentences with the correct prepositions.
  a He was born _on_ the tenth of May nineteen eighty-four.
  b He was born _____ the 20th century.
  c His wife was born _____ 1992.
  d His wife was born _____ summer.
  e His daughter was born _____ the 21st.
  f His son was born _____ October.
  g Shops in the UK open _____ 9 a.m.
  h Some shops in the UK close _____ Sunday.
  i Shops in the UK close _____ Christmas.
  j Some shops in the UK close _____ lunchtime.
  k Most shops in the UK close _____ night.
  l Post offices in the UK close _____ the evening.
  m Most banks in the UK close _____ the weekend.

PRONUNCIATION: WEAK FORMS OF *DOES, WAS, WERE, OF, AT, AND*

1 03.16 **Listen to these phrases. Note the stressed (underlined) words.**

What <u>time</u> does it <u>open</u>? What <u>time</u> does it <u>close</u>?
<u>When</u> were you <u>born</u>? I was <u>born</u> in <u>June</u>
The <u>tenth</u> of <u>July</u> The <u>fourteenth</u> of <u>August</u>
at <u>five thirty</u> at <u>Christmas</u>
two <u>hundred</u> and <u>thirty</u> five <u>thousand</u> and <u>forty</u>

Listen again. What do you notice about the pronunciation of the highlighted words? Practise saying the phrases. Remember, don't stress the highlighted words!

Listening and speaking

LISTENING 1: A PHONE CONVERSATION ABOUT MEETING

1 03.17 **Ellie, Ruby and Pete are friends. They want to meet next week.**

Listen to the conversation. Do they choose a day to meet?

2 03.17 **Listen again and fill in the phone numbers.**

	MOBILE	HOME PHONE
Ellie	04596 310352	
Ruby	a	
Pete	b	c

 What is the date next Tuesday?

LISTENING 2: UK AND US FESTIVALS AND CELEBRATIONS

1 Read the list of festivals. Match the words to the pictures.

> Christmas Easter Mother's Day
> US Independence Day Hallowe'en
> Thanksgiving

a   b   c

d   e   f

 Which festivals do you celebrate in your country?
What dates are Thanksgiving and Mother's Day this year?

2 03.18 **Listen to someone talking about the festivals and celebrations. Two festivals are only in the US, not in the UK. Which ones?**

SPEAKING 1: ENROLLING FOR A COURSE

1 Read the information in the form.

London City Language School – enrolment form

Family name	Costa
Given names	Maria
Date of Birth (DD/MM/YYYY)	07/11/1992
Address	4, Cross Street, Millchester
Postcode	SK38 5RR
Phone number	0161 458 6950
Email	mariacosta567@gmail.sp
Nationality	Spanish

You are the student, Maria. Complete the answers to the receptionist's questions.

Receptionist:	Hello, can I help you?
Student:	Good morning. Can I enrol for the English conversation class?
Receptionist:	Yes, of course. You just need to complete the enrolment form. We can do that now if you like. What's your name?
Student:	a _____
Receptionist:	And your date of birth? What's your date of birth?
Student:	b _____
Receptionist:	And where do you live?
Student:	c _____
Receptionist:	And what's your postcode?
Student:	d _____
Receptionist:	Fine. And what's your phone number?
Student:	e _____

3 Numbers, times and dates

Receptionist:	Just two more questions ... have you got an email address?
Student:	**f** _____
Receptionist:	And where are you from, what's your nationality?
Student:	**g** _____
Receptionist:	Great. So if I could just take payment, that is all done and you can start on Monday.
Student:	Lovely. Thank you very much.
Receptionist:	See you Monday.

03.19 **Now listen to the complete conversation and check your answers.**

2 03.20 **You are Maria. Listen to the receptionist and answer his questions.**

3 03.20 **Play the audio again. Answer the receptionist's questions with information about you.**

SPEAKING 2: IN A TOURIST OFFICE

1 You are a tourist in a tourist information office. You want information about the times of an art gallery and a concert. Complete the questions a–e.

Advisor:	Good morning. Can I help you?
Tourist:	Yes, please. I'd like some information about the City Art Gallery. **a** _____ _____ _____ _____ ?
Advisor:	Ten o'clock in the morning.
Tourist:	**b** And _____ _____ _____ _____ _____ ?
Advisor:	Seven thirty in the evening.
Tourist:	Thank you. And there is a concert today in the Royal Albert Hall. **c** _____ _____ _____ _____ _____ ?
Advisor:	Six o'clock.
Tourist:	**d** Great, and _____ _____ _____ _____ _____ ?
Advisor:	About two hours.
Tourist:	**e** _____ _____ _____ _____ finish?
Advisor:	About eight thirty. There's an interval of about 30 minutes.
Tourist:	Thank you.

2 03.21 **Now you are the tourist. Listen to the advisor and have the conversation.**

Reading and writing

READING: TOURIST POSTERS

 1 You are in the tourist information office. Look at the posters and leaflets. What information is there? Choose *Yes* or *No*.
  a The opening times of local libraries   Yes/~~No~~
  b Film times at a local cinema   Yes/No
  c The opening times of a zoo   Yes/No
  d The opening time of an art exhibition   Yes/No
  e The start time for a firework display   Yes/No

 2 Is there information about New Year's Day (Thursday 1 January)? Choose *Yes* or *No*.
  a The Rex cinema poster   ~~Yes~~/No
  b The firework display poster   Yes/No
  c Cheshire libraries poster   Yes/No
  d Chester Zoo poster   Yes/No

REX CINEMA

CHESHIRE LEISURE PARK

Films for Fri 2 until Thurs 8 January
Summer of Love
2.50 p.m., 6.10 p.m., 9.10 p.m.
Shrek
12.20 p.m. (Sunday only)
The End of Time
Late show: 11.30 p.m. Sat 3

BOOK NOW • 08712 231 231

3 Numbers, times and dates

BUXTON TOWN COUNCIL
NEW YEAR'S DAY
FIREWORK DISPLAY

**Doors open 6 p.m.
Fireworks at 7.30 p.m.
Hot food stalls
Live music**

VICTORIA PARADE, BUXTON

**Adults £5
Children £3
Family tickets £12
(2 adults and 2 children)**

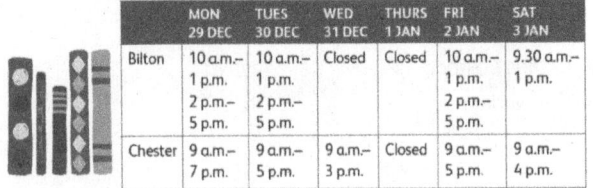

Cheshire Library
OPENING HOURS OVER NEW YEAR

	MON 29 DEC	TUES 30 DEC	WED 31 DEC	THURS 1 JAN	FRI 2 JAN	SAT 3 JAN
Bilton	10 a.m.–1 p.m. 2 p.m.–5 p.m.	10 a.m.–1 p.m. 2 p.m.–5 p.m.	Closed	Closed	10 a.m.–1 p.m. 2 p.m.–5 p.m.	9.30 a.m.–1 p.m.
Chester	9 a.m.–7 p.m.	9 a.m.–5 p.m.	9 a.m.–3 p.m.	Closed	9 a.m.–5 p.m.	9 a.m.–4 p.m.

For information or to renew your books outside of opening hours, please phone: 0845 148 0148.

Chester Zoo

	Opening time	Closing time
Mon 3 Nov to Tue 23 Dec	10 a.m.	4 p.m.
Wed 24 Dec	10 a.m.	3 p.m.
Christmas Day	Closed	Closed
Fri 26 Dec to Tues 30 Dec	10 a.m.	4 p.m.
New Year's Eve and New Year's Day	10 a.m.	3 p.m.
Fri 2 Jan to Sat 28 Feb	10 a.m.	4 p.m.

We're open every day from 10 a.m., except for Christmas Day, with FREE on-site parking.
Our opening hours change depending on the season and school holidays.
Don't forget – buy your tickets online and you can beat the queues with Fast Track admission.

3 Look at the information again and answer the questions.

a What day is the film 'Shrek'?   *Sunday*
b What time does 'Shrek' start?
c What day is the film 'Terminator'?
d What time does 'Terminator' start?
e What is the phone number for cinema tickets?
f What date is the firework display?
g What time does the firework display start?
h What is the phone number for tickets for the fireworks?
i What time does Chester library close on 29 December?
j What time does Chester library close on New Year's Eve?
k Does Bilton library open on New Year's Eve?
l What time does Bilton library close on 3 January?
m Does the zoo open on 25 December?
n Does the zoo open on 1 January?
o What time does the zoo close on 24 December?
p What time does the zoo open on 23 January?
q What time does the zoo close on 16 January?

WRITING 1: FESTIVALS AND CELEBRATIONS

Write about festivals and celebrations in your country.

Look at the audioscript from Listening 2 (download for free from the Teach Yourself Library app or www.library.teachyourself.com.) for ideas and help, then fill in the gaps.

Use the correct preposition – *in* + month or *on* + date.

Use capital letters for days and months.

Festivals and celebrations in _____ (your country)

The most important festivals and celebrations in _____ (your country) are probably _____ and _____ (the names of two important festivals). People also celebrate _____ and _____ (the names of two other festivals).

Some festivals happen on the same date each year. For example, _____ (name of the festival) is always on _____ (date)/in _____ (month).

The other festivals and celebrations happen on different dates each year. For example, this year, _____ (name of the festival) is on _____ (date). Last year, it was on _____ (date).

WRITING 2: GREETING CARDS

1 Look at the pictures of different festivals and celebrations.

What do we write on a greeting card for these festivals and celebrations? Match the phrases to the festivals.

Congratulations! *Happy Birthday!* *Happy Anniversary!*

Happy Mother's Day! *Happy New Year!* *Happy Diwali!*

Happy Thanksgiving! *Merry Christmas!*

 2 Look at the card. Choose a celebration or festival and write a card for a friend or someone in your family.

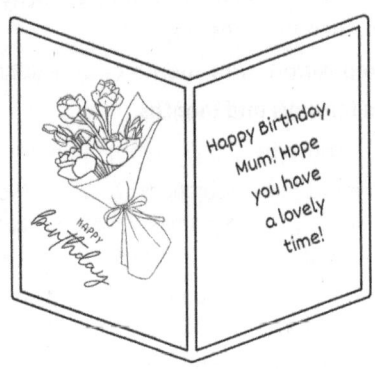

Test yourself

1 Put the words in the correct part of the table.

> ~~Tuesday~~ January summer
> morning March Monday
> afternoon autumn Wednesday
> Thursday December spring
> night April August evening
> Friday October winter Sunday

Days of the week	Months of the year	Seasons	Parts of the day
Tuesday			

2 Write the numbers in order, small to big.

Five hundred, ...

Five thousand five hundred
Five thousand five hundred and fifty
Five hundred and fifty
~~Five hundred~~
Five thousand
Five thousand and fifty-five
Five thousand and five
Five thousand and fifty
Five hundred and five
Five hundred and fifty-five

3 Read the sentences. The prepositions are not correct! Note the correct prepositions.

a He was born at *on* the 7th November 1986.
b His wife was born on _____ 1981.
c His daughter was born at _____ May.
d His daughter was born at _____ summer.
e Shops in the UK open on _____ ten o'clock.
f Shops in the UK open in _____ Sunday.
g Shops in the UK close on _____ night.
h Banks in the UK close on _____ the weekend.

4 Put the times in the correct part of the table.

> quarter past four 16.00
> twenty past five 5 p.m.
> twelve o'clock four thirty
> four in the morning four fifty

midnight	*twelve o'clock*
4 a.m.	
five o'clock in the afternoon	
half past four	
five twenty	
four o'clock in the afternoon	
ten to five	
4.15	

5 Write the dates in numbers and put them in order.

> 12th June 31st October
> 4th January 19th April
> 2nd December

4/1, ...

6 Fill in the gaps.
 a What time _____ it open?
 b How long does it _____?
 c When _____ you born?
 d What'_____ your phone number?

SELF CHECK

I CAN . . .
- . . . say numbers.
- . . . talk about the date and the time.
- . . . ask and answer questions about dates and times.

4

In this unit you will learn how to:
» speak and write about everyday routines and free time activities.
» speak and write about likes and dislikes.
» speak and write about ability using *can*.

Everyday life, sports and free time

Popular sports in the UK and the US

1 Which sports are popular in the UK? Which sports are popular in the US? What do you think? Look at the sports and complete the table.

> ice hockey swimming
> American football running
> cycling baseball basketball football

THE UK	THE US

2 Read the text and check your answers.

Sport is very popular in the United Kingdom. The number one sport is swimming, then running, then cycling and then football. About 25% of the UK population and over 50% of young people (16–25 years old) play sport once a week, but about 50% don't play any sport. A lot of people watch sport on television. People like watching football, rugby and tennis best. People all over the world watch English football with famous teams like Manchester United, Liverpool and Arsenal. 46% of English people watch football on television. Tennis is also popular. Wimbledon is the most famous tennis competition. It happens every year in June and nearly a quarter of people in the UK watch the final. In 2012 the Olympics were in the UK and 90% of the UK population watched some of it on television (51.9 million people). In the United States, the most popular sport is American football, then baseball, then basketball and then ice hockey. Not many people play these sports in the United Kingdom.

3 Complete the sentences with the correct numbers.

In the UK ...
- **a** _25%_ of people play sport once a week.
- **b** Over _____% of young people (16–25 years old) play sport once a week.
- **c** About _____% of people don't play any sport.
- **d** _____% of English people watch football on television.
- **e** _____% of people in the UK watch the Wimbledon final.
- **f** _____% of the UK population watched some of the 2012 Olympics on television.

04.01 **Listen and check your answers.**

Vocabulary builder

VOCABULARY 1: SPORTS

1 04.02 **Listen and repeat. Mark the stressed syllable, for example,** _football_. **Practise saying the words.**

| football | cricket | jogging | basketball | hockey | swimming |
| tennis | volleyball | baseball | rugby | golf | cycling |

2 Read the text on popular sports in the UK and the US again.

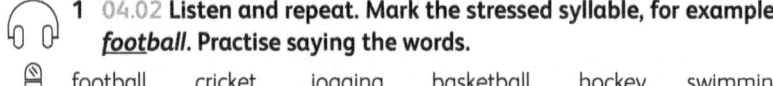

- **a** What is the most popular sport in the UK?   _swimming_
- **b** What is the most popular sport in the US?   _____
- **c** What is the most popular sport in your country?   _____

> **LANGUAGE TIP**
> We say play football, play cricket, play basketball, play hockey, but three sports in the list use a different verb. Which verb?

3 Complete the table. Match the sports with the correct verb.

play	football, *cricket, basketball, hockey* …
go	

VOCABULARY 2: OTHER LEISURE ACTIVITIES

1 Match the words to the pictures.

watch TV/television
go out with friends
listen to music
go shopping
~~read~~

go on the internet
go on social media
play computer games
go to the cinema
go to a museum/an art gallery

a   b   c   d   e

read

f   g   h   i   j

2 04.03 **Listen and repeat. Note the stressed syllable, for example, *watch TV*. Practise saying the words.**

What do you do in your free time?

4 Everyday life, sports and free time

Conversation 1: *Like/love/hate* + verb + *ing*

1 04.04 **Tom and Sandra are talking about free time. Listen to the conversation. Who has lots of free time?**

Sandra:	So Tom, what do you do in your free time?
Tom:	Well, I work every day and I don't have much free time during the week, but I spend the weekend relaxing. I love going to the cinema and I also like going out with friends. I don't like going to museums or art galleries but I love watching TV, particularly football. In the evenings, I am usually quite tired but I quite like reading and listening to music. I also like going on the internet but I hate playing computer games and I don't like using social media. What about you?
Sandra:	I don't work and so I have a lot more free time. I love going out with friends and family and I also quite like going to museums and art galleries. I like watching television but I don't like reading or listening to music. I have a new computer and I like going on the internet. I love going on Facebook™.

2 04.04 **Listen to the conversation again. Put or in the table.**

What do they like doing? ♡

What do they not like doing? ✖

Tom					
Sandra		♡			

Tom		♡		✖	
Sandra					

3 Match the sentences to the pictures.
  a ~~I quite like reading~~
  b I hate playing computer games.
  c I don't like using social media.
  d I like going on the internet.
  e I love going on Facebook™.

♡♡♡   _____

♡♡   _____

♡   *a I quite like reading.*

✖   _____

✖✖   _____

4 Look at the sentences in Exercise 3. What do we use after *love/like/hate*?

I	love like hate	verb + *ing*

4 Everyday life, sports and free time

04.05 **Look at the information in the table. Complete sentences a–g for Tom. Write sentences h–l for Sandra. Then listen and check your answers.**

	TOM	SANDRA
♡♡♡	a (talking with friends), b (watching TV)	h (having dinner with friends)
♡♡	c (having dinner with friends), d (using computer)	i (using computer)
♡	e (listening to music)	j (looking at art)
✗	f (looking at art)	k (reading), l (listening to music)
✗✗	g (playing video games)	

a I love *going to* the cinema.
b I _____ _____ TV.
c I _____ _____ _____ _____ friends.
d I _____ _____ _____ the internet.
e I _____ _____ _____ _____ music.
f I _____ _____ _____ _____ museums or art galleries.
g I _____ _____ computer games.

5 What about you? What do you like doing at the weekend? Finish the sentences.

I love _____

I like _____

I quite like _____

I don't like _____

I hate _____

VOCABULARY 3: EVERYDAY VERBS AND NOUNS

1 What do you do every day? Put the verbs in the correct part of the table for your days. Check any words you are not sure of in the dictionary.

~~get up~~

have a shower

get dressed

have breakfast

do the housework

have dinner

do the washing up

do the washing

go to bed

go to work

have lunch

do the cleaning

go out

do the shopping

get home

go online

MY DAYS		
every day	on working days	on days off (not working days)
get up		

Write the words in the every day column in the correct order for you.

4 Everyday life, sports and free time

2 **Match the times to the phrases.**

01.30   06.30   20.30   ~~10:00~~

get up early		go to bed early	
get up late	10:00	go to bed late	

3 04.06 **Listen and repeat. Note the stressed syllables, for example, _have_ a _shower_. Practise saying the words.**

4 **Cover the words in Exercise 1. Can you remember the verbs? Put the correct verb with each list in the table.**

		get	
the housework	a shower	up	to work
the cleaning	breakfast	dressed	out
the shopping	lunch	home	to bed
the washing	dinner	up early	to bed early
the washing up		up late	to bed late
			online

5 **Describe a typical day for you.**

VOCABULARY 4: HOW OFTEN?

Mon	Tues	Wed	Thurs	Fri	Sat	Sun
play tennis	do yoga		go to the gym	go out with friends	go to the cinema	watch football
Mon	**Tues**	**Wed**	**Thurs**	**Fri**	**Sat**	**Sun**
play tennis	do yoga		go to the gym	go out with friends	go out for lunch	
Mon	**Tues**	**Wed**	**Thurs**	**Fri**	**Sat**	**Sun**
	do yoga	play tennis	go to the gym	go out for lunch	go to the theatre	visit Mum and Dad
Mon	**Tues**	**Wed**	**Thurs**	**Fri**	**Sat**	**Sun**
play tennis	do yoga		go to the gym	go out with friends	visit Mum and Dad	go out for lunch

1 **Look at the calendar. Read the sentences. One is NOT true. Which one?**
   a I go out with friends three times a month.
   b I play tennis once a week.
   c I go out for lunch twice a month.
   d I always go to the gym on Thursday.
   e I usually play tennis on Monday.
   f I sometimes play tennis on Wednesday.
   g I never play tennis on Friday.

2 **How do we say *one time* in a week? How do we say *two times* in a month? Complete the table.**

_____ (one time)		day
_____ (two times)	a	week
three times		month

3 **Put the words in the correct part of the table.**

usually never always sometimes

	✓	✓	✓	✓
usually	✓	✓	✓	X
	✓	✓	X	X
	X	X	X	X

4 04.07 **Listen and repeat. Note the stressed syllables. How do we pronounce the word *a* in *once a month*? Practise saying the words.**

5 **Which sentences are correct English? Use the table to help you.**
   a I **always** cook dinner.
   b I cook dinner **always**.
   c I am **always** late.
   d I **always** am late.

4 Everyday life, sports and free time

	verb *to be*	always	**adjective**
I	am/is/are	usually	
You		sometimes	
He		never	late
She	always	**verb**	early
We	usually	cook/cooks dinner	
They	sometimes	go/goes to the gym	
	never	do/does the shopping	

6 Look at the table in Exercise 1. Complete the sentences.
a I go to the gym *once* a *week*.
b I visit my parents _____
c I _____ do yoga on Tuesday.
d I _____ go out with friends on Friday.
e I _____ go to the gym on Sunday.
f I _____ go out for lunch on Friday.

7 Complete sentences about you.
a I _____ once a day.
b I _____ twice a week.
c I _____ three times a day.
d I _____ once a month.
e At the weekend, I always _____
f I never _____
g I usually _____
h I am sometimes _____

VOCABULARY 5: SOCIAL MEDIA

1 Going online and using social media is a very popular way to spend free time. Choose the word to complete sentences about you.

I always / sometimes / never   go on Facebook.
I always / sometimes / never   go on Instagram.
I always / sometimes / never   watch videos on YouTube.
I always / sometimes / never   use WhatsApp.
I always / sometimes / never   use Snapchat.
I always / sometimes / never   go on TikTok.

2 What do you do on social media? Use the same words (always/sometimes/never) to complete sentences about you.

I _____ share, post or comment on social media posts.

I _____ look at and sometimes like photos, videos or posts.

I _____ send messages, chat or make calls.

I _____ follow friends or companies, celebrities or influencers.

I _____ find people who share my interests.

I _____ watch or upload content on video-sharing platforms such as YouTube or TikTok.

> **LANGUAGE TIP**
> Notice the different verbs we use with the different social media platforms.

Conversation 2: Present simple third person (*he* or *she*)

1 04.08 **Listen to the conversation about Joanna. Is it about a school day? Decide *Yes* or *No*.**

Tom:	Tell me about Joanna's typical day.
Sandra:	Well, she lives in London and she goes to school. She gets up early, at seven o'clock, and she goes to school at eight o'clock. She usually has lunch at school but sometimes she has lunch in a café. She gets home at about four o'clock.
Tom:	What does she do when she gets home?
Sandra:	Well, she often has a lot of homework and she usually finishes her homework before dinner. She never cooks dinner but she sometimes does the washing up. After dinner, she watches television or goes on the internet. She usually goes to bed at about ten o'clock.
Tom:	Does she like listening to music?
Sandra:	Oh yes, she listens to music all the time and she plays the piano quite well.

4 Everyday life, sports and free time

2 04.08 **Listen to the conversation again. Read the sentences and choose T (true) or F (false).**

Example: She goes to school at seven o'clock. T/F

a She always has lunch at school. T/F
b She has a lot of homework. T/F
c She doesn't cook dinner. T/F
d She finishes her homework after dinner. T/F
e She doesn't listen to music. T/F
f She goes to bed at eleven o'clock. T/F

3 Sandra tells us about Joanna's typical day. Use the correct verbs to complete spaces a–j in the table.

I YOU WE THEY	HE SHE + _____	I YOU WE THEY	HE SHE + _____	I YOU WE THEY	HE SHE + *IRREGULAR VERB*
play	a	watch	f	have	j
listen	b	finish	g		
live	c *lives*	do	h		
cook	d	go	i		
get	e				

88

4 How do we change verbs when we write about *he* and *she*? Put the rules in the correct place and complete the table in Exercise 3.

verb + s   verb + es (if the verb ends in *ss*, *x*, *ch*, *sh* or *o*)   ~~irregular verb~~

5 Fill in the table with more *he* or *she* verb forms.

I/YOU/WE/THEY	HE/SHE	I/YOU/WE/THEY	HE/SHE
use		say	
live		choose	
speak		know	
read	*reads*	decide	
write		see	
look		start	
practise		give	
put		help	

6 Look at the question and the negative sentence.

Do you speak French?   I don't speak Chinese.

a How do we make a question with *you* and *I*?
b How do we make a negative sentence with *you* and *I*?
c How do we make a question with *he* and *she*?
d How do we make a negative sentence with *he* and *she*?
e Fill in the gaps.

Does he _____ on social media?   He _____ go on social media.

> **LANGUAGE TIP**
>
> When we make questions or negatives, we use the simple form of the verb.
>
> Do you speaks English? ✗   Do you speak English? ✓
>
> He doesn't speaks French ✗   He doesn't speak French. ✓
>
> | + (add *s* to the verb for he/she) | – (don't add *s* to the verb) | ? (don't add *s* to the verb) |
> |---|---|---|
> | I/you/we/they + verb | I/you/we/they *don't* + verb | *Do* I/you/we/they + verb |
> | He/She/It + verb + *s* (or *es* or irregular) | He/She/It *doesn't* + verb | *Does* he/she/it + verb? |

7 Correct these sentences.
a He don't watch television.
b He doesn't listens to music.
c Do he use the computer?
d Does he goes to work early?

8 Look at the text. Change *I* to *she* and then change all the verbs.

I **get** up early and **go** to the gym at seven o'clock. I **have** a shower and breakfast and then I **go** to work. I **start** work at nine o'clock and **finish** at five thirty. I usually **have** lunch in a café near work. I **don't like** staying in the office for lunch. I sometimes **do** the shopping before I **go** home. I **get** home at about seven o'clock and **cook** dinner. In the evening, I usually **watch** television or **use** the computer. I **like** going on the internet. I don't **go** to bed late but I often **read** before I **go** to sleep.

Write some sentences about a friend or a person in your family.

CAN/CAN'T

1 Match the activities to the pictures a–i.

drive   ride a bike   sing   speak French
play the guitar   swim   cook
use a computer   use Microsoft Excel

a *play the guitar*   b _____   c _____

d _____   e _____   f _____

g _____   h _____   i _____

2 04.09 **Listen to Tom talking about his free time. Look at the three activities a–c. Tom can do one activity. Is it a, b or c?**

a   b   c

3 04.09 **Listen to Tom again. Are the sentences true (T) or false (F) about Tom?**

Example: He can drive.   T̶/F

a He can't play the guitar.   T/F
b He can't cook.   T/F
c He can use a computer.   T/F

4 Match the two sentences to the pictures.

> I can't do it.
> I can do it.

a _____   b _____

5 Look at the sentences. Correct the mistakes. Use the sentences about Tom and the table in Exercise 6 to help you.

Example: I can t̶o̶ swim.

a He cans cook.
b He can speaks French.
c I not can speak French.
d He no can ride a bike.
e You can play the piano?

4 Everyday life, sports and free time

6 Complete the table. Use the corrected sentences from Exercise 5.

		?
I You He/She/It **can** + verb We They	I You He/She/It **can't** + verb We They	I you **Can** he/she/it + verb? we they
I can swim.		

What activities can you do? Can you cook? Write sentences.

Listening, speaking and pronunciation

LISTENING: A JOURNALIST ASKS PEOPLE ABOUT THEIR EVERYDAY LIFE

1 04.10 **A journalist asks people about their everyday life for a TV programme. Listen to the conversations. Who doesn't work in the evening? Person 1, Person 2 or Person 3?**

2 04.10 **Listen to the conversations again. Read the sentences about Person 1 and Person 2. Choose T (true) or F (false).**

Person 1

- **a** She goes to the gym after work.   T/F
- **b** She finishes work at eight o'clock.   T/F
- **c** She cooks dinner every night.   T/F
- **d** She watches television in the evening.   T/F
- **e** She visits family at the weekend.   T/F
- **f** She loves going to the theatre.   T/F

Person 2

- **g** He gets up at four o'clock.   T/F
- **h** He finishes work at six o'clock.   T/F
- **i** His wife doesn't work.   T/F
- **j** His wife does the housework and the shopping.   T/F
- **k** He can play football well.   T/F
- **l** He loves listening to music and playing the guitar.   T/F

3 04.10 **Listen to the conversations again. Complete the sentences for Person 3.**

Example: She works _two_ evenings a week.
a She starts work at _____.
b She finishes work at about _____.
c She usually goes out on a _____ and _____ evening.
d She _____ football.
e She _____ Facebook™.

SPEAKING: TELLING SOMEONE ABOUT YOUR DAILY LIFE

A journalist asks you about your daily life. Answer the journalist's question for you.

We are asking people about their daily life. Can you tell me a little about yours?

PRONUNCIATION 1: THIRD PERSON SINGULAR VERB ENDINGS

1 04.11 **Listen to the pronunciation of these words:**

visits   plays   watches

How do we pronounce the final _s_?

2 04.12 **Listen to the verbs. Put them in the correct part of the table.**

reads watches visits
listens uses goes
takes gets finishes
stays starts plays

/S/	/Z/	/IZ/
visits	_plays_	_watches_

Practise saying the verbs.

PRONUNCIATION 2: *CAN* AND *CAN'T*

1 04.13 **Listen to the sentences. Which words are stressed?**

I can speak French but I can't speak Spanish. Can you?

Yes, I can, and I can speak Japanese. Can you speak Japanese?

No, I can't.

2 04.13 **Listen to the sentences again.**
How do we pronounce *can't*?
When do we pronounce *can* as /kæn/?
When do we pronounce *can* as /kən/?
Use the sentences to complete the table.

> No, I can't. I can speak French.
> Can you? I can't speak Spanish.
> Yes, I can.

affirmative		/kən/
question	*Can you?*	/kən/
negative		/kɑːnt/
short answer negative		/kɑːnt/
short answer affirmative		/kæn/

3 04.14 **Listen and repeat.**

PRONUNCIATION 3: QUESTIONS IN THE PRESENT SIMPLE

1 04.15 **Listen to the sentences. Which words are stressed?**

Where does he work?

What time does he start?

When do you go?

What do you cook?

2 04.15 **Listen to the sentences again.**
How do we pronounce *do* in questions?
How do we pronounce *does* in questions?
Practise saying the questions.

Put *do* and *does* in the correct part of the table.

Question word	Do/does	Subject	Main verb
When	____/də/	you	go?
What			cook?
Where	____/dəz/	he/she	work?
What time			start?

3 04.15 **Listen and repeat.**

Reading and writing

READING 1: A FREE TIME QUESTIONNAIRE

 1 Look at the questionnaire. Does the person do a lot of things in their free time?

Free time questionnaire – How do you spend your free time?					
How often do you do the following activities? Choose one answer for each question.					
	Every day	Three or more times a week	Once or twice a week	Once a month	Never
Watch television	✔				
Go shopping			✔		
Go to a museum or art gallery					✔
Read a book	✔				
Play a sport		✔			
Go out with friends		✔			
Go on the internet	✔				
Drive a car			✔		
Visit family				✔	
Go to the cinema				✔	

2 Look at the questionnaire again. Are the sentences true (T) or false (F)?

    a He plays a sport three or more times a week.   T/F
    b He never reads.   T/F
    c He watches television every day.   T/F
    d He plays sport every day.   T/F
    e He visits family once a month.   T/F
    f He goes to the cinema once or twice a week.   T/F

3 Fill in the questionnaire about you.

4 Everyday life, sports and free time

WRITING 1: FREE TIME

 Use your answers to the free time questionnaire. Write five sentences about your free time.

READING 2: A PERSONAL PROFILE

 1 Tina is a student from Portugal. She wants an English-speaking penfriend. She finds three profiles on a penfriend website. Match the profiles with the pictures.

a   b   c

Margaret

I live in London and I speak English. I want penfriends from the UK. I am retired and so I have a lot of free time. I love going out with friends and visiting family. I also love visiting museums and art galleries and going to the cinema. I don't like playing sports but I love watching sports, particularly tennis and athletics. I can't play the piano but I love listening to music. I can use a computer and I like going on the internet but I don't like using Facebook™.

Susan

I live in New York and work full-time for an IT company. I can speak German, English and Japanese but I can't speak French very well. I want to practise my French so I want a penfriend from a French-speaking country. I love going to the theatre and the cinema but I also like watching television in the evenings after work. I don't like cooking but I love going out with friends to restaurants. I listen to music every day and I love listening to jazz music in particular. I play tennis once a week and go swimming three or four times a week. I work with computers so when I come home I don't like using the computer or going online.

Tracy

I live in Canada and I can speak English but I can't speak French. I want penfriends from all over the world. I love animals. I have a cat and a horse and I ride every day. I play lots of other sports, usually tennis and football and at the weekend I sometimes go fishing with my Dad. I love going on the internet and playing computer games but I don't really like watching television. I can't play the guitar very well, but I love playing and listening to music.

2 Read the profiles again and complete the table.

	MARGARET	SUSAN	TRACY
♡	going out with friends		
✗			
			speak English
??		speak French	

3 Who does Tina choose? Margaret, Susan or Tracy?

WRITING 2: A PERSONAL PROFILE

1 Write your personal profile. Use the examples for help and ideas. Write about what you love doing, what you like doing, what you don't like doing, what you can do and what you can't do.

2 Look online at a real penfriend website and register. Writing to a penfriend helps your English! Look at:

www.globalpenfriends.com

http://usa.ipfpenfriends.com/

www.penpalworld.com/

Test yourself

1 Correct the spelling mistakes in the sports.
- **a** footbal
- **b** criket
- **c** joging
- **d** basketbal
- **e** hocky
- **f** swiming
- **g** tenis
- **h** vollyball
- **i** basball
- **j** rogby
- **k** gof
- **l** cyclng

2 How many activities and everyday verbs can you remember? Fill in the table.

DO	HAVE	GET	GO
the washing	breakfast	home	jogging
___	___	___	___
___	___	___	___
___	___	___	___

3 Write the sentences in correct English.

Example: I get up usually at seven o'clock.   *I usually get up at seven o'clock.*
- **a** I am have breakfast at eight o'clock.
- **b** I go to English classes one time per week.
- **c** I never am late.
- **d** I love to learn English.
- **e** I not like do homework.
- **f** I can't to speak English very well.
- **g** My teacher help me a lot.
- **h** My girlfriend speak English very well.

4 Use the information in brackets. Complete the sentences. X = negative.

Examples: (She/watch) *She watches* television every evening.

(She/X go shopping) *She doesn't go shopping* on Mondays.
- **a** (She/go) _____ to the gym every day.
- **b** (He/have) _____ breakfast at eight o'clock.
- **c** (He/ X work) _____ in the evening.
- **d** I play tennis (two times/week) _____
- **e** I (♡ go) _____ to the cinema.
- **f** He (✗ cook) _____ dinner.

g He (♡♡♡ watch) _____ TV.
h She (✘ go) _____ on Facebook™.
i I (play) _____ the piano.
j He (play) _____ the guitar.

5 Look at the sentences. Change *I* to *he* and then change all the verbs.
  a I love going out with friends. _____
  b I quite like going to the cinema. _____
  c I don't like using social media. _____
  d I hate doing the housework. _____
  e I always get up early in the summer. _____
  f I don't have breakfast at home. _____
  g I have lunch at work. _____
  h I sometimes go to bed after midnight. _____
  i I go to the gym twice a week. _____
  j I am never late for work. _____
  k I go out for lunch on Sunday. _____
  l I don't go to the gym at the weekend. _____
  m I can speak Portuguese. _____
  n I can't use a computer very well. _____
  o I usually finish work late. _____
  p I cook dinner every night. _____
  q I start work at seven o'clock in the morning. _____
  r I watch television every evening. _____

6 Complete the sentences with the correct word or phrase

> cook   cooking   cooks

a I can _____.
b I like _____.
c Does he _____?
d I _____ dinner every night.
e I don't _____ at the weekend.
f They often _____ lunch on Sunday.
g He _____ lunch every day.
h She doesn't like _____.
i Do you _____ after work?
j He can't _____ very well.
k I sometimes _____ dinner.
l He loves _____.
m She doesn't _____ very well.
n She never _____ lunch.
o He doesn't _____.

SELF CHECK

I CAN ...

- ... speak and write about everyday routines and free-time activities.
- ... speak and write about likes and dislikes.
- ... speak and write about ability using *can*.

5

In this unit you will learn how to:
» ask how people feel.
» say how you are.
» talk about plans and preferences.
» make and respond to suggestions and invitations.

Going out

My progress tracker

Popular places for going out

1 When people go out, where do they go?

What do you think? Put pictures a–c in order from the most popular (1) to the least popular (3).

a   b   c

2 When people go to a pub or restaurant, what do they do?

What do you think? Read the sentences and choose T (true) or F (false).

a	People can smoke in British pubs.	T/F
b	Children can buy an alcoholic drink in a pub in the UK.	T/F
c	If the meal cost £40, people usually leave a tip of about £7.	T/F
d	People sometimes leave a tip in pubs.	T/F
e	People usually go out at about eleven o'clock at night.	T/F
f	People never have a meal at the pub.	T/F

3 Now read the text and check your answers.

● GOING OUT

A lot of people in the UK like going out with friends or family. The most popular activity is going to a restaurant. Going to a pub is very popular and going to the cinema is also quite popular. In the evening, people often go out at between 8 and 9 p.m. Many pubs and restaurants close at around 11 p.m. so this is often the time that people go home. If you have something to eat in a restaurant, you usually leave a tip of 10% of your bill. People don't always leave a tip in cafés or pubs. In pubs, cafés and restaurants in the UK, you can't smoke. You can't buy an alcoholic drink in a pub or restaurant until you are 18 years old. When people go to the pub they don't always have a meal. Sometimes they just have a drink.

Vocabulary builder

VOCABULARY 1: ASKING HOW PEOPLE ARE AND RESPONDING

1 Put the conversation in the correct order. Start with c.
   a Very well.
   b How are you?
   c Hello Amy!
   d Fine, thank you. How are you?
   e Hello.

2 A friend asks *How are you?*

Put 🙂 or 🙂🙂 or 🙂🙂🙂 for each answer.
   a Fine.   🙂🙂
   b So-so.   _____
   c I'm good, thanks.   _____
   d Not bad.   _____
   e Very well.   _____
   f I'm OK.   _____

3 05.01 **Listen to the question and the answers. Note the stress, for example, *How are you?* Practise saying the question and the answers.**

What about you? How are you today?

VOCABULARY 2: SOCIAL ACTIVITIES

1 Match the activities and the pictures.

go to the pub

go to the cinema

go to the theatre

go to an art gallery

go to a restaurant or a café

go to someone's house for a meal

go to a concert

2 There are different ways to say some of the activities. Put four of the phrases from Exercise 1 next to the phrases with a similar meaning.

a go out for a meal/dinner/lunch/something to eat _____
b go round for dinner or lunch _____
c go and see a film _____
d go out for a drink _____

3 05.02 **Listen and repeat. Note the stress, for example, _go_ to a _concert_. Practise saying the words.**

4 Correct the mistakes in the sentences.
a I like going to a cinema.   *I like going to the cinema.*
b He like going out for a dinner.
c She like going the theatre.
d I like going to pub.
e I like going to the restaurant.
f They like go out for meal.

When you go out, what do you like doing?

5 Cover the list of social activities in Exercise 1. Look at the pictures. Can you remember how to say them?

VOCABULARY 3: TIME PHRASES

1 Look at the tables. Fill in the gaps a–f.

today	Monday
a *yesterday*	Sunday
b	Tuesday
the day before yesterday	Saturday
the day after tomorrow	**c**

today	Friday
yesterday	**d**
e	Wednesday
tomorrow	**f**
the day after tomorrow	**g**

2 Today is Monday 10th July. Complete sentences a-c. Put one word in each gap. Use the table to help you.

a _____ Monday is 17th July.
b _____ Monday was 3rd July.
c _____ Thursday is 13th July.

last ←	Monday, Tuesday, Wednesday …
	weekend
this	week
	month
⟶ next	year

3 Today is Wednesday 3rd September. Put the missing dates in the table.

Last Monday	a
Next Monday	b
This Friday	c
Last Friday	d
Next Wednesday	e
This Thursday	f

4 05.03 **Listen and repeat. Note the stress, for example, _yes_terday. Practise saying the words.**

Conversation 1: Making, accepting and declining an invitation

1 05.04 **Read and listen to three conversations. What do they decide to do and when? Fill in the table.**

a Linda and Paula

Linda:	Hi Paula. How are you?
Paula:	I'm very well, thanks Linda. How are you?
Linda:	I'm OK. Would you like to go to the cinema next weekend?
Paula:	Yes, that would be great. When?
Linda:	Is Friday evening any good?
Paula:	I'm really sorry, I can't do Friday. Are you free on Saturday?
Linda:	Yes, Saturday is fine.

b Sam and Pete

Sam:	Hi Pete. How are you?
Pete:	I'm good. And you?
Sam:	Yes, very well. Do you fancy going to the pub sometime?
Pete:	Yes, I'd love to. When?
Sam:	How about tomorrow?
Pete:	I'm afraid I can't. Tomorrow is no good. Are you doing anything the day after tomorrow?
Sam:	Let's see, that's Friday. Yes, Friday's great.

c Maria and Susana

Maria:	Hello Susana.
Susana:	Hi Maria.
Maria:	How are you?
Susana:	Well. How about you?
Maria:	Not bad. A bit tired. I had a really long day yesterday – and the day before yesterday!
Susana:	Do you want to go for a coffee?
Maria:	Yes, I'd love to. Now?
Susana:	Yes. There's a really nice café near here. Are you ready?
Maria:	Let's go!

		WHAT	WHEN
a	Linda and Paula	*go to the cinema*	
b	Sam and Pete		*Friday*
c	Maria and Susana		

 2 05.04 **Listen again. How do Linda, Sam and Susana invite their friends to do something? Fill in the gaps.**

Linda	**a** _Would_ you like **b** _____ **c** _____ to the cinema?
Sam	**d** _____ you **e** _____ **f** _____ to the pub?
Susana	**g** _____ you want **h** _____ **i** _____ for a coffee?

3 Complete a–c in the table with either *to do* or *doing*.

a	Would		like _____	
b	Do	you	fancy _____	something?
c	Do		want _____	

4 Look at the different ways to invite people to do something in Exercise 3. Which one is the most polite? Which two are informal (with friends)?

5 05.05 Listen to the invitations. Note the stress, for example, *Would you like to go to the cinema?* Practise saying the invitations.

6 **Invite a close friend. Complete the invitations with the missing words.**
   a _____ for a coffee?
   b _____ for dinner?
   c _____ and see a film?

7 **Now invite someone you don't know well (for example, a work colleague) to do the same activities. Complete the questions in Exercise 6.**

8 **How do people answer? Complete the conversations.**

SAYING YES 😃	
Yes, ____ *would* _____ ____ (Paula)	
Yes, ____ ____ ____ (Pete and Maria)	

SAYING NO 😃	
I'm ____ ____ *I can't*. (Paula)	
I'm *afraid* ____ ____ (Pete)	
	time/date
I ____ *do*	Friday next week eight thirty the morning April 4
time/date	
Thursday Next week Six o'clock The evening July 23	____ ____ *good.*

9 05.06 Listen to the answers. Note the stress, for example, *Yes, that would be great.* Practise saying the answers.

10 05.07 **Here is your diary. Listen to the different invitations and answer 😊. For example:**

You hear: Would you like to go for coffee on Sunday morning?

You look at the diary and say: Yes, I'd love to.

11 Look at your diary again. Invite a friend to do different things. You already have some ideas (?) in your diary.

Then invite a colleague to go out. Use the ideas in your diary, or different ideas!

Vocabulary builder

VOCABULARY 4: USING *IT'S TOO* + ADJECTIVE

1 Can you remember these adjectives from Units 1–4? Fill in the missing letters.

Example: sm _all_

a n_c_
b q_ _ _t
c lov_ _y
d b_ _ _tiful
e gr_ _t
f n_w
g t_p_c_l
h n_ _sy
i b_g

2 Complete the table with these adjectives.

bad expensive good cheap

Cost or price	££££££££££££ **a** It's _____	£ **c** It's _____
In general	😐 **b** It's _____	🙂 **d** It's _____

3 Look at these sentences. Which one is negative?

It's quite big. It's really big.
It's very big. It's too big.

> **LANGUAGE TIP**
>
> *Too* + adjective has a negative (not good) meaning 😐.

4 Look at the pictures. Finish the sentences using the adjectives:

noisy expensive small big

a It's too big.

b It's _____ _____

c It's _____ _____!

d It's _____ _____

5 05.08 Listen to the adjectives and phrases. Note the stress, for example, *expensive*, *too big*. Practise saying the words.

Conversation 2: Making suggestions and arrangements

1 05.09 **It's Saturday night and Janet and Martin are at home. Listen to the conversation and answer the questions.**
  a Does Janet go out?
  b Does Martin go out?

Janet:	It's Saturday evening. I don't know what to do.
Martin:	How about going out for a meal?
Janet:	No, I'm not very hungry.
Martin:	Why don't we go to the cinema?
Janet:	No, it's too expensive.
Martin:	Let's watch TV.
Janet:	No, it's not very interesting.
Martin:	How about a drink?
Janet:	No, it's too noisy at the pub and I'm too tired.
Martin:	Fine. You stay here. I'm going out on my own!

2 Read the conversation. Note the phrases Martin uses to make suggestions. Fill in the gaps a–c with the words from the conversation.

a _Why don't we_	go to the cinema?	d _____
b _____	going out for a meal? a drink?	e _____
c _____	watch TV	f _____

Now put the three different ways of making suggestions in the correct spaces d–f.

How about + verb + *ing* or noun?

Why don't we + verb?

Let's + verb

> **LANGUAGE TIP**
>
> Janet says *no* 🙂 to everything! Here are phrases for saying *yes* 🙂:
>
> *That's a <u>good</u> idea.   That sounds <u>good</u>.*

3 Look at Units 1–4. Find positive adjectives and complete the gaps to say *yes*.

That's a _____ idea. That sounds _____

4 05.10 Listen and repeat. Note the stress, for example, <u>How</u> about going <u>out</u> for a <u>meal</u>? Practise saying the suggestions and answers.

5 Correct the mistakes.
   a Let's going out for lunch.
   b Why we don't meeting at the train station?
   c That's sounding great. Let's meet two o'clock.
   d Why not we go out for a drink?
   e How about meet in The King's Head at seven tomorrow?

6 Make suggestions about going out.
   a How about/go out for lunch
   b Let's/the Manchester Deli/one o'clock
   c Why don't we/film
   d How about/in front of the cinema/six o'clock

Conversation 3: Talking about preferences

1 05.11 Listen to the conversation. Do they decide to go to a pub or to a café?

2 05.11 Listen to the conversation again and read the sentences. Choose T (true) or F (false).
   a Kevin and Shona decide to go out for lunch.   T/F
   b Kevin is happy to have a meal.   T/F
   c Kevin is happy to go to The Coffee Shop.   T/F
   d Kevin likes the Downtown Deli more than The Coffee Shop. T/F

Kevin:	Let's go out for lunch.
Shona:	That's a good idea. Do you want to have a meal at the pub?
Kevin:	I like the pub but it's too expensive. I'd prefer to have a sandwich at a café.
Shona:	Yes, me too. There's a really lovely café near here.
Kevin:	The Coffee Shop?
Shona:	Yes.
Kevin:	Mmm. It's OK but it's too busy. I'd rather go to the Downtown Deli. It's really nice and quiet.
Shona:	OK. Let's go.

3 **Read the conversation again. Find two phrases for saying you want one thing more than another thing. Then complete these sentences.**

a The pub ☺ is OK but I _____ _____ _____ go to a café ☺ ☺.

b A meal ☺ is OK but I _____ _____ _____ have a sandwich ☺ ☺.

c The Coffee Shop ☺ is OK but I _____ _____ go to the Downtown Deli ☺ ☺.

4 **Look at the sentences. What do we say after *would prefer*? What do we say after *would rather*? Fill in the gaps in the table.**

> How about a meal at the pub?

I You He She We They	would 'd	prefer _____ _____ a sandwich.
		rather _____ a sandwich.

5 Going out

5 Read the sentences. Only one is correct. Find the correct sentence.
  a He rather to go to a café.
  b I would prefer go to the cinema.
  c They'd prefer to go in the evening.
  d I'd prefer to going on Monday.

6 05.12 **Listen and repeat. Note the stress, for example, *I'd prefer to go to the cinema*. Practise saying the sentences.**

7 Make sentences using *prefer* and *rather*.

Example: A sandwich is OK but I'd rather have a meal.

☺	☺ ☺
a a sandwich	a meal
b a glass of water	a glass of wine
c a restaurant	the pub
d a cup of coffee	a cup of tea
e the TV	the cinema

Conversation 4: Using the present continuous for plans

1 05.13 **Listen to the conversation. What does Sam suggest?**

Sam:	Hi Linda. How are you?
Linda:	I'm very well. How are you?
Sam:	I'm good, thanks. Do you fancy going to the cinema sometime this week?
Linda:	Yes, that would be great. When?
Sam:	Are you doing anything on Friday?
Linda:	I'm really sorry, I can't do Friday because my mum is coming to London for the day and we are going out for lunch. Is Saturday any good?
Sam:	I can't do Saturday because I'm going to a concert with my brother. How about Sunday? Are you free on Sunday?
Linda:	Sunday is great.

2 05.13 **Listen again and read the conversation. Answer the questions.**
  a Which day **can't** Linda go to the cinema?
  b Which day **can't** Sam go to the cinema?
  c Which day **can** they go to the cinema?
  d What word do Linda and Sam use **just before** they say **why** they can't go out?

  ... _____ my mum is coming to London.

  ... _____ I'm going to a concert.

> **LANGUAGE TIP**
> Use the word *because* for an answer to the question *Why...?*

3 05.13 **Listen again. Answer the questions by filling in the gaps.**
  a Why can't Linda go to the cinema on Friday? What does she say about her plans?
     My mum _____ _____ to London for the day and we _____ _____ out for lunch.
  b Why can't Sam go to the cinema on Saturday? What does he say about his plans?
     I _____ _____ to a concert with my brother.

4 Complete spaces a–f in the table.

SUBJECT	VERB *TO BE*	VERB + *ING*	
My mum g_____ h_____	a _____	b _____	to London for the day.
We i_____ j_____	c _____	d _____	out for lunch.
I	e _____	f _____	to a concert with my brother.

Now complete spaces g–j by putting *he*, *she*, *you* and *they* in the correct place in the subject column.

5 Look at the sentences about the grammar. Choose T (true) or F (false).
  a This is the present continuous tense.   T/F
  b We make it with *am*, *is* or *are* + verb + *ing*.   T/F
  c We use it to talk about planned and arranged activities in the future.   T/F
  d Planned or arranged usually means other people know about it, or it is in our diary or on a calendar.   T/F

6 05.14 **Listen and repeat. Note the stress, for example, *My mum is coming to London*. How do we pronounce the words *am* and *are*?**

We are /ə/ going out for lunch.

I am /əm/ going to a concert.

Practise saying the sentences.

7 Look at the diary. We can use present continuous for most of the things but not all. Which activities can't we describe with present continuous and why?

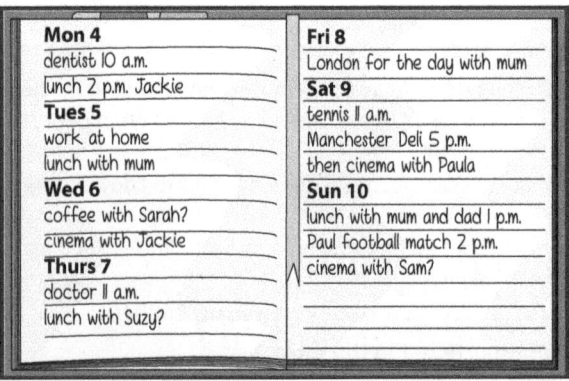

8 Look at Linda's sentences about her plans and arrangements for next week. Correct the mistakes. There are two mistakes in each sentence.

 a On Tuesday I going to the dentist.
 b On Wednesday I am work at home.
 c On Tuesday I having lunch with dad.
 d On Thursday Mum and I are go to London for the day.
 e On Friday I meet Paula at the Manchester Deli.
 f On Saturday morning we is going to the cinema.
 g On Saturday I have lunch with mum and dad at one o'clock.
 h On Monday afternoon Paul playing football at three o'clock.

9 Complete the sentences about Linda's plans and arrangements for next week.

 a On Monday, she is _____ and she _____.
 b On Wednesday, Jackie and Linda _____.
 c On Thursday _____.
 d On Saturday morning _____.
 e On Sunday she _____

10 Look again at Linda and Sam's conversation. Complete Sam's question.

a _____ anything on Friday?

Use the words in the box to make three more questions with a similar meaning.

> Friday Sunday Saturday free
> good about you any on

b Is _____?
c Are _____?
d How _____?

11 05.15 Listen and repeat. Note the stress, for example, *Are you doing anything on Friday?* Practise saying the questions.

Listening and speaking

LISTENING 1: PLANNING TO MEET

1 05.16 Listen to two friends, Jack and Rachel.
a What do they decide to do?
b When and where are they meeting?

2 Listen again and read the sentences. Choose T (true) or F (false).

a Rachel is very well. T/F
b Jack suggests going to see a film. T/F
c Jack is working on Tuesday and Thursday evening. T/F
d Rachel's brother is coming for dinner on Wednesday. T/F
e Jack can go to the cinema at the weekend but he would prefer to go on Monday. T/F
f Rachel is not free on Monday. T/F
g Jack doesn't want to spend too much money. T/F
h Jack suggests the Black Dog pub. T/F
i The Black Dog is cheap. T/F
j The café is cheap if you eat before six o'clock. T/F

LISTENING 2: PLANS AND ARRANGEMENTS

1 05.17 Listen to two friends (Simon and Paula).
a What do they decide to do?
b When and where are they meeting?

2 05.17 **Listen again and choose the correct answer.**
a Simon is **OK/good**.
b Simon is free on **Tuesday/Wednesday**.
c Paula is going out for lunch on **Tuesday/Saturday**.
d Simon would rather go to the gallery **at the weekend/on Wednesday**.
e Paula **is/isn't** free on Wednesday.
f **Simon/Paula** doesn't want to spend too much money.
g **Simon/Paula** doesn't like noisy places.
h **Simon/Paula** suggests going to a café.

SPEAKING 1: YOUR FRIEND INVITES YOU OUT

1 You meet Susan and arrange to go out. Read the conversation and prepare your answers.

Susan:	Hi. How are you?
You:	**Reply and ask how Susan is.**
Susan:	I'm very well. Hey, do you fancy going out sometime?
You:	**Say yes and ask what she wants to do.**
Susan:	How about going to the cinema? There's a really good film on at the moment.
You:	**Say yes and ask when.**
Susan:	Is this Thursday any good? I am working Tuesday and Wednesday evening but I am free on Thursday.
You:	**Say no, explain why and suggest the weekend.**
Susan:	Mmm, maybe, but tickets are more expensive at the weekend. I'd rather go during the week. How about next Monday? Are you free on Monday?
You:	**Say yes, and suggest going out for something to eat.**
Susan:	Great idea.
You:	**Suggest Pizza House near the cinema, ask if Susan knows it.**
Susan:	Yes, I do. It's very nice but it's quite expensive and too noisy.
You:	**Agree and ask what she suggests.**
Susan:	There's a really nice little café near the cinema called Dinner Time. I think it's really cheap if you eat before seven o'clock. I'd prefer to go there.
You:	**Agree.**
Susan:	How about meeting there at six?
You:	**Agree.**

2 05.18 **Listen to Susan and have the conversation. Then try to have the conversation without looking at the text.**

SPEAKING 2: INVITING YOUR FRIEND TO GO OUT

1 Now you meet Paul and arrange to go out. Read the conversation and prepare your answers.

You:	**Say hello and ask how Paul is.**
Paul:	I'm OK thanks. How about you?
You:	**Say how you are and ask if he wants to go out.**
Paul:	Yes! That would be great. What do you fancy doing?
You:	**Suggest going to an art gallery.**
Paul:	That's a brilliant idea. I'd love to. When?
You:	**Say you are working Monday and Wednesday and suggest Tuesday.**
Paul:	I'm really sorry I can't, because I'm going out for lunch. How about Saturday?
You:	**Say you would prefer to go next week, say why.**
Paul:	No problem, which day is good for you?
You:	**Suggest Wednesday.**
Paul:	Wednesday is fine. How about going out for something to eat first? There's a really nice restaurant about five minutes away, Brad's Diner, do you know it?
You:	**Say yes, you know it but say why you don't like it.**
Paul:	Mmm, yes, maybe... So what do you suggest?
You:	**Suggest the café in the gallery, say why you would rather go there.**
Paul:	Yes, that sounds better.
You:	**Suggest meeting at twelve.**
Paul:	Great. See you then.

2 05.19 **Listen to Paul and have the conversation. Start by saying** *Hello* **and asking Paul how he is. Practise until you can have the conversation with your book closed!**

Reading and writing

READING: A PARTY INVITATION

1 Match the words to the pictures of different types of celebration.

birthday wedding New Year

a   b   c

2 Look at the two invitations and the replies. Read the sentences and choose T (true) or F (false).

a The invitations are for the same day. T/F
b The celebrations are in different towns. T/F
c Louise can go to the 40th birthday party and the wedding. T/F
d There is dinner at the 40th birthday celebration. T/F
e The wedding celebration is at a pub. T/F
f 'RSVP' means please reply and tell me if you are coming or not. T/F
g Louise is going to the birthday party. T/F

Party
Joanna is 40!
Please come and celebrate my birthday!

Drinks at The Swan Inn, Malmsbury
on Saturday April 28
From 9pm onwards
RSVP

Wedding!
Robin and Alice
are getting married
on Saturday 28 April.
Please come and celebrate
with us
at the Royal Ship Hotel, Telsford
7pm for dinner at 8pm
RSVP

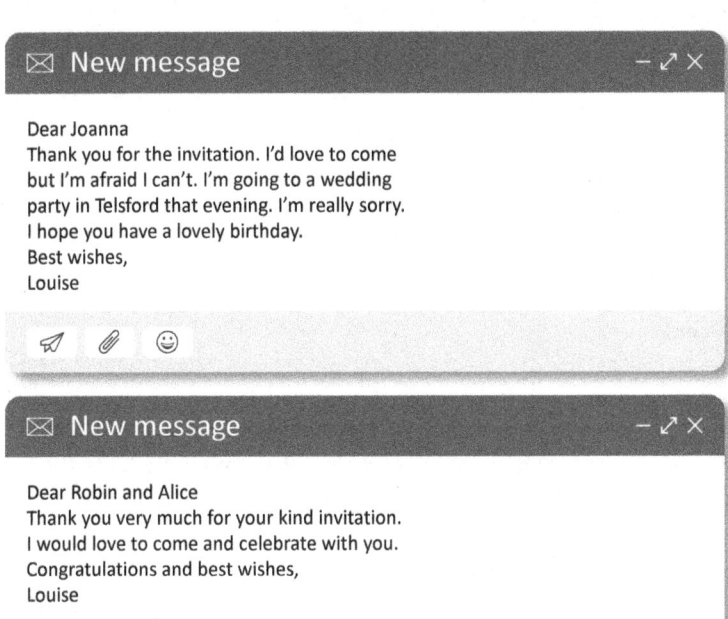

WRITING: EMAIL INVITATIONS: MAKING AND CHANGING PLANS

1 Read the emails.

a Who wrote the first email and who wrote the second email?
b What do Linda and Paula want to do?
c When do they arrange to meet?

> ✉ New message
>
> Hi Paula. Good to hear from you 😊! **I'm very well.**
> I'd love to go for a coffee. **I can't do Thursday** because I'm going to the dentist 😖 but Friday is great. Yes, I know Coffee City ... it's OK but it's quite expensive. **I'd prefer to go** to the little café on New Street, The Tea Pot. It's lovely.
> What do you think? **Why don't we meet at 11 on Friday?**
> Linda

2 There are some highlighted phrases in the emails. Re-write the emails. Change the highlighted phrases but don't change the meaning.

Example: I'm very well: *I'm fine, thanks.*

How many different ways you can think of to say the same thing?

3 Now write a reply to Paula's email (use Linda's email to help you).
- Say you would love to go for coffee.
- Explain you can't do Friday (think of a different reason why).
- Agree to Thursday.
- Explain why you don't want to go to Coffee City (think of a different reason why).
- Suggest the new café next to the market, Central Stop, and say why.
- Explain you would prefer to go in the afternoon (think of a reason why).
- Suggest a time on Thursday afternoon.

4 Write an email inviting a friend to go out. Use Paula's email to help you.
- Ask how she is.
- Invite her for a drink.
- Explain you are working every day this week but not next week.
- Ask if she can meet on Tuesday or Wednesday next week.
- Suggest the pub near the train station, The Red Lion.
- Explain you would prefer lunchtime.
- Suggest 12 p.m.

Test yourself

1 How many different answers can you remember to the question **How are you?**
2 Look at the pictures. Complete the activities. Some (*) have more than one way of saying the same thing. Use the key words to help you.

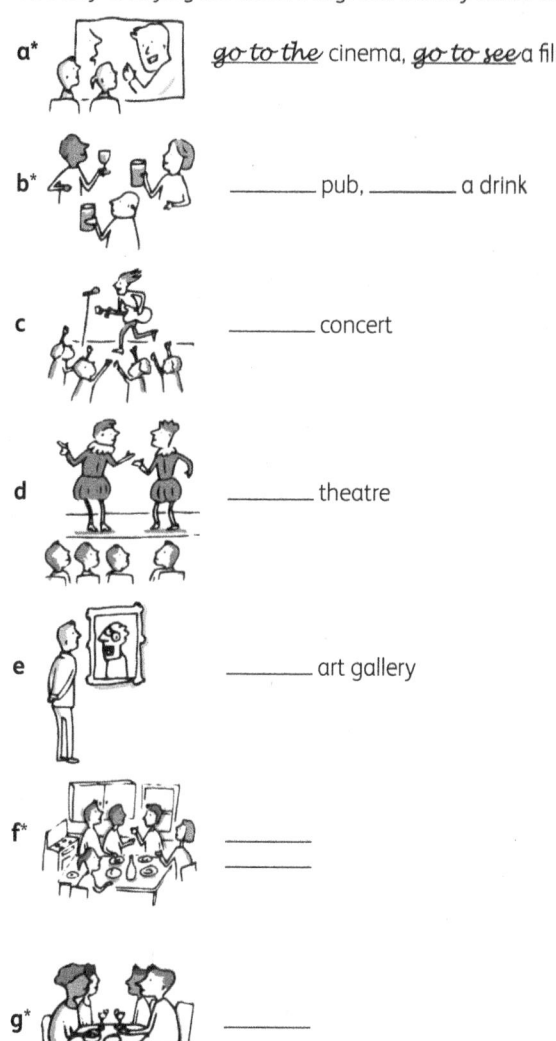

a* _go to the_ cinema, _go to see_ a film

b* _____ pub, _____ a drink

c _____ concert

d _____ theatre

e _____ art gallery

f* _____
   _____

g* _____

3 Fill in the gaps.

a _____ you like _____ out for a meal?
😊 Yes, I _____ _____ to.

b _____ you fancy _____ for a coffee?
😊 I'm _____ _____, I _____.

c Do you _____ to _____ to the cinema?
😊 Yes, _____ _____ _____ great.

d _____ you fancy a meal?
☹️ _____ afraid I _____ _____ _____ have a cup of coffee.

e Would you _____ a cup of tea?
_____ _____ _____ have a meal.

f _____ _____ fancy a sandwich?

g How _____ meeting on Friday?
☹️ _____ _____ do Friday.

h _____ meet at six o'clock.
☹️ Six o'clock _____ no _____.

i _____ _____ _____ meet at the train station?
😊 That's _____ _____ _____.

j How _____ a café?
😊 _____ _____ great.

k _____ meet in The Queen's Head.
☹️ No, it's _____ noisy.

l _____ _____ The Red Lion?
☹️ No, it's _____ expensive.

m _____ you _____ on Tuesday?
☹️ _____ _____, I can't do Tuesday. _____ _____ meeting my dad.

n _____ you _____ anything at the weekend?
My brother _____ visiting us.

o _____ _____ Monday?
We _____ _____ out for dinner.

4 Look at the calendar. Today is Thursday 14th. Complete the table.

Mon	Tues	Weds	Thurs	Fri	Sat	Sun
4	5	6	7	8	9	10
11	12	13	(14)	15	16	17
18	19	20	21	22	23	24
25	26	27	28	29	30	31

a	Fri 15th
The day after tomorrow	b
Yesterday	c
d	Tues 12th
e	Mon 11th
This Saturday	f
g	Sat 23rd
Last Tuesday	h
This Friday	i
j	Fri 22nd

SELF CHECK

I CAN ...
- ○ ... ask how people feel.
- ○ ... say how I am.
- ○ ... talk about plans and preferences.
- ○ ... make and respond to suggestions and invitations.

5 Going out

R1 Review 1

This Review tests the main vocabulary and language from Units 1–5. Each task has a number of points. Do all the tasks. When you finish, check your answers. How many points can you get? There is a table at the end of the test. It tells you your score.

1 Can you write five different ways to complete the sentence and say how you are?

Example: *fine*

I'm _____, thanks.

Points: ___/5

2 Complete the lists with the missing words.

Example: One, two, ***three***, four, five, six

a Monday, _____, Wednesday, _____
b _____, today, tomorrow, _____
c March, April, May, June, _____

Points: ___/5

3 Make sentences: match the phrases.

Example: a *He is Russian.*

a	He is	too noisy.
b	I live in	Russian.
c	I live in a	tired.
d	It's	in a factory.
e	I am really	detached house.
f	He works	England.

Points: ___/5

4 How do we say these dates? Say and write the dates in words.

Example: 12/09/2001 *The twelfth of September two thousand and one*

a 01/02/1956
b 22/12/2002
c 05/01/1999
d 30/10/2010
e 14/08/2016

Points: ___/5

5 Read the paragraph about when people were born. Fill in the gaps with the correct preposition: *in*, *on* or *at*.

I was born in London **a** _____ 1999. My mother says it was **b** _____ about four o'clock **c** _____ the afternoon. My daughter was born **d** _____ summer, on the same date as my father. Their birthday is **e** _____ 31st July. My son was born **f** _____ 3rd September. He was born **g** _____ night, at about 2 a.m. My mother was born **h** _____ December and she celebrates her birthday **i** _____ Christmas, because she was born **j** _____ 25th December!

05.20 **Listen and check your answers.**

Points: _____ /10

6 05.21 **Listen to the sentences and fill in the times.**

a b c

d e

Points: _____ /5

7 Write the plural of the underlined words in the sentences.
  a 260 <u>baby</u> are born every minute in the world.
  b More <u>boy</u> are born than <u>girl</u>.
  c 25% of the world's population is <u>child</u>.
  d There are 19.5 million <u>family</u> in the UK.
  e There are 55 <u>city</u> in England.
  f There are 9.5 million <u>person</u> in London.
  g There are more than 50 <u>country</u> in Europe.
  h There are more <u>man</u> than <u>woman</u> in the world.

Points: _____ /10

8 05.22 **Listen and note down the website and email addresses you hear.**

a _____
b _____
c _____

Points: _____ /3

9 Spell the email addresses and websites.
 a www.uktourist.org/advice
 b mareko.yumi357@yahoo.com

05.23 **Listen to the audio to check your answers.**

Points: _____ /2

10 Read the answers. Use the key words and write the questions.

Example:	He's from Portugal.	from	*Where's he from?*
a	It starts at five o'clock.	time	
b	It lasts about three hours.	last	
c	28th April 1963.	born	
d	I am 52.	old	
e	28th April	birthday	
f	05694 340 865	number	
g	WR10 5CD	postcode	
h	22, High Street, Wendon	what	
i	Jane Smith	your	
j	I'm from London.	where	
k	I live in Madrid.	you	
l	Miguel Silva	his	
m	He lives in London.	where	
n	No, he speaks Portuguese.	English	
o	Yes, two.	children	

Points: _____ /15

11 Make the sentences negative.

Example: I speak Spanish.   I *don't speak Spanish.*
 a They live in New York.   They _____
 b I like listening to music.   I _____
 c He gets up early.   He _____
 d She speaks Japanese.   She _____
 e There are a lot of people.   There _____
 f He's from New Zealand.   He _____
 g It's very beautiful.   It _____

128

h He can speak French. He _____
i He's got a car. He _____
j I've got a lot of free time. I _____

Points: _____/10

12 Complete the sentences. Use the words in the box and the information in the table.

| too |
| there is/are |
| there isn't/aren't |
| a/an/any |
| a lot of |
| quite/really |

MY VILLAGE	
a café	no
a pub	yes
a bank	no
cinema	no
tourists	yes, a lot
a shop	yes, two
5G coverage	no

I live in a village. It's **a** _____ small and **b** _____ beautiful ☺ but it's **c** _____ quiet ☹.

d _____ a pub and **e** _____ two shops but **f** _____ bank and **g** _____ cafés. In the summer, **h** _____ tourists. I love my village but I also like going to see films and **i** _____ cinema here. I like going on social media and the internet connection is quite good but **j** _____ 5G coverage ☹.

Points: _____/10

13 Read the conversation and fill in the gaps. Use one word for each gap.

Marilyn:	Do you **a** _____ _____ out sometime?
David:	I'd like **b** _____ _____ and see the new Bond film.
Marilyn:	That's **c** _____ _____ _____.
David:	How **d** _____ this weekend?
Marilyn:	This weekend **e** _____ _____ good because **f** _____ _____ working all day Saturday and all day Sunday, so I'm afraid I can't.

David:	**g** _____ _____ _____ next Monday?
Marilyn:	Yes, Monday is good. Actually, I'd **h** _____ _____ go on Monday because it is quiet.
David:	Yes, there are too many people at the weekend. Do you want **i** _____ _____ out for a meal first?
Marilyn:	Well, food is a good idea but I'd **j** _____ have a sandwich in a pub or something.
David:	Let's **k** _____ at five at the cinema. The Queen's Arms is two minutes from the cinema and it's a really nice pub and not too expensive.
Marilyn:	The Queen's Arms **l** _____ perfect but five is **m** _____ early. I finish work at five thirty.
David:	Oh, OK, so why **n** _____ _____ _____ at six?
Marilyn:	Six sounds **o** _____ See you then.

Points: _____/15

14 Read about Mike and then write about him. Change the highlighted words. Start: *His name is Mike and he lives ...*

My name is Mike and I live in Brazil. **a** I am a teacher and **b** I work in a language school in Sao Paulo. **c** I love living in Brazil. It's a beautiful country and the people are very friendly. **d** I've got a lot of friends and **e** I can speak Portuguese. **f** I love my job but **g** I haven't got any free time during the week and **h** I can't usually go out. The weekend is different. **i** I usually go to the beach in the morning and **j** play football with some friends and then **k** go home for lunch. **l** I often cook fish on the barbecue but **m** I don't like eating a lot when it is hot. In the afternoon **n** I sometimes go to the café or **o** I go round to a friend's house, but **p** I sometimes have homework to mark. In the evening, **q** I usually go to a bar or the cinema. **r** I stay up quite late on Friday and Saturday but on Sunday **s** I don't go out. On Monday morning **t** I'm back at work!

Points: _____/20

15 Make sentences using the words and pictures.

a He _____ _____ English.

b I _____ _____ Japanese.

c He _____ friendly.

d They _____ hard-working.

e This is my family. I _____ _____ three children.

f This is Anna's family. She _____ _____ two sisters.

g She ✗ _____ _____

h She ♡ _____ _____

Sun 10
lunch with mum and dad 1 p.m. Paul football match 2 p.m.

---

i On Sunday I _____ _____ _____ with mum and dad.

j On Sunday Paul _____ _____ _____ at 2 o'clock.

Points: _____ /10

Check your answers in the Answer key. How many points did you get?

Look at the table. Is your score excellent, very good, quite good or not too bad? Do you need some more practice before you start Unit 6?

100–130	Excellent – congratulations! You are ready to start Unit 6.
80–99	Very good. You understand a lot of English and can use a lot of vocabulary and language from Units 1–5. Note the things that are difficult. Practise them again.
60–79	Quite good. You understand some English and can remember some of the vocabulary and language from Units 1–5. It is a good idea to look at the difficult points and practise them again, before you start Unit 6.
59 or less	Not too bad! English can be difficult to learn. It is a good idea to read Units 1–5 again and repeat some of the exercises for more practice. When you feel more confident, do the test again and then start Unit 6.

6

In this unit you will learn how to:
» talk about travel and transport.
» buy tickets and ask about journey times and distance.
» understand simple instructions and announcements.
» ask for and give directions.

Transport and directions

My progress tracker

Travelling by public transport

1 **Read the text about travelling in the UK. Look at the pictures in Vocabulary 1. Find the three kinds of transport in the text.**

People often use trains to travel around the UK. There are a lot of different train companies, but a good place to find information and buy a ticket for any journey is online at National Rail Enquiries. Train tickets can be very expensive but they can also be very cheap. For example, do you want to travel from London to Manchester? It is expensive when you travel first class, buy the ticket just before you go or travel early in the morning. It is often cheap when you travel standard class, buy the ticket a few weeks before you travel and leave after ten o'clock in the morning.

Travelling by coach is always a cheap way of travelling. It is possible to find very, very cheap tickets but the journeys take quite a long time.

How about travelling by plane? Some people use budget airlines for long journeys in the UK, for example when they travel from London to Scotland. It is sometimes cheap and the flight is very quick but the journey to the airport and check-in and security can take a lot of time.

2 Read the text again and decide if the advice below is correct. Choose Yes or No.

a Find out information about train tickets online from National Rail Enquiries. Yes/No
b For cheap train tickets, buy your ticket a few weeks before you travel and don't leave early in the morning. Yes/No
c For a quick journey, travel by coach. Yes/No
d For a very cheap journey, travel by coach. Yes/No
e For a long journey, flying can be quick and cheap. Yes/No

Vocabulary builder

VOCABULARY 1: TRAVEL AND PLACES

1 Match the different forms of transport and the pictures.

train   underground (in London, 'tube')   bus   plane   coach
taxi (or minicab)   car   ferry   bicycle (bike)   foot

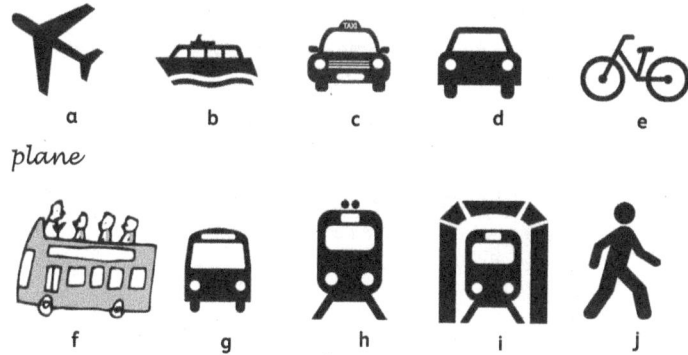

a — *plane*
b
c
d
e
f
g
h
i
j

6 Transport and directions

2 **Where do we catch a plane? Match some of the different forms of transport with the correct places.**

| plane | ferry | train | bus | coach | taxi |

a airport _____
b station _____
c taxi rank _____
d bus stop _____
e coach station _____
f ferry port *ferry*

> **LANGUAGE TIP**
> We usually say by + a form of transport. For example, I travel by car or I often go by bicycle.

3 **We say *on* for one of the forms of transport in Exercise 1. Which?**

4 06.01 **Listen and repeat. Note the stress, for example, *ferry*, *coach* station. Practise saying the forms of transport and places.**

5 **Answer for you. What forms of transport do you usually use ...**
a ... when you go to work?
b ... when you go on holiday?
c ... when you go out at the weekend?

6 **Cover the words in Exercises 1 and 2 and look at the pictures. Can you remember the words?**

VOCABULARY 2: PUBLIC TRANSPORT

1 **Use words from the box to complete the sentences. Check the meaning of any words you don't know in a dictionary.**

> delayed cancelled check-in
> book gate passport leave arrive
> security boarding card
> hold luggage hand luggage
> single (ticket)
> return (ticket) platform

Example: You say hello when you *arrive* and goodbye when you *leave*.

a You can _____ a ticket online. Do you want a _____ ticket or a _____ ticket?
b A small suitcase can be _____ but a large suitcase is _____.
c You go to an airport to catch a plane. First you go to _____ then to _____, then you go to a departure _____.

d At check-in, you show your passport and they give you a _____. Some people check in online and download their _____ to their phone.

e When you arrive in a different country, you usually have to show your _____.

f The 8.15 train is late. It's _____ and is now arriving at 8.45.

g The 10.30 coach is not going. It's _____.

h It's important to know which _____ your train is leaving from.

 2 06.02 **Listen and repeat. Note the stress, for example, de*lay*ed. Practise saying the words and phrases.**

VOCABULARY 3: PREPOSITIONS OF PLACE AND MOVEMENT

1 Here are some announcements on a plane. Read the text and note the prepositions.

> Please put your hand luggage in the overhead lockers **above** your seat.
>
> Life vests are located **under** your seat.
>
> The safety information card is located **in** the seat pocket **in front of** you.
>
> Please take a few moments to locate your nearest emergency exit. Remember that your nearest exit may be **behind** you.
>
> If you are seated **next to** an emergency exit, you are expected to assist in the opening of the emergency door.
>
> There is no smoking anywhere **on** the aircraft.

2 Match the prepositions to the correct pictures.

in   on   next to   in front of
behind   above   under

a   b   c   d   e   f   g

 3 06.03 **Listen to the prepositions. Note the stress, for example *be*hind. Practise saying the prepositions.**

6 Transport and directions   135

4 Look at the picture and complete the sentences.

  a There are three people _____ the carriage.
  b A woman is _____ the window.
  c A man is _____ the woman.
  d A child is _____ the woman.
  e The suitcases are _____ the luggage rack _____ their heads.
  f There is a newspaper _____ the seat.

5 Look at the sentences and the underlined verbs and prepositions. Are they correct? Note Yes or No.
  a The train <u>arrives to</u> Liverpool <u>at</u> six o'clock.
  b The train <u>gets to</u> Liverpool <u>at</u> six o'clock.
  c We <u>leave to</u> Manchester tonight.
  d We are <u>going to</u> Scotland next week.
  e We are <u>going to home</u> tomorrow.
  f We are <u>flying to</u> Tokyo the day after tomorrow.
  g We are <u>travelling to</u> Brazil next month.
  h We are <u>visiting to</u> Istanbul next year.

6 Look at the table. Put in the correct preposition *in* or *to* where necessary.

	+ place e.g. *London*	at	time
a arrive _____			
b get _____			
c leave _____			
d go _____			
e fly _____			
f travel _____			
g visit _____			

> **LANGUAGE TIP**
> When we talk about home, there is no preposition, for example: *We are going to home, flying to home, travelling to home.* (with "to" crossed out)

PRONUNCIATION 1: SENTENCE STRESS, /ə/ FOR *A* AND *AN* AND LINKING

1 06.04 Look at the sentences and listen to the pronunciation.

Mark the stressed words and syllables. In English, we usually stress the most important words in the sentence.

Can you remember how to pronounce *a* and *an* in a sentence? Mark /ə/ next to *a* and *an*.

Note where one word links to the next word.

> **LANGUAGE TIP**
> Remember, if a word ends with a consonant sound and the next word begins with a vowel sound, we usually say them together and it sounds like one word. For example, *Have you got a boarding card?* <u>Have</u> you got_a/ə/ <u>boarding</u> <u>card</u>?

a Can I have a return ticket, please?
b I'd like to book a flight.
c The flight is cancelled.
d The train is delayed.
e Which platform is it?
f How much is a first class ticket?
g It's above the seat.
h I've got a single ticket.
i Quick! The flight is boarding!
j The train arrives in London at ten o'clock.

2 Practise saying the sentences. Use the correct sentence stress, the weak forms of *a* and *an* and the linking between words.

PRONUNCIATION 2: THE WORD *TO*

1 06.05 Listen and notice how we pronounce the word *to*. Choose the correct answer, /tə/ or /tu:/.

a get to London, fly to Spain, travel to Japan, go to China
In all these phrases do we say /tə/ or /tu:/?

b travel to Italy, get to Argentina, go to England, fly to Australia
In all these phrases do we say /tə/ or /tu:/?

> **LANGUAGE TIP**
>
> When the word after **to** begins with a consonant sound, we usually say /tə/. When the word after **to** begins with a vowel sound, we usually say /tu:/.

2 Look at the places, decide if we say /tə/ or /tu:/ and put the places in the correct part of the table.

> London East London England
> Manchester America
> New York Oxford San Francisco
> Dallas Edinburgh

/tə/	/tu:/

3 06.06 **Listen, check your answers and practise.**

Conversation 1: Questions about travel

1 06.07 **A tourist is in a tourist information centre in London asking about travelling in the UK. Listen to the conversation and answer the questions.**
 a Where does the tourist want to go?
 b How far is it?

Tourist:	Good morning
Advisor:	Good morning. Can I help you?
Tourist:	Yes. I want to travel to Scotland, to Edinburgh. What's the best way to get there?
Advisor:	Well, you can hire a car and drive, but that takes about eight hours and it is very expensive.
Tourist:	How far is it?
Advisor:	It's about 400 miles.
Tourist:	Mmm ...
Advisor:	Or you can go by coach. Coach tickets are usually very cheap.
Tourist:	How long does it take by coach?

Advisor:	It takes about ten hours ....
Tourist:	Wow ... what time does it leave?
Advisor:	Very early in the morning ... yes, it leaves at six o'clock.
Tourist:	Wow, that is early ... what about the train?
Advisor:	The train usually takes about five hours. If you book tickets in advance, you can get them quite cheaply.
Tourist:	Can I fly?
Advisor:	Yes, there are flights from Heathrow and Gatwick, so for example, there is a flight at ten o'clock in the morning.
Tourist:	OK ... and what time does it arrive?
Advisor:	That flight arrives an hour and fifteen minutes later at 11.15.
Tourist:	Wow, that's quick ... and how much is a ticket?
Advisor:	Tickets can be quite expensive. But they can be very cheap if you book in advance. Use one of the budget airlines and check-in online.
Tourist:	OK, well a cheap flight would be great. Can I go online here to try and book a ticket?
Advisor:	Yes, of course. Let me know if you've got any problems.

2 06.07 **Listen to the conversation again and complete the table.**

WAYS OF TRAVELLING	JOURNEY TIME	JOURNEY COST
a hire a car		
b	about ten hours	
c		quite cheap if you book in advance
d	an hour and 15 minutes	

3 The tourist asks a lot of useful questions. Here are the answers. What are the questions?

    a _____ Just over 400 miles.
    b _____ £20.
    c _____ Six o'clock in the morning.
    d _____ About twelve hours later.
    e _____ About three hours.
    f _____ Probably by train, it is quick and cheap.

4 06.08 **Listen and repeat. Note the stress, for example, *How far is it?* Note where one word links to the next word, for example *How far is it?***

Practise saying the questions.

5 06.09 **Listen to the answers. Say the correct question – you will hear the answer again.**

Conversation 2: Using *can/can't* for permission

1 06.10 **Listen to the conversation. Answer the questions.**
   a Where are the two people?
   b Does the passenger want to go to Manchester?

Train manager:	Good morning.
Passenger:	Good morning.
Train manager:	Excuse me sir ... you can't smoke on the train.
Passenger:	Oh, OK. I'm sorry.
Train manager:	And you can't use your phone in this carriage. It's a quiet carriage.
Passenger:	Sorry. Can I use my phone in the next carriage?
Train manager:	Yes, no problem.
Passenger:	OK I think I will go and sit in the next carriage then ...
Ten minutes later ...	
Train manager:	Hello again.
Passenger:	Hello.
Train manager:	I'm afraid you can't sit here.
Passenger:	Oh. Why?
Train manager:	This seat is reserved.
Passenger:	Oh. OK. Can I sit here?
Train manager:	Yes, this seat is free, but you can't put your bags on the floor. People can't walk past.
Passenger:	Right. Where can I put them?
Train manager:	You can put them in the rack above your seat or on the left there at the end of the carriage. Can I see your ticket, please?
Passenger:	Yes, of course ... um ... it's ... um ... mmm ... I can't find it ...

Train manager: You can't travel on the train without a ticket.
Passenger: Yes, I know that. Can I buy one from you?
Train manager: Yes, of course. Where are you going?
Passenger: Reading.
Train manager: Oh dear ... this is the Manchester train ... we don't go to Reading ...

2 06.10 **The passenger does five things that it is not OK to do on the train. Listen to and read the conversation. Put the five things in part B of the table (use the pictures to help you).**

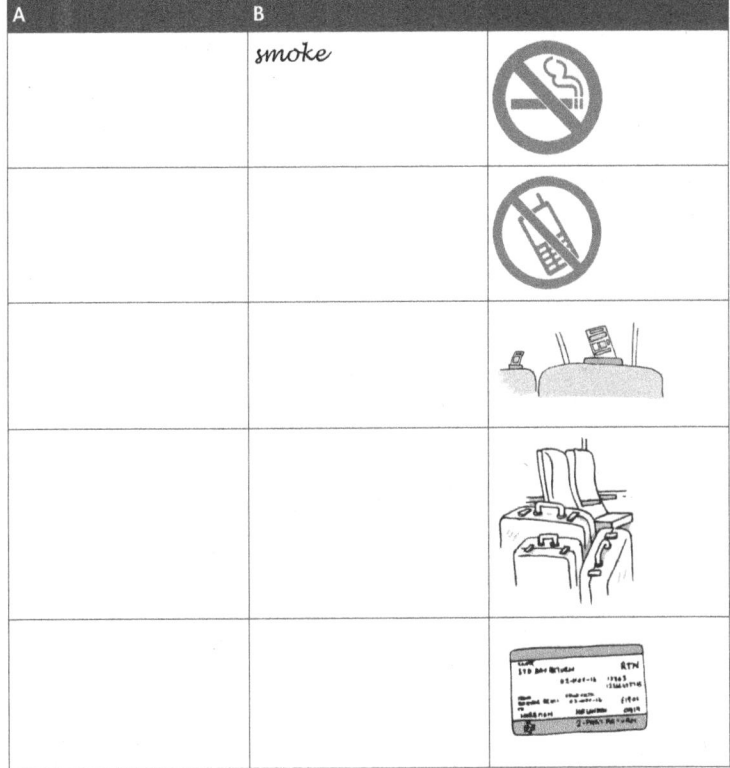

A	B	
	smoke	

3 06.10 **Listen again to the conversation. What words does the train manager use to say it is not OK to do something? Put the words in Part A of the table.**

6 Transport and directions

> **LANGUAGE TIP**
> We use *can* and *can't* to say it is OK or it is not OK to do something. It is the same word we used in Unit 4 (*I can cook*, *I can sing*) but this is a different meaning. Here we are using it for rules and permission.

4 Look at the icons. Choose the correct phrase and make a sentence about what you can't do in a place.

Example: a *You can't park here.*

> drink alcohol   take photographs
> eat or drink   run   smoke   park
> swim   use a mobile

a

b

c

d

e

f

g

h

5 How does the passenger ask if it is OK to do something? Fill in the gaps.
  a _____ I use my phone in the next carriage?
  b _____ I sit here?
  c Where _____ I put my suitcase?
  d _____ I buy one from you?

6 Use the icons and the words in the table to make questions and ask permission.

Example: *Can I pay by credit card?*

a   b   c

d   e

use	pay	this ticket	cash
smoke	park	by card	here
pay		here	

ASKING FOR AND GIVING DIRECTIONS

1 You want to go to the train station but you don't know where it is. Look at the different questions. One is more polite. Is it a or b?
  a Where is the train station?
  b Could you tell me where the train station is?

2 06.11 Listen to someone asking for directions to the train station. Find the station on the map. Choose the correct letter.

Tourist:	Excuse me ...
Person in the street:	Yes?
Tourist:	Could you tell me where the train station is? Is it a long way?
Person in the street:	Oh, no, it's not far. If you go along this road and take the first right, it's on the right, in front of the big supermarket.
Tourist:	Thank you very much.

3 06.12 **Listen to three tourists asking for directions. Find the places on the map. Note the places and the correct letters.**

4 **Read the directions. You are the tourist on the map. Note the places.**

Example: a *the taxi rank*

- **a** Take the first left. Then take the second right. Go along the road for about 50 metres. It's on the right.
- **b** Take the first right and it's on your left next to the supermarket.
- **c** Take the second right, then take the first left. It's on your right.
- **d** Go along this street and take the second left. Then take the first right. It's on the left. It's about five minutes from here.

 5 06.13 **Listen and repeat. Note the stress, for example, *It's on the left*. Note where one word links to the next word, for example *It's on the left*. Practise saying the question and the directions.**

6 **Look at the map in Exercise 3. Complete the text about how to get to the places.**

- **a** The post office

  _____ along the road _____ _____ 50 metres and _____ the _____ _____, it's on the _____, _____ _____ the cinema.

b The taxi rank

_____ the _____ left, then take _____ _____ _____, _____ _____ the road _____ about 50–100 metres. _____ on _____ right. It's _____ five _____ _____ _____.

7 Look again at the map in Exercise 3. Describe how to get to …
   a The bus station
   b The Station Hotel

Listening and speaking

LISTENING 1: AIRPORT ANNOUNCEMENTS

 1 06.14 **Listen to the airport announcements. Are all the flights leaving on time?**

 2 06.14 **Listen again to the airport announcements. Read the sentences and choose T (true) or F (false).**
   a Flight TP409 to Lisbon leaves from gate 49. T/F
   b Flight TP409 is leaving in a few hours. T/F
   c Flight BA4369 to New York leaves from gate 34. T/F
   d Passengers can get on flight BA4369 to New York now. T/F
   e Flight VA345 to Rio leaves from gate 70. T/F
   f Passengers with children can get onto Flight VA345. T/F
   g Flight TE549 is going to Hong Kong. T/F
   h Passengers can't get on flight TE549 because it is cancelled. T/F

LISTENING 2: PUBLIC TRANSPORT IN LONDON

 1 06.15 **Listen to the people talking about travelling around London by public transport. Look at the pictures of transport in Vocabulary 1. Note the ones you hear.**

 2 06.15 **Listen again. Use the words in the box to complete the summary about travelling around London by public transport.**

> can can can't can't underground
> travel card ticket bus bus
> bus bus tube tube tube

6 Transport and directions   145

Most people travel around London by **a** _____ or **b** _____ (called the **c** _____). The **d** _____ is quick, but a lot of it is under the ground so you **e** _____ see London. On a **f** _____ you **g** _____ see a lot of the famous places in London. You **h** _____ pay for a **i** _____ on a **j** _____ with cash so it is a good idea to buy a visitor **k** _____. You then add money to (or top up) the card and you **l** _____ do all the journeys you want to on the **m** _____ or **n** _____.

SPEAKING: PUBLIC TRANSPORT IN A CITY IN YOUR COUNTRY

1 Imagine you are telling some tourists about how to travel around a city in your country. Change the text to describe your city.

There are a lot of different ways to travel around London. Two good ways are by bus or underground train (called 'the tube').

Do you want to go across London? The tube is great because it is quick. You can travel across London, for example from Knightsbridge (and Harrods) to Tower Hill (and the Tower of London) and the journey takes 30 minutes.

Or do you want to see the sights in the centre of London? Travelling by bus is a good way to see famous London sights. You can take a bus that goes next to the river or in front of the Houses of Parliament or Buckingham Palace.

2 Cover your complete text. Look again at the text in Exercise 1. Can you give the talk, remembering the words you added?

3 Cover Exercise 1 and your completed text. Can you give the talk?

Reading and writing

READING 1: A WEB PAGE ABOUT HEATHROW AIRPORT

1 Read the information from a web page about what you can do at Heathrow Airport. Look at pictures a–j. What does the web page say you can do? Choose the correct pictures.

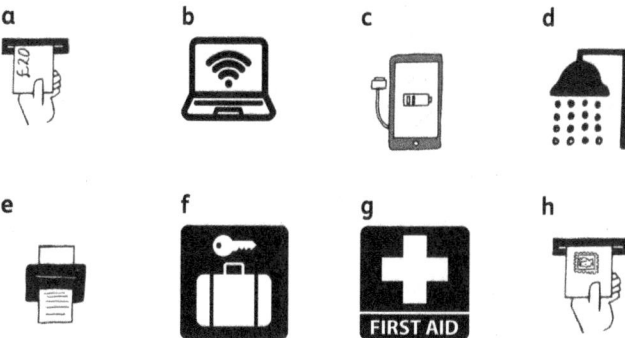

Heathrow terminal facilities and services

You can access Wi-Fi in the terminal to help you stay in touch.

You can buy stamps from coin-operated stamp machines in each terminal.

You can withdraw money from ATMs both before and after security in every terminal at Heathrow.

You can leave bags at the left luggage/luggage storage facilities in each terminal at Heathrow Airport.

You can charge your phone at one of the free mobile charging stations before and after security.

2 Have a look online at the website and read about more things you can do at Heathrow.

heathrow.com/at-the-airport/terminal-facilities

3 What do you know about plane travel? Read the sentences and choose T (true) or F (false).
   a You can't take a large suitcase as hand luggage. T/F
   b You can't take liquids in containers over 100 ml in hand luggage. T/F
   c You can take a 125 ml bottle of perfume in hold luggage. T/F
   d You can take a 75 ml bottle of perfume in hand luggage. T/F
   e You can't take a bottle of water through security. T/F
   f You can take liquids in containers over 100 ml in hold luggage. T/F

g You can take a 125 ml tube of toothpaste in hand luggage. T/F
h You can take a laptop in your hand luggage. T/F
i You can take lots of bags as hand luggage. T/F
j You can travel from London to Scotland without your passport. T/F

WRITING: DIRECTIONS IN AN EMAIL

 1 Cristina is coming to London to visit Joanna. Joanna writes her an email. What is the email about? Choose the correct answer.
   a Things they can do in London.
   b How Cristina can find Joanna's flat.
   c Advice about packing her suitcase.

✉ New message

Hi Cristina!

I am so happy you are coming to London and I am really sorry that I can't meet you at the airport when you arrive because I am working all day but it is easy to get to my house.

At the airport, look for signs to the train station. It is easy to find and not far from Arrivals. Take any train to London Victoria. There is one every 15 minutes. It takes about 30 minutes and you can buy a ticket on the train. I think it costs about £20.

When you get to London Victoria, you can walk to my flat. It is very near the train station. Come out of the station and turn left. Go along the road (Victoria Street) for about 100 metres and then take the second right. It is a little street called Brook Place. Go along Brook Place for about 200 metres and then take the first left. My building is on the right. It is called Orchardson House and my flat is number 9.

I usually get home from work at about five o'clock. Your flight arrives at four o'clock and we can meet at the flat at five o'clock, but don't worry if you are late! See you next week!

Love Joanna

2 Read the email again and answer the questions.
 a Can Joanna meet Cristina at the airport?
 b What's the best way to get from the airport to London Victoria?
 c How long does it take to get from the airport to London Victoria?
 d Can Cristina get her ticket on the train?
 e How much is a ticket?
 f Is Joanna's flat near London Victoria?
 g What's the best way to get from London Victoria to Joanna's flat?
 h Does Joanna live in Brook Place?
 i Does Joanna live in Orchardson House?
 j What time does Cristina's flight arrive?
 k What time does Joanna get home?
 l How long does it take to get from the airport to Joanna's house?

3 Write a similar email to a friend giving information about how to get from the airport to your house. In your email, fill in the gaps, and give the information for questions a–c. Use Joanna's words as much as possible.

✉ **New message**   – ⤢ ×

Hi_____

I am so happy you are coming to _____ and I am really sorry that I can't meet you at the airport when you arrive because but it is easy to get to my house.

 a Describe how to get from the airport to the city/town/village where you live, say when the transport leaves, how long it takes, where you can buy a ticket and how much is costs.

 b Give directions to your house/flat, say if it is near or far and say where your house is.

 c Say how long the journey from the airport to your house/flat takes.

See you next week!

Love_____

✈ 📎 ☺

6 Transport and directions

Test yourself

1 Add the words to the table.

> first class gate a single ticket
> a return ticket check-in delayed
> underground cancelled
> hold luggage security
> boarding card airport station
> passport hand luggage platform

PLANES	PLANES AND TRAINS	TRAINS
gate	first class	

2 Read the instructions. Draw the picture.

Draw a car. <u>Behind</u> the car, draw a house. <u>In front of</u> the car, draw a man. <u>Next to</u> the man, draw a child. <u>In</u> the car, draw a woman. <u>On</u> the car, draw a suitcase. <u>Under</u> the car, draw a cat. <u>Above</u> the house, draw a plane.

3 Fill in the gaps.

a Could you _____ _____ _____ the station _____, please?
b _____ _____ first left.
c It's _____ _____ left.
d Go _____ the road _____ about 100 metres.
e How far _____ _____?
f It's _____ _____, only about 50 metres.
g It's about five minutes _____ here.
h How _____ _____ _____ return ticket?
i What _____ _____ it leave?
j How long _____ it _____?
k What's the best _____ to get to Edinburgh?
l We arrive _____ London at 10 p.m.
m We get _____ Paris in the morning.
n We _____ home tomorrow.

4 **Re-write the underlined sentences. Use *can* or *can't*.**
   a <u>It isn't OK to smoke here.</u> This is a no-smoking area.
   b <u>It isn't OK to sit here.</u> This is a reserved seat.
   c **A:** <u>Is it OK to pay by card?</u>
      B: Yes, of course. We take cash or credit cards.
   d <u>It's OK to take a drink into the theatre.</u>

SELF CHECK

I CAN ...
... talk about travel and transport.
... buy tickets and ask about journey times and distance.
... understand simple instructions and announcements.
... ask for and give directions.

7

In this unit you will learn how to:
» manage simple business in hotels.
» complain about problems politely.
» make requests.

Hotels and accommodation

Types of accommodation

When you travel what type of accommodation do you stay in?

 1 Read the text about holiday accommodation and label the pictures.

> budget hotel B+B youth hostel
> full English breakfast ~~expensive hotel~~
> continental breakfast

a *expensive hotel*

b _____

c _____

d _____

e _____

f _____

152

There are a lot of different types of accommodation in the UK. You can stay in an **expensive hotel** or **a budget hotel**, or in a **B+B** (bed and breakfast). The cheapest accommodation is probably a **youth hostel**. You usually share a large room with other people (either all women or all men) and cook your own meals in a shared kitchen.

Staying in accommodation and paying for your room but no meals is called **room only**. Paying for a room and breakfast is **bed and breakfast**. Paying for a room, breakfast and one other meal (usually dinner) is **half board**. A room, breakfast, lunch and dinner is **full board**. If a B+B has got rooms available, there is a sign saying *Vacancies*. If they are fully booked, there is a sign saying *No vacancies*. Most hotels, guesthouses and B+Bs will offer you either a **full English breakfast** or a **continental breakfast**.

2 Read the text again. Match the accommodation to the prices. Then match the meals information to the correct phrase.

£	expensive hotel
££	youth hostel
£££	B+B or budget hotel

no meals	full board
one meal (breakfast)	room only
two meals (breakfast and dinner)	half board
three meals (breakfast, lunch and dinner)	bed and breakfast

Vocabulary builder

VOCABULARY 1: SERVICES AND FACILITIES

Look at the icons a–h and match them with the words 1–8.

Example: a 8

Which are important to you when you choose a hotel?

1 a restaurant
2 a bar
3 a gym
4 a laundry service
5 a pool
6 parking
7 a lift/elevator
8 internet/Wi-Fi

VOCABULARY 2: DESCRIBING ACCOMMODATION

1 Look at the table. There are positive and negative words to describe hotels.

POSITIVE (GOOD 😊)	NEGATIVE (BAD 😠)
about the hotel and the rooms amazing, good, brilliant, fantastic, excellent, comfy, quiet	**about the hotel and the rooms** awful, expensive, dirty, noisy
about the staff polite, friendly	**about the staff** unfriendly, rude

Add the words in the box to the correct part of the table (use a dictionary if necessary).

> clean comfortable excellent value
> helpful basic central great

2 Look at the table in Exercise 1 again. Find words for the following meanings.
   a a lot of money
   b not clean
   c not quiet
   d not friendly
   e not polite
   f very bad

3 07.01 Listen and repeat. Note the stressed syllables, for example, _comfortable_. Practise saying the words.

4 Look at some hotel reviews online (www.tripadvisor.co.uk). Find some more positive and negative words and add them to the table in Exercise 1.

VOCABULARY 3: DESCRIBING ROOMS

1 Look at the pictures a–g and match them with the words 1–7.

a   1 a single room

b   2 a double room

c   3 a twin-bedded room

d   4 a family room

e   5 a cot

f   6 an en suite room

g   7 a room with a view

2 07.02 **Listen and repeat. Note the stressed syllables, for example, a _single_ room. Practise saying the words.**

VOCABULARY 4: BOOKING ACCOMMODATION

1 Look at the expressions. Put them in the correct part of the table.

a ~~What time is **check-out**?~~
b From **Monday 10th July** to **Wednesday 12th July**.
c For **three** nights.
d Does the price include **breakfast**?
e Where is **breakfast** served?
f It's on the **first** floor.
g I'd like to book a **twin-bedded** room.
h For **three** people.
i I've got a reservation.
j Have you got any vacancies?
k We are fully booked.
l Do I need to pay a deposit?
m I'd like to make a reservation.

WHEN YOU MAKE A BOOKING	WHEN YOU ARRIVE AT THE HOTEL
	What time is check-out?

2 You can replace the words in bold in Exercise 1 with other words. Can you think of any examples?

Example: a *What time is breakfast?*

3 07.03 Look at some of the phrases from Exercise 1 and listen to the pronunciation.

▶ Note the stressed words and syllables.
▶ Note where a vowel is pronounced /ə/. Remember, we often use /ə/ for ***to*** /tə/ and ***a*** /ə/ and ***does*** /dəz/. We can also use it for words like ***from*** /frəm/ and ***for*** /fə/ and ***have*** /həv/.
▶ Note where one word links to the next word.

Example: a Have /həv/ you got any vacancies?

a Have you got any vacancies?
b Do I need to pay a deposit?
c What time is check-out?
d Does the price include breakfast?
e Where is breakfast served?
f I've got a reservation.
g From Monday 10th of July to Wednesday 12th of July.
h For three nights.
i I'd like to make a reservation.
j I'd like to book a twin-bedded room.

Conversation 1: Complaining about problems

Sometimes things are not working or there are things missing (not there).

1 Look at the words and add them to the correct part of the table. Check any words you are not sure of in your dictionary.

> shower soap clean sheets
> air-conditioning TV
> clean towels toilet paper
> hairdryer lights radio heating
> pillows internet lift/elevator

THINGS NOT WORKING	THINGS MISSING
shower	soap

2 07.04 Listen to some guests complaining about problems in their room and read the conversations. Is the receptionist helpful?

Guest 1

Guest 1: Hello? I'm calling from room 245. I'm afraid there isn't any soap and there isn't a hairdryer.

Receptionist: Oh, I'm so sorry. I'll see to it straight away.

Guest 1: Hello? I'm calling from room 245 again. I'm afraid the shower isn't working.

Receptionist: Oh, I'm so sorry. I'll deal with it immediately.

Guest 2

Guest 2: Hello? It's room 96. I'm afraid the lights aren't working.

Receptionist: Oh, I'm so sorry. I'll sort it out straight away.

Guest 2: Hello? It's room 96 again. I'm afraid there aren't any clean towels.

Receptionist: Oh, I'm so sorry. I'll send some up immediately.

7 Hotels and accommodation

3 **07.04 Listen to the conversations again. What are the problems?**
   a What things aren't working?
   b What things are missing?

4 **07.04 How do the guests describe the problems? Fill in the gaps.**
   a The shower _____ working. (*isn't* for singular or uncountable noun)
   b The lights _____ working. (*aren't* for plural _____)
   c _____ _____ _____ hairdryer. (*there isn't a/an* + singular noun)
   d _____ _____ _____ soap. (*there isn't any* + _____ noun)
   e _____ _____ _____ clean towels. (*there aren't any* + _____ noun)

5 **Look at the conversations again.**
   a What small phrase do the guests use to be more polite?
   b What words tell you that the receptionist wants to do something about the problem quickly?

 6 **Use the words in Exercise 1 and practise describing the problems.**

Conversation 2: Making requests

A hotel receptionist often helps guests.

1 **What can a receptionist help you with? Use the words in the box to complete the sentences.**

> directions taxi tickets
> reservation theatre
> airport tour luggage car

He or she can . . .
   a ... make a *reservation* in a restaurant.
   b ... book _____ or concert _____.
   c ... arrange a sightseeing _____.
   d ... arrange _____ hire.
   e ... give you _____.
   f ... help you get to the _____.
   g ... look after your _____ until you leave.
   h ... call you a _____.

2 07.05 **Some guests ask a receptionist to help them. Listen to and read the conversations. Are the guests in a hotel, a B+B or a youth hostel?**

Guest 1
Guest: Hello. Could you help me, please?
Receptionist: Yes, of course, sir. What can I do for you?
Guest: Well, my family and I would like to rent a car. Could you arrange car hire for us?
Receptionist: Yes of course, sir.

Guest 2
Receptionist: Good morning. How can I help you?
Guest: Well, my flight leaves this evening and I am checking-out now. Could you look after my luggage until I leave?
Receptionist: Yes, of course, sir.

Guest 3
Guest: Good morning.
Receptionist: Good morning.
Guest: Could you help me, please?
Receptionist: Yes, of course, madam. What can I do for you?
Guest: Could you call me a taxi?
Receptionist: Yes, of course, madam.

3 07.05 **Listen to the conversation again. Which things from Exercise 1 does the receptionist help with? Note the correct letters from Exercise 1.**

4 Look at the conversation. What words do the guests use to ask the receptionist to help them?

a _____ help me?
b _____ arrange car hire?
c _____ look after my luggage?
d _____ call me a taxi?

> **LANGUAGE TIP**
> They use the words *Could you* before the verb because they are asking someone to help them. It is a polite way of making a request.

7 Hotels and accommodation

5 07.06 **Listen to the requests. Note the stress, for example, *Could you <u>help</u> me?* Note the intonation and practise saying the requests in the same way. It sounds polite.**

 6 **Practise making more requests by saying *Could you* in front of the things in Exercise 1.**

Listening and speaking

LISTENING 1: MAKING A BOOKING AND ARRIVING WITH A BOOKING

 1 07.07 **You will hear a conversation at the reception desk of a hotel. Listen and decide. How many different people does the receptionist talk to?**

 2 07.07 **Listen again and read sentences a–f. Choose T (true) or F (false).**

a The first person wants to book a double room. T/F
b He wants the room for three nights from Monday 28th April. T/F
c The hotel is fully booked. T/F
d The second person has got a family room for seven nights. T/F
e He is in room 508. T/F
f He would like a newspaper in the morning. T/F

 3 07.08 **Listen to the person making a booking on the phone. Choose the correct answers.**

a What kind of room does he want? single/double/family
b For how many people? 2/4/5
c Which day are they arriving? Tuesday/Wednesday/Thursday
d What date are they arriving? 1st September/3rd September/13th September
e How many nights are they staying? 2/10/12

SPEAKING 1: MAKING A BOOKING

1 07.08 **Listen again to the person making a hotel booking. Listen carefully to the intonation. Pause the audio and repeat.**

2 07.09 **Use the prompts to make a booking. Practise what you are going to say then play the audio and respond to what the receptionist says. Use the same audio for each booking.**

a Family room/four people/Thursday 3rd September/ten nights/your name

b Double room/two people/Tuesday 4th August/four nights/your name

c Twin-bedded room/two people/Friday 28th April/one week/your name

d Double room with a cot/two adults and a baby/Thursday 7th November/five nights/your name

Receptionist: Good evening.
You: Good evening. I'd like to ...

3 07.09 **Now try to do it without looking.**

LISTENING 2: COMPLAINING ABOUT THE ROOM

1 07.10 **Listen to a telephone conversation between a guest and the receptionist. The guest is complaining about his room. How many different things does he complain about?**

2 07.10 **Listen again. Note the two things that are missing and the two things that are not working.**

3 07.10 **Listen again and answer the questions.**

a What does Mr Lopes ask the receptionist to do about the things that are missing?

b What does Mr Lopes want someone to do about the things that are not working?

c What does the hotel do to say sorry for all the problems in the room?

SPEAKING 2: COMPLAINING ABOUT THE ROOM

 1 Say the words of Mr Lopes. Try to remember what goes in the gaps.

a

Mr Lopes	_____? I'm _____ _____ _____ 408. I'm _____ the television _____ _____ _____ someone sort it out?
Receptionist	Oh, I'm so sorry. I'll deal with it straight away.

b

Mr Lopes	_____? It's _____ 408 _____. I'm _____ _____ _____ _____ clean towels. _____ _____ send some up?
Receptionist	Oh, I'm so sorry. I'll send some up immediately.

c

Mr Lopes	_____? I'm _____ _____ _____ _____ _____. _____ _____ the lights _____ _____. _____ _____ _____ it out?
Receptionist	Oh, I'm so sorry. I'll see to it immediately.

d

Mr Lopes	_____? It's _____ _____ _____ _____ _____ _____ toilet paper. _____ _____ _____ some up?
Receptionist	Oh I'm so sorry. I'll sort it out straight away.

e

Receptionist:	Hello? Is that Mr Lopes in room 408?
Mr Lopes:	_____.
Receptionist:	Is everything OK now Mr Lopes?
Mr Lopes:	Yes, _____ _____. Everything _____ _____.
Receptionist:	Mr Lopes, I am so sorry about all the problems with your room. The hotel would like to offer your family a free lunch or dinner. Would you like to have dinner this evening?
Mr Lopes:	That _____ _____ lovely, thank _____ _____ _____. What _____ _____ dinner?
Receptionist:	From six o'clock. We look forward to seeing you in the dining room later.

2 07.10 **Listen again and check your answers to Exercise 1.**

3 You are in room 34. Phone the receptionist and use the picture prompts to make complaints about your room.

a   b   c

d   e

 4 07.11 **Listen to the example answers. Did you say the same thing?**

Reading and writing

READING: BOOKING.COM

 1 Read the text about booking.com. Read the sentences and choose T (true) or F (false)
 a There are only hotels on booking.com
 b You can see photos, reviews and the location
 c You can limit your search to places with a swimming pool only
 d You can change the language of Booking.com to English

7 Hotels and accommodation

A lot of people book hotels on websites. The most visited travel and tourism website is booking.com with 514 million visits worldwide each year. The booking platform has hotels, apartments, hostels and guest houses all over the world. You can see photos and choose a room only, or a room and breakfast (bed and breakfast) or a room with breakfast and dinner (half board) or an apartment. You can read reviews and see where it is on a map. You can use filters to look for accommodation with different facilities (for example somewhere with a swimming pool, with parking, in front of the beach, with a sea view, with a private bathroom). You can save your favourite places in a list and then sort (or organise) your list so you can see the cheapest first, or the most popular or the place with the best reviews or highest ratings (for example, five stars) first.

2 Go to Booking.com. Change the language to English (click on the flag at the top of your page and choose English). Choose a destination and accommodation and practise reading.

READING: DESCRIPTIONS AND REVIEWS

 1 Look at the pictures, then the information, then the reviews. Which hotel would you choose?

The Victoria Hotel

A privately-owned hotel and bistro in a peaceful setting only minutes away by metrolink from city centre Manchester

Facilities: bar, free parking, restaurant, free Wi-Fi, laundry service
Price per night inc. taxes and fees: £140

'I really liked my stay here and I would definitely recommend this hotel. The room was lovely and big and the breakfast was very good. It took a long time to get to the centre because the metrolink wasn't working but it was lovely and peaceful in the hotel.'

'The staff were really friendly and the room was very clean but there was no soap in the bathroom. It was nice to have free Wi-Fi. Recommended.'

'The hotel had a lovely garden and it was easy to park the car. We had a really nice meal in the evening but it was quite expensive.'

2 Read the text again and complete the table with Yes or No.

	HOTEL IRIS	THE VICTORIA HOTEL
central location	Yes	No
free internet		
free parking		
laundry service		
restaurant		
expensive		
recommended		

3 Read the reviews again. Are the sentences true (T) or false (F)?

a The breakfast at the Iris is good. T/F
b The breakfast at the Victoria Hotel is good. T/F
c The rooms at the Iris are clean. T/F
d The rooms at the Victoria Hotel are clean. T/F
e The rooms at the Iris are big. T/F
f The rooms at the Victoria Hotel are big. T/F
g The rooms at the Iris are quiet. T/F
h The rooms at the Victoria Hotel are quiet. T/F

i	The staff at the Iris are friendly.	T/F
j	The staff at the Victoria Hotel are friendly.	T/F

WRITING 1: AN EMAIL BOOKING

 1 Read the email from Mr Lopes to the Sandy Bay Hotel. He wants to book a room. Answer the questions.

a What kind of room does he want?
b Does he want half board?
c How many people is the room for?
d How many nights are they staying for?
e When do they arrive?

> ✉ **New message** — ⤢ ×
>
> Dear Sir/Madam,
>
> I would like to book bed and breakfast in a family room with a sea view at The Sandy Bay Hotel. The booking is for seven nights, from Monday 10th July to Monday 17th July for four people, two adults and two children (aged eight and eleven). Could you tell me if I need to send a deposit?
> I look forward to hearing from you.
>
> Best regards,
> Mr Jose Lopes
>
>

2 Read Mr Lopes' email again. Now write a booking for you. Complete the email.

> ✉ New message − ↗ ×
>
> Dear Sir/Madam,
>
> I would like to book _____ in a _____ room at the Victoria Hotel.
>
> The booking is for _____ nights, from _____ to _____ for _____ people.
>
> Could you tell me if I need to send _____?
>
> _____
>
> Best regards,
>
> _____

WRITING 2: A HOTEL REGISTRATION FORM

Look at the hotel registration form for Mr Lopes. Complete the form with the missing information.

Hotel   Hotel

REGISTRATION CARD			
Name		Nationality	Spanish
Address	Rua de la Frontera 29, Vila Real, 4306-435 9 Valegio, Spain		
City or town	Vila Real	Car registration Number	HO 23 42 81 P
Date of arrival		Date of departure	
Method of payment	Credit card ☒	Cheque ☐	Cash ☐
Room rate	Full board ☐	Bed and breakfast ☐	Room only ☐
Signature		Room number	

7 Hotels and accommodation

Test yourself

1 Complete the table of positive and negative words to describe accommodation and staff.

😀	☹
quiet	c
a	dirty
b	expensive
fantastic	d
polite	e
friendly	f

2 Match the two halves of the sentences.

a The rooms
b The staff
c The hotel
d There are
e The lift

1 are unfriendly and rude.
2 are clean and comfy.
3 isn't working.
4 no clean towels in the room.
5 is excellent value.

3 Match the questions and responses.

a Have you got any vacancies?
b I'd like to book a family room.
c How much is the deposit?
d Does the price include breakfast and dinner?
e I've got a reservation.
f Where is breakfast served?
g What time is check-out?

1 On the ground floor.
2 At ten o'clock.
3 Yes, it is half board.
4 For how many people?
5 I am sorry, we are fully booked.
6 £50.
7 In which name?

4 Fill in the gaps.

A man arrives at a hotel. He talks to the receptionist.

a I' _____ _____ a reservation. My name's Johnson.
b _____ you _____ a room with a sea view?
c _____ the price _____ breakfast?
d What time _____ dinner?

There are a few problems with his room so he calls reception ...

e There _____ _____ soap.
f _____ _____ _____ towels.
g The lights _____ _____.
h The Wi-Fi _____ _____.

He is still not happy and says to the receptionist ...

i _____ _____ call me a taxi?

SELF CHECK

I CAN ...
... manage simple business in hotels.
... complain about problems politely.
... make requests.

8

In this unit you will learn how to:
» make recommendations.
» talk about the weather.
» talk about the past.
» compare things.

Sightseeing and the weather

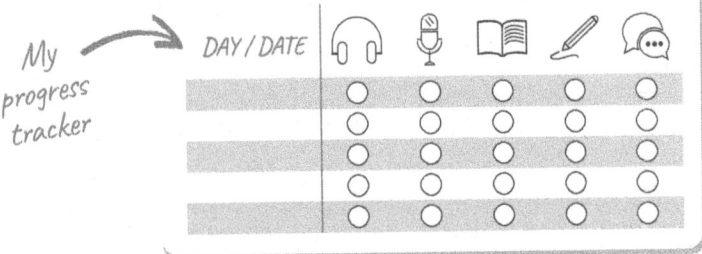

My progress tracker

Coming to the UK on holiday

 1 Read the text. Find the places on a map of the UK and London.

When you arrive in the UK, you should visit a tourist information centre where you can get information and maps. **London** is the capital and there are a lot of famous sights such as **Buckingham Palace** and the **Tower of London**. You should take a trip on the **River Thames** and see landmarks such as **Big Ben** and the **Houses of Parliament**, the **London Eye** and **St Paul's Cathedral**. London's got a lot of museums and art galleries such as the **British Museum** and **Madame Tussaud's**.

London is a great place to go shopping or see a show. It's also well worth going on an excursion (a short trip) to places such as **Windsor Castle**, the oldest and largest inhabited castle in the world. Or do you prefer the countryside? I'd recommend visiting **Stonehenge**, the villages of the **Cotswolds** or the mountains of **Scotland** or **Wales**. For the seaside, one of the loveliest regions is the **south-west of England**.

2 Find the tourist attractions in the text. Put them into the correct part of the table.

MUSEUM OR ART GALLERY	CHURCH OR CATHEDRAL	MONUMENT, CASTLE OR PALACE	CITY, COUNTRY OR REGION	OTHER ATTRACTION

3 Put these famous tourist destinations in the USA into the table. Add some tourist destinations in your country.

New York City   The Grand Canyon   Niagara Falls

The Statue of Liberty   Yellowstone National Park   The White House

The Empire State Building   Museum of Modern Art, New York

4 Find five phrases in the text for making recommendations. Complete the sentences. Then replace the underlined words with information about your own country.
  a Joining a guided tour ___ ___ ___ ___.
  b You ___ take a trip <u>on the River Thames</u>.
  c <u>London</u> is ___ ___ ___ ___ go shopping.
  d It's ___ ___ going on an excursion to places such as <u>Windsor Castle</u>.
  e I'd ___ ___ <u>Stonehenge</u>.

Vocabulary builder

VOCABULARY 1: THE WEATHER

1 Put these weather phrases in order from cold to hot.

It's chilly.
It's warm.
It's cold.
It's boiling.
It's freezing.
It's hot.

  ___ ___ ___ ___

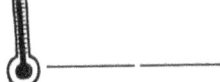 ___ ___

2 **What's the weather like? Match the pictures a–g with the descriptions.**

It's raining.   It's showery.   It's cloudy.   It's stormy.

It's snowing.   It's sunny.   It's windy.

3 **Match the weather phrases with the clothing. Put them in the correct part of the table.**

It's really sunny.   It's pouring with rain.

It's quite windy.   What terrible weather!

~~It's very cold.~~   What miserable weather!

It's a really nice day.   ~~What a lovely day!~~

It's absolutely freezing!   It's a beautiful day.

~~It's really wet.~~

4 Add the words from Exercises 1 and 2 to the table.

5 08.01 **Listen and repeat: Note the stressed syllable. Practise saying the words.**

> **LANGUAGE TIP**
> Talking about the weather is a good way to start a conversation.
> It's a nice (lovely, beautiful) day, isn't it?
> It's terrible (miserable, awful) weather, isn't it?

VOCABULARY 2: COMPARING

1 Which of these are true about the weather in the UK?
- There is a lot of rain throughout the year.
- It is wetter in the north and west than in the south and east.
- The coldest months are December and January.
- It is generally warmer in England than in Scotland.
- London is one the warmest places in the UK.
- The average summer temperature in the UK is 22°C.
- In the summer tourists can get a week of rain or a week of wonderful sunshine.
- The weather is often more miserable in the autumn than in the summer.
- The weather is the most miserable in winter – cold and wet!
- The weather in the summer is usually better than the weather in the winter.
- In the spring the weather is sometimes nicer than in the summer.

In fact, they are all true!

2 Look at the temperatures. Use *hotter* or *the hottest* to complete each sentence.

Edinburgh 20°C   Manchester 22°C   London 25°C

a It is _____ in Manchester than in Edinburgh.
b London is the _____ place.

> **LANGUAGE TIP**
> To compare two things we use the **comparative** form of the adjective.
> To say something is *more* x than all other things, we use the **superlative** form.

8 Sightseeing and the weather

3 Make a list of the comparative adjectives and the superlative adjectives in the sentences in Exercise 1. What do you notice? Complete the rules.

   a You usually add _____ to make the comparative form of the adjective.

   b You usually add *the* and _____ to make the superlative form.

4 Complete the comparative or superlative forms in the gaps in the table. Look at the instructions to help you with the spelling.

ADJECTIVE	COMPARATIVE	SUPERLATIVE
cold	*colder*	*the coldest*
warm	_____	_____
nic**e** (ends in *e*)	(+ r) _____	(+ st) _____
h**o**t (ends in vowel and consonant)	(double the consonant and + er) _____	(double the consonant and + est) _____
wet	_____	_____
sunn**y** (ends in *y*)	(change the *y* to *i* and + er) _____	(change the *y* to *i* and + est) *the sunniest*
dry	_____	_____

Two adjectives are irregular:

good	**better**	**the best**
bad	**worse**	**the worst**

If the adjective has more than two syllables, we use *more* or *the most*.

beautiful	*more beautiful*	*the most beautiful*
miserable		

5 Find the English mistakes in these sentences. Correct the sentences.

   a It is usually more hot in July than in January.

   b The weather in summer is usually beautifuller than the weather in winter.

   c It is more wetter in spring than in summer.

   d January is the most cold month.

   e August is the most hot month.

   f The better month for dry weather is July.

Which of these sentences are true about the weather in your country?

Compare the weather in your country with the weather in the UK. Use comparative words from Exercise 4.

Conversation 1: Past simple

1 08.02 **Read and listen to this conversation. Nina is telling her colleague about her holiday. Was it a good holiday?**

Susana:	Hi there, Nina! You look very well!
Nina:	I am very well, thanks, Susana. We came back from holiday yesterday!
Susana:	Oh, I see! Where did you go?
Nina:	We got a cheap flight and we went to Portugal. We had a brilliant time.
Susana:	I'd love to go to Portugal. What was it like? What did you do?
Nina:	We flew to Lisbon and we stayed in a lovely hotel in the centre of the city. We didn't know Lisbon so we went to the Tourist Information Centre. They gave us some good ideas about different things to do. We did so much in just one week and we were never bored! We met some really nice people, we went to the beach, we saw some amazing buildings and monuments and we visited a couple of museums. It was really interesting and I took a lot of photos.
Susana:	That sounds lovely! What about the food? Was the food nice?
Nina:	The food was really good. We found some nice little restaurants in the old part of the city. They were lovely but they weren't expensive. We ate out nearly every night.
Susana:	Did you hire a car?
Nina:	No, we didn't, we used the local transport and it was fine.
Susana:	Did you spend a lot of money?
Nina:	I didn't spend too much, but we bought a lot of souvenirs. I wanted to buy more but we didn't have room in our suitcase!

8 Sightseeing and the weather

Susana:	Was the weather good?
Nina:	The weather was really good for the whole week apart from one day when it rained a bit. When we left it was a lovely day and I felt so sad saying goodbye to Lisbon. I was really tired but I didn't want to go home!
Susana:	It sounds like the holiday was amazing!
Nina:	It was. I even tried to learn some Portuguese and yesterday I enrolled on a Portuguese course! We are going back next year!

2 08.02 **Read and listen to the conversation again. Choose the true sentences.**

a They had a good holiday. They had a miserable holiday.
b They travelled by plane. They travelled by train.
c They didn't do much. They did a lot of things.
d They were bored. They weren't bored.
e The food was quite cheap. The food wasn't cheap.
f They ate in restaurants. They ate in the hotel.
g They hired a car. They didn't hire a car.
h It poured with rain all week. It rained once.

3 Find the past tense of these verbs in the Conversation.

a come *came*
b get
c go
d have
e be (I, she, he, it)
f fly
g stay
h give
i do
j be (you, we, they)
k meet
l see
m visit
n take
o find
p eat
q use
r buy
s want
t rain
u leave
v feel
w try
x enrol

Some verbs are regular – which ones?

How do we make the past tense of regular verbs?

4 Write the past tense of these other regular verbs.

a ask
b work
c arrive
d look
e enjoy
f start

> **LANGUAGE TIP**
> When do we change y to i and add ed for verbs ending in y?
> stay – stayed   try – tried   enjoy – enjoyed
> It's when the verb ends in a consonant + y.

5 Look at the underlined words in the sentences. They are irregular verbs in the past tense. Complete the table with the simple form of the verbs.

I didn't have a good holiday last year. I went to France but I <u>forgot</u> my driving licence, I <u>lost</u> my passport and I <u>spent</u> a lot of money. I <u>knew</u> how to speak French and they <u>told</u> me it was easy to understand people, but I <u>made</u> a lot of mistakes and I was very embarrassed!

a	*forget*	forgot
b		lost
c		spent
d		knew
e		told
f		made

> **LANGUAGE TIP**
> It's important to learn irregular verbs. They are very useful! Try to learn and remember all the irregular verbs from Exercises 3 and 5.

Look at the questions and the negative sentences from the conversation.
How do we make questions and negative sentences in the past?

QUESTIONS				
What	did	you	do?	
Where			go?	
	Did	you	hire	a car?

NEGATIVE SENTENCES			
		know	Lisbon.
We	didn't	spend	too much.
		have	room.

When we make questions or negatives, we use the simple form of the verb (not the past form).

Did you went to New York? ✗   *Did you go to New York?* ✓

I didn't enjoyed it. ✗   *I didn't enjoy it.* ✓

8 Sightseeing and the weather

Look at the questions and the negative sentences from the conversation.
How do we make questions and negative sentences in the past?

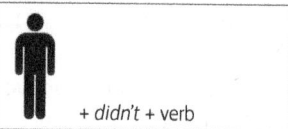

6 How do we make questions and negatives with the verb *to be* in the past? Fill in the gaps in these sentences from the conversation.

　a _____ the people friendly?
　b They _____ expensive.
　c _____ the weather good?

> **LANGUAGE TIP**
>
> To make a question with *to be*, swap the order of the subject and the verb.
> *He was here.*　　*Was he here?*
> To make a negative with *to be*, add *not* or *n't* after the verb.
> *He was here.*　　*He wasn't here.*

7 Look at the example sentences. Complete the questions.

EXAMPLE SENTENCES	QUESTIONS
a We came home yesterday.	When _____ home?
b We went to Warsaw.	Where _____ go?
c We did a lot of things.	What _____ do?
d We met some nice people.	Who _____?
e We saw some monuments.	What _____?
f I took a lot of photos.	How many photos _____?
g We ate in little restaurants.	Where _____?
h We bought a lot of clothes.	What _____?
i We left yesterday.	When _____?
j I spent a lot of money.	How much _____?

 8 Cover the example sentences in Exercise 7. Write the answers to the questions.

9 Put the verbs in brackets into the past simple.

We _____ (**come**) back yesterday. We _____ (**get**) a cheap flight and we _____ (**go**) to Portugal. We _____ (**have**) a brilliant time. We _____ (**fly**) to Lisbon and we _____ (**stay**) in a lovely hotel in the centre of the city. We _____ (**not know**) Lisbon so we _____ (**go**) to the Tourist Information Centre. They _____ (**give**) us some good ideas about different things to do. We _____ (**do**) so much in just one week. We _____ (**meet**) some really nice people, we _____ (**go**) to the seaside, we _____ (**see**) some amazing buildings and monuments and we _____ (**visit**) a couple of museums. I _____ (**took**) a lot of photos. We _____ (**find**) some lovely little restaurants in the old part of the city and we _____ (**eat**) out nearly every night. We _____ (**not hire**) a car. We _____ (**use**) the local transport and it _____ (**be**) fine. I _____ (**not spend**) too much money but we _____ (**buy**) a lot of souvenirs. I _____ (**want**) to buy more but we _____ (**not have**) room in our suitcase! The weather _____ (**be**) really good for the whole week apart from one day when it _____ (**rain**) a bit. When we _____ (**leave**) it was a lovely day and I _____ (**feel**) so sad saying goodbye to Lisbon. I _____ (**not want**) to go home! I _____ (**try**) to learn some Portuguese and yesterday I _____ (**enrol**) on a Portuguese course!

10 Can you remember the questions Susana asked?

a What _____ _____ like?
b What _____ _____ do?
c Where _____ _____ go?
d _____ the food nice?
e _____ _____ _____ a car?
f _____ _____ _____ a lot of money?
g _____ the weather good?

11 Look at the verbs in the table. Find the regular verbs. There are five.

come	stay	visit	want	buy	see	enjoy
get	meet	have	rain	eat	fly	forget
go	do	find	leave	be	lose	spend

12 Answer Susana's questions about your last holiday. Try to use all the verbs in the table in the past.

-ED AND -ING ADJECTIVE ENDINGS

1 Look at these sentences from the conversation between Nina and Susana.

We were never bored. It was really interesting. I was really tired. The holiday was amazing.

Some adjectives have two endings, -ed or -ing. For example, interesting and interested. Complete the table with the correct spelling of the words.

-ed	-ing
	amazing
bored	
tired	
	interesting
	disappointing
	worrying
excited	
	frightening

2 Why do we say *the holiday was amazing* and not *the holiday was amazed*?

Why do we say *I was really tired* and not *I was really tiring*? Complete the words.

a We use the *-ed* ending to describe how a person feels. *I was bor_____.*

b We use the *-ing* ending to describe what a person or a thing is like. *It's really excit_____!*

3 08.03 Listen and repeat: Note the stressed syllable. Practise saying the words.

4 Which of the following sentences are correct English?
   a I am very interested in sport.
   b The film was very frightening.
   c I was very frightened.
   d My holiday was amazed.
   e The weather was very disappointing.
   f There was nothing to do so I felt very boring.

5 Fill in the gaps.
a The journey was very tir _____ so I felt very tir _____.
b The film was amaz _____.
c She talked about the same thing all day. She was very bor _____!

6 When was the last time you were tired? Bored? Frightened? Disappointed?

Can you think of someone or something that is interesting? Boring? Exciting?

> **LANGUAGE TIP**
> **Be careful!**
> *I am very tired* means I am very tired **now** (because of the word *am*).
> The *-ed* ending doesn't mean the past (it **isn't** the past simple).
> If you want to talk about the past, you say *I **was** very tired*.

PRONUNCIATION 1: *-ED* VERB ENDINGS

1 08.04 Look at the three groups of regular past tense verbs. Listen to their pronunciation. Can you hear the different ways we pronounce the 'ed' ending?

/t/	/d/	/id/
worked	tried	visited
stopped	stayed	wanted
looked	arrived	started

> **LANGUAGE TIP**
> When do we pronounce the *-ed* ending as /t/, when as /d/ and when as /id/?
> ▶ /t/ if you say the last sound in the verb without using your voice (for example, /k/ as**k**)
> ▶ /d/ if you say the last sound in the verb using your voice (for example /ei/ s**tay** or /v/ lo**ve**)
> ▶ /id/ if the last sound in the verb is /t/ or /d/ (for example /t/ wan**t** or /d/ deci**de**)

2 08.05 How do you pronounce these regular verbs in the past tense? Put the verbs into the correct part of the table in Exercise 1. Listen and check your answers. Practise saying the words.

8 Sightseeing and the weather

| talked | loved | needed | liked | waited | played | enjoyed |
| used | asked | watched | helped | studied | rained | started |

PRONUNCIATION 2: IRREGULAR PAST SIMPLE VERBS

 1 08.06 **Look at the verbs. Can you remember the past form? Listen and check. Practise saying the words.**

 come, get, go, have, fly, give, do, meet, see, take, find, eat, buy, leave, feel, forget, lose, spend, know, tell, make

Listening and speaking

LISTENING 1: A CONVERSATION ABOUT THE WEATHER

 1 08.07 **Listen to Nina and her friend from work, Peter, talking about the weather. Put ☺ for good weather or ☹ for not good weather.**
   a Today
   b When Anna was in Portugal
   c When Anna's friends were in Portugal
   d When Anna was in Dubai
   e Last week
   f Next week

2 08.07 **Listen to the conversation again. Cross out any words that are not true and add any extra information you hear.**

TODAY	WHEN NINA WAS IN PORTUGAL	WHEN NINA'S FRIENDS WERE IN PORTUGAL	WHEN NINA WAS IN DUBAI	LAST WEEK	NEXT WEEK
chilly windy	fantastic boiling	it rained every day cloudy	really sunny 36 degrees too hot to go out	miserable poured with rain windy chilly cloudy	good lovely sunny

LISTENING 2: A CONVERSATION ABOUT A HOLIDAY

1 08.08 **Mark is going to New York next week, and Julie went to New York last year. Listen to their conversation. Did Julie have a good holiday in New York?**

2 Listen again to the conversation and choose the correct answers.
a How long is Mark in New York for?   one week/two weeks
b Which attractions does Julie recommend?

The Statue of Liberty	Rockefeller Centre
The Chrysler Building	Times Square
The Brooklyn Bridge	The Empire State Building
The Metropolitan Museum of Art	Chinatown Coney Island
Museum of Modern Art	Central Park
	Grand Central Station

c How long does a guided tour of the city take?   three hours/four hours
d Does Julie recommend eating in the hotel?   Yes/No
e Did Julie recommend hiring a car?   Yes/No

SPEAKING: TALKING ABOUT A HOLIDAY

1 Mark asked Julie a lot of questions. Complete questions a–f.

Mark:	We don't really know where to go or what to do.
	a _____?
Julie:	I'd recommend going on a cruise to see the Statue of Liberty.
Mark:	**b** _____?
Julie:	Yes. Going on a guided tour is a great way to see the main sights.
Mark:	**c** _____?
Julie:	Most nights we went out. I think that's the best idea.
Mark:	What about getting around? **d** _____?
Julie:	No. I didn't like the idea of driving in New York! We travelled by subway.

8 Sightseeing and the weather

Mark:	e _____ _____ _____ _____?
Julie:	Good. It was a lot better than I expected and sunnier and warmer than London.
Mark:	f _____ _____ _____ _____ _____?
Julie:	If you are not sure of anything, just ask! Everyone was friendly and helpful.

 2 08.09 **Listen to the questions, note the stress and practise saying them.**

 3 08.10 **Imagine you are Mark. Ask questions a–f and wait for the answer.**

 4 08.11 **Listen to how Julie uses phrases for making recommendations. Note the stress and practise saying the phrases.**

 5 08.12 **Now imagine someone is asking YOU similar questions about where YOU are from. Plan your answers to the same questions. Try to use the phrases for making recommendations. Then play the audio, listen to the question and give your answer.**

Reading and writing

READING: A TOURIST INFORMATION LEAFLET

 1 Look at the tourist information. Find two interesting places for each person.
   a A child
   b Someone who likes art, old clothes and furniture
   c Someone who likes shopping
   d Someone who loves eating

 2 Look at the information again. Read the sentences and choose T (true) or F (false).
   a The National Gallery closes at 7 p.m.
   b Children are usually bored at the National Gallery.
   c Saturday is the best day to visit Portobello Market.
   d You cannot go to Hyde Park at night.
   e There is late night shopping on Oxford Street on a Wednesday night.

Great free things to do in London

National Gallery (nearest tube Charing Cross)

The National Gallery is an art museum on Trafalgar Square in London. There are over 2,300 paintings dating from 1250 to 1900. You can see paintings by Leonardo da Vinci, Michelangelo, Rembrandt, Turner, Van Gogh, Claude Monet and lots of other famous artists. It also has lots of exciting activities for children!

Open daily 10 a.m.–6 p.m. (closed 1 January and 24–6 December)

Portobello Market (nearest tube Ladbroke Grove or Notting Hill Gate)

Portobello Road market is one of the most famous markets in the world. You can find interesting antiques, vintage clothes, food, lots of craft stalls and independent shops as well as souvenirs. It is open every day from 8 a.m. but the busiest and most interesting day is Saturday.

Hyde Park (nearest tube Marble Arch)

Hyde Park is one of the largest parks in London and many people think it is one of the most beautiful. There is a children's play area, a lake where you can go swimming or hire a boat, and lots of cafés and places to have a snack. Hyde Park is open from 5 a.m. until midnight all year round.

Oxford Street (nearest tube Oxford Street)

Oxford Street is the busiest shopping street in Europe. There are over 300 shops of all kinds, from very cheap to very expensive. If you are interested in fashion, this is the place to visit. Shops are generally open until 8 p.m. Monday to Saturday and later on a Thursday when they close at 9 or 10 p.m. but the best time to go is just after 9 a.m. when it is usually quiet. Later on it gets very busy.

WRITING: DESCRIBING A HOLIDAY

1 Look quickly at this social media post from someone describing her holiday in Edinburgh. Is she having a good time?

 AileenM

Hi there!

This is to tell you about our visit to Scotland. We spend three days in the Highlands and it be absolutely beautiful. We stay in a small guest house and spend most of the time walking. I want to see Ben Nevis, the tall mountain in Scotland, but it be cloudy and it rain for the first two days. Then on our last day the weather be good, the rain stop and we see Ben Nevis ! I not climb to the top but we walk for about three hours! I be really tired! We meet some lovely people and they tell us about a little pub in the village so we go there for dinner on our last evening and have a fantastic time. I really enjoy it. Edinburgh be also lovely but it be busy than the mountains (and expensive!). We spend two days there. I forget my driving licence so we not hire a car but travel by bus. In fact, using public transport be probably easy than driving. I lose my bag on the second day and I be really worried but someone find it in the hotel bar and take it to the hotel reception. We also visit Edinburgh Castle and I take a lot of photos and I get some great pictures. Someone tell me the view from Edinburgh Castle be well worth seeing and he be right. It be amazing.

We are now in a hotel by Loch Ness. I can't wait until tomorrow as we are going on a boat trip.

1,989 likes
View all 204 comments
2 DAYS AGO

2 Now correct the description, changing the highlighted words. Put the verbs into the past tense and the adjectives into the comparative or superlative form.

3 **Think about your last holiday and write a similar description. Fill in the gaps in the sentences and answer the questions.**

 Username

Hi there!

This is to tell you about our visit to _____. We spent _____ days in _____ and it was _____.

- **Describe where you stayed.**
- **Describe what you did** (for example, go shopping, buy a lot of souvenirs, visit places, take photos).
- **Describe where you went** (for example, to a museum, to the beach, on a guided tour).
- **Describe how you felt** (for example, bored, tired, disappointed, excited).
- **Describe what the weather was like** (for example, chilly, boiling, pouring with rain).
- **Describe what places were like** (for example, boring, interesting, tiring, amazing, frightening, exciting).
- **Compare it with another place and use the comparative form of adjectives** (for example, busy, noisy, beautiful, expensive, cheap, interesting, nice, small, big, quiet).
- **Describe a problem** (use forget or lose) and describe how you felt (for example, worried, frightened).
- **Describe how you travelled around** (for example, hire a car, use public transport, walk, travel by bus).
- **Describe something that was well worth doing or something someone recommended doing.**
- *We are now in a hotel _____. I can't wait until tomorrow because we are _____.*

See you soon!

1,989 likes
View all 204 comments
2 DAYS AGO

8 Sightseeing and the weather

Test yourself

1 Note in the table all the words you can remember for weather.

GOOD WEATHER 😊	BAD WEATHER 😣

2 What is the past simple tense of these verbs?
   a go
   b have
   c enjoy
   d be (x2)
   e want
   f get
   g do
   h come
   i arrive
   j take

3 Correct the mistakes in these sentences.
   a Did you went to Scotland last year?
   b I not see him yesterday.
   c They wasn't here last week.
   d You were on holiday last week?
   e I were in New York.
   f I taked a lot of photos.
   g Did you lost your passport?
   h I am forgot my money.
   i He not buy any souvenirs.
   j I spending a lot of money.
   k We really enjoied it.
   l I tryed to learn Spanish.

4 Complete the sentences.
   a London is hot but Mexico City is hot_____.
   b Paris is cold but Oslo is c_____.
   c A 3 star hotel is good but a 4 star hotel is _____ and a 5 star hotel is _____.
   d A 2 star hotel is bad but a 1 star hotel is _____.
   e A 3 star hotel is expensive but a 4 star hotel is _____.

5 Choose the correct form.
   a I'd recommend **to visit/visiting** The Empire State Building.
   b You should **visit/visiting** Times Square.
   c It's well worth **do/doing** a guided tour.
   d **Travelling/Travel** by public transport is a good idea.
   e I went everywhere on foot and I was really **tiring/tired**.
   f Some of the museums are a bit **boring/bored**.
   g The weather was very **disappointing/disappointed**.
   h I am very **exciting/excited** about visiting London.

SELF CHECK

I CAN ...
... make recommendations.
... talk about the weather.
... talk about the past.
... compare things.

9

In this unit you will learn how to:
» talk about food and drink.
» describe food and restaurants.
» manage conversations in cafés and restaurants.

Restaurants and food

Food in the UK

 1 Read the text. For each topic a–c choose the correct paragraph 1–3.
  a Snacks and sandwiches
  c Traditional British food
  b International food

  1 In the UK you can eat food from all over the world. The British love Chinese and Thai food (like noodles, sweet and sour chicken and fried rice), Indian food (like curry), Italian food (such as pizza and pasta) and American food (for example, burgers, chips and fried chicken).

  2 Traditionally, there is a lot of meat (chicken, beef, lamb and pork) or fish, potatoes, flour, butter and eggs in British cooking. The most famous British dishes, are fish and chips, roast beef, cream teas, and a cooked breakfast (bacon, sausages and eggs). The British also love pies (meat pies and fruit pies) and steaks, and puddings such as treacle pudding.

  3 Between meals, a lot of people have snacks: 64% of people under 20 eat something between breakfast and lunch or lunch and dinner, like a packet of crisps, biscuits and chocolate as well as fizzy drinks (like coke). A lot of snacks are not very healthy because they contain a lot of sugar or salt or fat. Another very popular food in the UK is the sandwich, particularly for lunch. People in the UK eat 11 billion sandwiches every year!

2 Read the text again and match the food and the picture.

a cream tea   a Chinese meal   roast beef
fish and chips   a packet of crisps   a cheese sandwich

a   b   c   d   e   f

3 Choose your five favourite things to eat from the foods in the text.

HEALTHY EATING

 1 Read the text.

A lot of people in the UK try to eat fewer processed foods, less meat and more fresh fruit and vegetables often because of health reasons or lifestyle choices.

Over 10% of the UK population follow a plant-based diet (which means mainly fruits, vegetables, grains, nuts and seeds but sometimes a portion of eggs, fish or meat). About 10% of the population follow a gluten-free diet (so no traditional bread, pasta or cereal) and some people (about 5%) follow a dairy-free diet (so no cream, cheese or butter and not cow's milk but almond or oat milk as an alternative)

2 What do you eat? Write always, usually, sometimes or never in the table

Processed food		A gluten-free diet	
Eggs, fish and meat		Bread, pasta and cereal	
A plant-based diet		A dairy-free diet	
Fresh fruit and vegetables		Cream, cheese, butter and cow's milk	
Grains, nuts and seeds		Almond or oat milk	

 3 Practise writing sentences.

Example: I never drink almond or oat milk but I sometimes eat bread, pasta and cereal

Vocabulary builder

VOCABULARY 1: TYPES OF FOOD

1 Use the letters to make the correct spelling of the words.

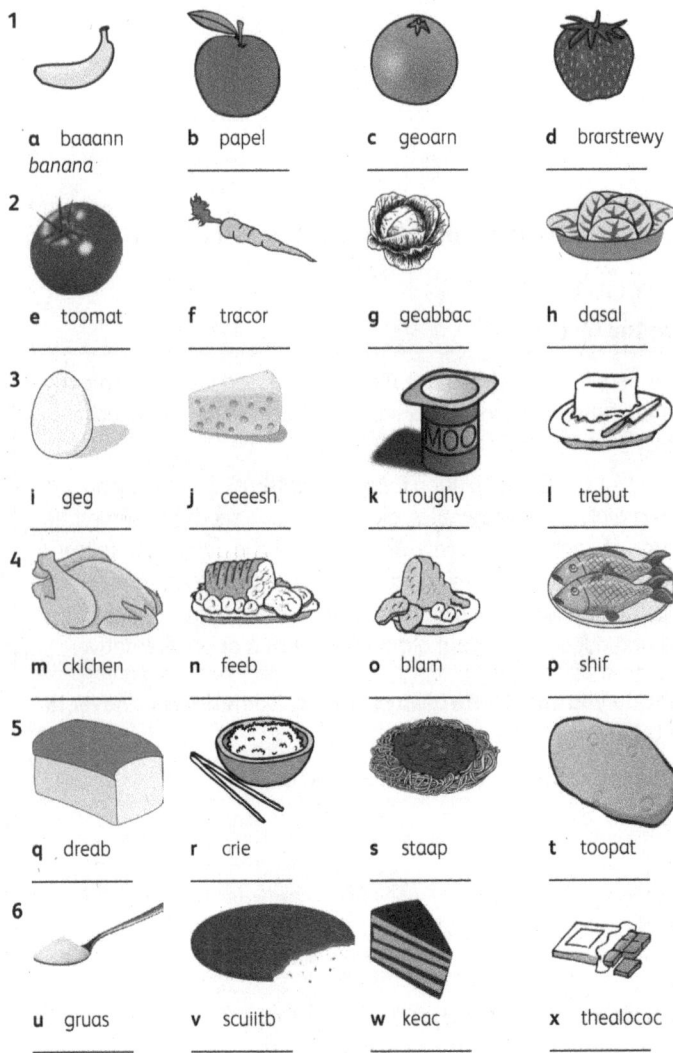

1
- **a** baaann
  banana
- **b** papel
  _____
- **c** geoarn
  _____
- **d** brarstrewy
  _____

2
- **e** toomat
  _____
- **f** tracor
  _____
- **g** geabbac
  _____
- **h** dasal
  _____

3
- **i** geg
  _____
- **j** ceeesh
  _____
- **k** troughy
  _____
- **l** trebut
  _____

4
- **m** ckichen
  _____
- **n** feeb
  _____
- **o** blam
  _____
- **p** shif
  _____

5
- **q** dreab
  _____
- **r** crie
  _____
- **s** staap
  _____
- **t** toopat
  _____

6
- **u** gruas
  _____
- **v** scuiitb
  _____
- **w** keac
  _____
- **x** thealococ
  _____

2 Choose the correct titles for parts A–D of the table.

Sugary foods Fruit Dairy foods Carbohydrates Vegetables Meat and fish

3 09.01 **Listen and repeat. Note the stressed syllable. Practise saying the food items.**

> **LANGUAGE TIP**
> Some of the food nouns are uncountable. Uncountable nouns are nouns which have no plural and we can't count them.

4 List the uncountable nouns in Exercise 1.

> **LANGUAGE TIP**
> The other foods in the table are countable. We usually add an s to make the plural, but not always.

5 Write the plural forms of the countable nouns in Exercise 1. Then check your answers. What do you notice? Complete the rules.

If a word ends in *y*, we change the *y* to _____ and add _____.

If a word ends in *o*, we add _____.

6 Read the rules and fill in the gaps in the examples.

With countable nouns, we can say:

  a *a* or *an* (+ singular noun)   I'd like _____ **apple**.
  b a number (+ _____ noun)   Can I have **two eggs**?
  c *some* (+ plural noun)   I ate _____ **carrots**.

With uncountable nouns, we use:

  d *some* (+ uncountable noun) I'd like _____ **bread**. Can I have _____ **rice**?

With some nouns (countable and uncountable), we can also use the following phrases:

a packet of _____	a piece of _____	a small/big portion of _____
crisps	cake	rice

7 Add more food items from Exercise 1 to the correct part of the table.

VOCABULARY 2: DRINKS

1 Look at these drinks and answer questions a–c. Put Yes or No in the table.

	a Do we usually drink it hot?	**b** Is it an alcoholic drink?	**c** Is it good for you?
milk	*no*	*no*	*yes*
coffee			
tea			
orange juice			
coke			
water			
beer			
wine			

2 With drinks, we often use these words for containers and quantities. Put the words under the pictures d–h in the table.

glass bottle cup can pint (UK)/litre

1 pint = 570ml

	d ___	e ___	f ___	g *glass*	h ___
milk					
coffee					
tea					
orange juice					
coke					
water					
beer					
wine					

3 Which words from Exercise 2 do we use with which drinks? Put Yes or No in the table.

PRONUNCIATION: CONTAINERS AND QUANTITIES

1 09.02 **Listen to the containers and food and drinks and note the stressed syllable. When we say the phrase, how do we pronounce *a* and *of*? Which words are stressed? Note where one word links to the next word, for example, *a packet‿of biscuits*. Listen again and practise.**

A/AN	CONTAINER	OF	FOOD OR DRINK
	packet		biscuits
a	glass	of	milk
/ə/	piece	/əv/	cake
	cup		tea

2 09.03 **Listen to more phrases and practise saying them.**

Conversation 1: Countable and uncountable nouns + *much/many*

1 09.04 **Joanna and Peter are in a café. They are talking about food. Joanna likes to keep fit and she prefers healthy food. Read and listen to the conversation. What did Joanna eat? Make a list.**

Peter: Hello Joanna! How are you?
Joanna: Hi Peter! I'm hungry!
Peter: Hungry?
Joanna: Yes, I'm trying to eat just good, healthy food and it's really difficult in a café like this with all the cakes and biscuits.
Peter: Oh, because you can't have any sugary foods?
Joanna: Exactly!
Peter: So what can you eat?
Joanna: Well, I eat a little of most things but not too much. I eat a lot of fruit.
Peter: How much fruit?
Joanna: Well, I probably have six pieces of fruit each day.
Peter: Wow! And what about things like potatoes and pasta?
Joanna: Yes, I can eat carbohydrates but not too many potatoes and only a small portion of rice or pasta with each meal.

9 Restaurants and food

Peter:	And what about meat?
Joanna:	Meat is OK but not too much red meat like beef, pork and lamb. That's fine because I like eating chicken. And fish. Fish is one of the best things you can eat. The worst things are fizzy drinks. Do you know how many grams of sugar are in the average fizzy drink?
Peter:	Ten? Twenty?
Joanna:	No, 35!
Peter:	Wow! So no fizzy drinks then! What did you have for breakfast this morning?
Joanna:	Well, I had some orange juice, a cup of coffee, some yoghurt, some strawberries, an egg and some toast.
Peter:	How much toast did you have?
Joanna:	Two small pieces!
Peter:	Sounds good. And what about dinner last night? What did you have for dinner?
Joanna:	Chicken, rice and salad.
Peter:	How much rice?
Joanna:	A small portion! And it was brown rice!
Peter:	Very good!
Joanna:	Yes, that was good but my daughter made some biscuits in the afternoon ...
Peter:	Oh dear ... how many biscuits did you have?
Joanna:	Well, only one ... in the afternoon ... and a couple more in the evening!
Peter:	Mmmm ... so are there any left?
Joanna:	I hope not!

2 Look at the questions from the conversation. Put *much* or *many* in the gaps and then look at the conversation and check your answers.

   a How _____ fruit?
   b How _____ grams of sugar?
   c How _____ toast?
   d How _____ rice?
   e How _____ biscuits?

3 **When do we say *how much* and when do we say *how many*? Fill in the gaps in these questions.**
   a How _____ pieces of fruit?
   b How _____ apples?
   c How _____ sugar?
   d How _____ pieces of toast?
   e How _____ pasta?
   f How _____ grams of rice?

4 **We can also use *much* and *many* in negative sentences and phrases. Put *much* or *many* in the gaps in the table.**

WITH UNCOUNTABLE NOUNS	
There isn't	
I can't have	
He doesn't want	_____ rice.
They didn't eat	
You haven't got	
I ate too	
Not too	

WITH PLURAL, COUNTABLE NOUNS	
There aren't	
I can't have	
He doesn't want	_____ potatoes.
They didn't eat	
You haven't got	
I ate too	
Not too	

5 **There are mistakes in six of the sentences. Find the mistakes and correct them.**
   a I'd like some salad but not too many, please.
   b The meal was fantastic but I ate too much pasta.
   c There isn't much wine. Let's get another bottle.
   d I'm on a diet. I can't have too much potatoes.
   e The restaurant was very good but there weren't much people there.
   f I haven't got much money. Is it expensive?
   g We haven't got many time. Is the restaurant near here?
   h I don't want much carrots, thank you. Just some cabbage.
   i Can I have a banana? Yes, but only one. There aren't many.
   j Would you like some coffee? Yes, thank you but not too much.
   k I didn't eat much biscuits, really!

9 Restaurants and food

Conversation 2: Phrases to use in a restaurant

1 09.05 **Sam and Anna are having dinner in a restaurant. Put the different parts of their conversations in order and find all the phrases that the waiter says. Then listen and check your answers.**

a

What are you having?
Mmm. I'm not sure. What do you fancy?
I don't know. It all looks very good. How about a burger?
I think I'd prefer to have fish. I fancy the salmon.
Well I'm really hungry. I'm having a burger, and let's get some extra chips!

b

Excuse me ... I'm sorry but I think there is a mistake with the bill. We didn't have any wine.
I'm so sorry. I'll see to it straight away.

c

My burger was lovely. How was your salmon?
It was delicious.
Excuse me. Can I have the bill, please?

d

Here you are. I'm sorry about the mistake.
That's OK. Never mind. Is service included?
No, people can leave a tip if they think the service was good.

e

Here's the menu and the wine list. Someone will be with you shortly to take your order. Can I get you any drinks while you look at the menu?
Yes, please. Can we have a large bottle of sparkling mineral water?

f

Are you ready to order?
Yes.
What would you like?
Can I have a burger?
Certainly.
I'd like the salmon.
Good choice. Would you like any side orders or salads?
Yes, please. Can we have a green salad and some extra chips?

g

Good evening.
Good evening. We'd like a table for two, please.
Certainly. Come this way.

h

Excuse me ... I'm sorry but we ordered some extra chips. We haven't got them yet.
And I ordered a green salad.
I'm so sorry. I'll sort it out immediately.

2 Read and listen to the conversations again and answer the questions.

  a Did they have a good meal?
  b What did they order?

3 Read the conversation again.

  a Find two ways of asking what someone wants.
  b Find two ways of saying what you want.
  c Find one way of making a suggestion. Can you remember another way?
  d Find one way of saying what you prefer. Can you remember another way?
  e Find three adjectives they use to describe food. Can you remember any other adjectives from Units 1 to 8 that you can use to describe food?

4 Fill in the gaps in the useful restaurant phrases from the conversations.

THE PHRASE	WHEN TO USE IT
a We'_____ _____ _____ _____ _____ _____, please.	when you go in to a restaurant
b What _____ you _____?	to see if someone knows what they want
c _____ I _____ + (the food). _____ _____ + (the food).	to order food
d _____ _____ + (the food)?	to find out if someone's food was good
e _____ me ... I'_____ _____ but ... + (the problem).	to introduce a complaint
f _____ _____ _____ the bill, _____?	to ask for the bill
g Is _____ included?	to ask about leaving a tip
h I'm sorry but _____ _____ _____ _____ the bill.	to say the bill is not correct
i I'm _____ _____	to apologize
j That's _____ _____ mind.	to say the mistake is not a problem

> **LANGUAGE TIP**
> We can use *too* + (adjective) or *not* + (adjective) + *enough* to complain in a restaurant.

5 Fill in the gaps in the phrases in the table.

THE PROBLEM	HOW YOU SAY IT
a The table is very near the kitchen/ the toilets.	The table is _____ near the kitchen. The table is _____ near the toilets.
b There is a lot of salt/sugar in the food.	This/It is _____ salty. This/It is _____ sweet.
c The food is cold.	This/It is _____ hot _____.

6 09.06 **Listen and repeat. Note the stress, for example, _What_ do you _fancy_? Mark /ə/ (remember, we often use /ə/ for *to* /tə/, *a* /ə/, *can* /cən/, *was* /wəz/, *are* /ə/, and /ən/ and for /fə/).**

Note where one word links to the next word, for example _steak and chips_?

Practise saying the phrases.

Listening and speaking

LISTENING 1: IN A CAFÉ

1 09.07 **Two friends are shopping and they go to a café. Listen to the conversation. Do they want a meal or a snack?**

2 09.07 **Listen to the conversation again. Read the sentences and choose T (true) or F (false).**
   a There are a lot of people in the café.   T/F
   b They choose a table near the window.   T/F
   c An Americano is smaller than an espresso.   T/F
   d They think a sandwich is a good idea.   T/F
   e They both fancy something sweet.   T/F
   f They both pay for their own food and drink.   T/F

LISTENING 2: IN A RESTAURANT

1 09.08 **It's Steve's birthday. Jenny and Steve go to a restaurant. Listen to the conversation. Do they have a good meal?**

2 09.08 **Listen to the conversation again. Answer the questions.**
   a What do they usually do to celebrate Steve's birthday?
   b What food and drink do they order?
   c What are two problems with the food and one other problem?
   d How much do they pay for their champagne?
   e Where do Jenny and Steve have dinner?

9 Restaurants and food

SPEAKING: IN A RESTAURANT

1 Imagine you are in a restaurant. Look at the menu in Reading 2: A restaurant website. Read the questions and prepare your answers.

The waiter:	Here's the menu and the wine list. Someone will be with you shortly to take your order. Can I get you any drinks while you look at the menu?
Your friend:	What are you having?
The waiter:	Are you ready to order?
The waiter:	What would you like?
The waiter:	Would you like any side orders or salads?
Your friend:	How was your meal?

2 09.09 Now listen and answer the questions. Use answers from Exercise 1. Can you do it without looking at your answers?

3 Look at the list of problems. Prepare what you say to the waiter. Use *Excuse me, I'm sorry but ...*
  a The table is very near the toilets and your glass is not clean.
  b There is a lot of salt in the salad and the soup is cold.
  c They brought red wine and you ordered white wine.
  d They didn't bring the bread.
  e The bill is not correct because they charged you for the burger twice (and you only had one).

4 09.10 Listen to the answers to Exercise 3. Then practise. Can you explain the problems without looking at the answers?

Reading and writing

READING 1: RESTAURANT DESCRIPTIONS AND REVIEWS

1 Read the descriptions of places to eat and drink. Match the names to the type of place.
  a A café/snack bar *Coffee Time*
  b A riverside pub with a garden
  c A busy city centre pub
  d A restaurant

sergio1109

The Red Lion (closed Mondays) Peter Street

This is a fantastic city centre pub serving traditional, good quality British meals with a wide selection of wines and beers from around the world. It can get very busy at lunchtime with local office workers and it isn't cheap but the service is excellent and quick and the people are very friendly. The dining room is open at lunchtime and in the evening until 10 p.m.

 Charlie M

Coffee Time (Mon–Sat until 7 p.m.) Black Lane

Popular with mums and kids after school, and a favourite with college students, this friendly snack bar and cafe is usually very busy, especially in the afternoon. The coffee is great, you can buy a wide selection of good home-made cakes, biscuits and sandwiches as well as hot snacks and everything is very cheap. Coffee Time is a great place for a coffee or a quick snack but it is a ten-minute bus ride from the city centre, near the college.

 London girl

The King's Head (open every day) Greenall Road

This is a small, traditional country-style pub. There is a good selection of British beers and lagers as well as some excellent whiskeys from Ireland. You can buy some delicious and very reasonably-priced sandwiches and other bar snacks at lunchtime but there is no food available in the evenings. It is usually quiet as it is about ten minutes on foot from the city centre but it's well worth the walk! It's a lovely place to have a drink and sit by the river on a warm, summer evening

 Katie5489

City Deli (Mon–Sat 11 a.m. till late) Arnott Square

This restaurant serves great European food, either eat-in or takeaway. You can buy snacks and sandwiches or a meal or just have a quiet coffee and enjoy the wonderful atmosphere of this fantastic modern space. The food is expensive and you sometimes have to wait a long time but it is very good. It's quiet. The staff are OK but not always very friendly. The City Deli is located in the city centre in the main shopping area.

2 Read the descriptions again. Match the reviews to the four places.

a 'A lovely place to have a fantastic lunch if you've got a lot of time and money.'
b 'This is a great place to have a cheap cup of coffee but it's popular with students and families and can be very busy and noisy. Not very central.'
c 'It was a long walk but I really enjoyed my pint of beer and cheese sandwich in this typically British pub.'
d 'We had an excellent, traditional British dinner of roast lamb with a lovely bottle of Portuguese wine.'

3 Read the reviews again and fill in the gaps in the table.

	THE RED LION	KING'S HEAD	COFFEE TIME	THE CITY DELI
Where is it?		ten-minute walk from the city centre, by the river		in the city centre in the main shopping area
What kind of food is there?		sandwiches, bar snacks	cakes, biscuits sandwiches, hot snacks	
What's the food like?			good, home-made	
When is it open?				Monday–Saturday 11 a.m.–late
What's it like?	fantastic, busy, excellent and quick service, very friendly staff			
Is it cheap or expensive?	not cheap			

4 **Look at the situations and choose the best place. You want:**
   a A traditional British meal such as a pie or fish and chips
   b To try a pint of British beer
   c A special celebration lunch with friends
   d A takeaway lunch while shopping
   e Somewhere peaceful to have a drink on a sunny afternoon
   f A quiet cup of coffee after shopping
   g A cheap cup of coffee and something to eat
   h Dinner with friends at 9 p.m. on a Sunday

WRITING: A REVIEW

1 **Write a review of a pub, restaurant or café you know. Use the questions in the table in Reading 1: Exercise 3. Here are some sentence starters you can use. Look for more ideas in the reviews in Reading 1: Exercise 1.**

This is a ...

It is a short walk from ...

It serves ...

The food is ...

It is open ...

Username

2 **Look on TripAdvisor for more ideas and then add your review to www.tripadvisor.co.uk!**

READING 2: A RESTAURANT WEBSITE

1 Look at the information about The National Café from a tourist information website. Can you find the café on a map of London?

> ### Where to eat in London ...
> **The National Café in the National Gallery, Trafalgar Square**
>
> (Monday–Friday 8 a.m.–11 p.m., Saturday 9 a.m.–11 p.m., Sunday 9 a.m.–6 p.m.)
>
> The National Café is a great place for breakfast, lunch, afternoon tea or dinner and well worth a visit. Its location makes it an excellent choice for anyone in central London, people who work near Trafalgar Square, shoppers and tourists visiting the Houses of Parliament or Westminster Abbey.
>
> Why not drop in for breakfast? We are open early every weekday morning. We also make a great lunch destination and our glorious afternoon teas are hard to beat. The café menu features a selection of regional dishes and includes a children's menu. We also have vegetarian, vegan and gluten and dairy free options. You can choose from a selection of cakes, pastries and baguettes or soups, salads and puddings as well as a range of hot and cold drinks.
>
> 'Grab and Go' is our self-service takeaway café, open from 10 a.m.–6 p.m., offering coffee, tea and a superb selection of freshly made sandwiches, salads and cakes.
>
> The National Café is the perfect place for a pre-theatre dinner. We offer a pre-theatre dinner menu for a special reduced price. The offer is available 5.30–7.30 p.m.
>
> ### Pre-Theatre Dinner Menu
>
> **Starters**
> Spring vegetable soup
> Roast chicken, lettuce, bacon & tomato salad
>
> **Mains**
> Wild mushroom omelette
> Beef burger with cheese and fries
> Fish of the day, broccoli and buttered carrots
>
> **Side Orders**
> Green salad
> Garlic bread
>
> **Desserts**
> Apple crumble, custard
> Vanilla ice cream, gingerbread biscuit
> Fresh melon
> A selection of teas and coffees

2 Read the information again. Read the sentences and choose true (T) or false (F).

a The National Café is in the centre of London. T/F
b It is open at 8.30 a.m. on a Tuesday morning. T/F
c There are a lot of different things to choose from for lunch. T/F
d You can buy a takeaway coffee at 9 a.m. T/F
e You can buy fish and chips to take away. T/F
f The pre-theatre menu is cheaper than the normal dinner menu. T/F
g You can have the special pre-theatre menu if you arrive at 5 p.m. T/F
h You can have breakfast on Sunday at 8.30. T/F

3 Look at the sample menu.

a What can a vegetarian eat?
b What would you choose from the menu?

Test yourself

1 Put the words into the correct part of the table.

> salad beer pasta a hamburger
> a cheese sandwich chocolate
> tomatoes potatoes bread an apple
> milk a banana roast beef a biscuit
> a packet of crisps fried chicken tea
> water rice fish and chips

FRUIT AND VEGETABLES	SNACKS	DRINKS	CARBOHYDRATES	MEALS

2 Look at the phrases. Note the phrases we don't usually say.
- **a** A can of milk
- **b** A piece of egg
- **c** A cup of tea
- **d** A glass of water
- **e** A piece of fish
- **f** A piece of salad
- **g** A litre of coffee
- **h** A packet of yoghurt
- **i** A bottle of orange juice
- **j** A pint of tea
- **k** A portion of rice
- **l** A can of water

3 Write sentences for things to say in a restaurant. You want ...
  a ... a table for five people.
  b ... to order a steak and chips.
  c ... to know if your friend's fish is good.
  d ... to complain because your meal is not very hot.
  e ... the bill.
  f ... to know if it is a good idea to leave a tip.
  g ... to say the bill is not correct.
  h ... to say the mistake is not a problem.
  i ... to know the number of millilitres there are in a pint.
  j ... to know the price of an Americano coffee.

4 Complete the matching sentence. Use *too* or *enough*.

a My soup is too cold.	My soup is not _____
b This portion _____	This portion is not big enough.
c The service is too slow.	_____
d _____	The restaurant isn't cheap enough.

5 Complete the opposite sentence.

a I want a lot of potatoes.	I don't want _____
b They can have a lot of rice.	They can't _____
c There was a lot of wine.	There _____
d He's got a lot of biscuits.	_____
e I didn't eat enough pasta.	_____

SELF CHECK

I CAN ...
○ ... talk about food and drink.
○ ... describe food and restaurants.
○ ... manage conversations in cafes and restaurants.

10

In this unit you will learn how to:
» manage simple business in shops.
» shop online.
» return products to shops.

Shopping and money

Shops and shopping in the UK

1 Read the text. Choose the correct word for each picture.

chemist   newsagent

shopping centre   supermarket

department store   market

a

b

c

d

e

f

Shopping is one of the most popular free-time activities in the UK and there are a lot of different places to go shopping. Some people like going to **shopping centres** where there are a lot of different shops in one building. In a shopping centre there are probably shops you know from your country.

Some people like shopping in a **market**. You can find a lot of things in markets. Markets are usually cheaper than shops and they are usually outside. Markets often sell fruit and vegetables, but a lot of markets sell other things, such as clothes, and they are usually interesting to walk around.

There are also some very famous **department stores** in the UK, such as Selfridges or Harrods. A department store sells a lot of different things but it is just one (very big) shop.

Most people in the UK do their food shopping in supermarkets because they are sometimes quite cheap. All supermarkets sell food and drink, but most supermarkets also sell other things, including clothes, health and beauty products and books and CDs.

People also buy things from newsagent's and chemist's shops. **A newsagent** sells newspapers and magazines, cigarettes, drinks, sweets and crisps. At a **chemist's** you can get medicines but also health and beauty products, for example, shampoo, soap or suncream.

Complete the table. Put *Yes, No* or *Sometimes* for each question.

	IS IT CHEAP?	CAN YOU BUY FOOD AND DRINK?	CAN YOU BUY CLOTHES?	CAN YOU BUY HEALTH AND BEAUTY PRODUCTS?
shopping centre				
department store				
market				
supermarket				
chemist				
newsagent				

2 What about you? Where do you buy clothes? Where do you buy food and drink?

SHOPPING ONLINE

3 Look at the questions. What do you think?
  a What is the most popular item to buy online?
  b What is the most popular website?
  c What are the best things about shopping online?
  d What is one of the bad things about shopping online?

4 Read the text and check your answers.

Nowadays, about 30% of shopping is online. Clothing is the most popular item and Amazon is the most popular site with over 300 million monthly visits. Many people like the convenience of online shopping and prices are often very competitive but delivery is usually not free and same-day or next-day delivery is sometimes very expensive. Some people like to 'buy online and pick up in store' (in the shop) to save delivery charges and some people take out a subscription, for example, to Amazon Prime, to get free and fast delivery (or shipping).

5 Answer the questions about you.
  a Do you shop online or in store or both?
  b When you shop online, do you pay for same-day or next-day delivery?
  c Do you have a subscription to an online retailer?
  d Which of the following do you buy online? Which do you buy in store?
  ▶ Clothes
  ▶ Electronic goods
  ▶ Beauty products
  ▶ Furniture
  ▶ Household appliances
  ▶ Groceries
  ▶ Books
  ▶ Shoes

Vocabulary builder

VOCABULARY 1: CLOTHES AND COLOURS

1 Choose the correct phrase for each picture.

> a pair of red shoes   some gold rings   a pair of white trousers
> a silver bag   ~~a pair of black jeans~~   a grey coat
> a green dress   a pink jacket   a blue T-shirt
> a purple shirt   a brown skirt   a blue and yellow jumper

a *a pair of black jeans* b _____ c _____ d _____

e _____ f _____ g _____ h _____

i _____ j _____ k _____ l _____

2 10.01 **Say your answers to Exercise 1. Then listen and repeat. Note the stressed syllables.**

3 Where do we put the colour adjective? Before the noun or after the noun? Look at Exercise 1 and decide.

VOCABULARY 2: SHOPPING ONLINE

1 Look at the different sections of a website. You want to buy the items in pictures a–j. Which website section do you click on?

> entertainment and books   health and beauty
> jewellery and watches   home and garden
> technology   sport and leisure   food and wine
> clothing   baby and child   flowers and gifts

10 Shopping and money

2 Describe the pictures in Exercise 1. Use *a*, *some* or *a pair of*. Say the colour of the item.

Example: a *some green soap*

VOCABULARY 3: IN THE SUPERMARKET

1 Complete the text. Use the pictures and the words in the box.

| barcode | receipt | trolley | basket | aisle | shelf |
| carrier bag | change | pay for | checkout | | |

Use a **a** basket or a **b** _____. Walk along each

c _____ and take the things you want off each

d _____. When you have got everything you want, go to the

e _____ where the assistant scans the **f** _____ on

each item. Put everything in a **g** _____. You can

h _____ your shopping by credit card, by debit card or in cash. If you use cash, you sometimes get i _____. The assistant then gives you a j _____.

VOCABULARY 4: MONEY

1 Choose the correct word or phrase for each picture.

| cash | coins | credit card | debit card | gift card |
| purse | wallet | get some money out/use an ATM | | |

a   b   c   d

_____ _____ _____ _____

e   f   g   h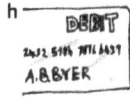

_____ _____ _____ _____

2 10.02 **Listen and repeat. Note the stressed syllable. Practise saying the words.**

3 Answer the questions for you.
   a How do you usually pay for your food shopping?
   b How do you usually pay for things in a market?
   c How do you usually pay for a holiday?
   d Have you got a purse or a wallet?
   e Have you got a lot of coins in your purse or wallet?
   f Do you like getting gift cards as presents? Why/Why not?
   g How often do you use an ATM to get some money out?
   h When you shop online, do you pay by debit card or credit card?

4 Cover the words and look at the pictures. Can you remember the words?

VOCABULARY 5: SPECIAL OFFERS

1 T-shirts are £12 each and you want to buy three. Look at the special offers. How much do you pay for three T-shirts? Complete the table.

SPECIAL OFFERS	HOW MUCH ARE THREE T-SHIRTS?
a Buy two get one free!	
b Buy two for £15!	
c Three for two on T-shirts!	
d Buy three save 20%!	
e 50% off when you buy two or more!	
f Save 1/3 on T-shirts!	
g Save £3 on all T-shirts!	
h Half price T-shirts (maximum two per customer)!	

2 Look at the completed table in Exercise 1. Which is the best offer?

Listening

LISTENING 1: BUYING SOUVENIRS

1 10.03 Listen to someone talking about five places to buy souvenirs in the UK. Put the places in the order she talks about them.

department stores   supermarkets
clothes shops   museum shops
souvenir shops

2 10.03 Listen again and look at pictures a–e. Where does she recommend buying these things?

a   b c   d   e

LISTENING 2: ENGLISH MONEY

1 10.04 **Listen to a student asking his teacher about English money. Read sentences a–f and decide if they are correct or incorrect. Correct the incorrect sentences.**
a There are £1, £2, £5, £10, £20 and £50 notes (paper money).
b There are 1p, 2p, 10p, 20p, 50p and £1 coins.
c £1 coins are gold and silver in colour.
d A fiver is the same as £50.
e A tenner is the same as £100.
f Five quid is the same as £5.

2 10.05 **Listen and note the prices a–l. Choose from the prices in the box.**

£4.28	£428	28p	£28	42p	£4	£10
	£10.28	10p	£4.10	£41	41p	

a _____   g _____
b _____   h _____
c _____   i _____
d _____   j _____
e _____   k _____
f _____   l _____

3 10.06 **Listen to the prices a–h. Are the prices more or less than £6.50? Listen and put *less* or *more*.**
a _____   e _____
b _____   f _____
c _____   g _____
d _____   h _____

4 10.06 **Listen again and note the prices.**
a _____   e _____
b _____   f _____
c _____   g _____
d _____   h _____

Conversation 1: Buying clothes

1 10.07 **Listen to eight customers in a clothes shop. Match the situations a–h with the customers 1–8.**

a She wants to pay by card.
b She wants a bigger size.
c She wants the trousers but she doesn't want the dress.
d She wants a different colour.
e She wants to try something on.
f She wants to know the price.
g She can't find trousers.
h She wants an umbrella.

2 Now read the conversations and look at the highlighted phrases. Put the phrases in the correct part of the table.

<u>Customer 1</u>
Customer: Excuse me. I'm looking for some red trousers.
Shop assistant: All our jeans and trousers are over there by the window.
Customer: Thank you.

<u>Customer 2</u>
Customer: Hello. Can you help me? Have you got this in a bigger size?
Shop assistant: Let me see ... No, I'm sorry.
Customer: Oh. OK.

<u>Customer 3</u>
Customer: Excuse me. Can you help me? Have you got this in a different colour?
Shop assistant: Yes, it comes in black, white or blue. Here you are.
Customer: Oh great, thanks.

<u>Customer 4</u>
Customer: Excuse me. Can I try this on?
Shop assistant: Yes, of course.
Customer: Where are the fitting rooms?
Shop assistant: Just over there.
Customer: Oh, thank you

Customer 5

Shop assistant: How were they? Any good?
Customer: Well, the trousers are really nice but the dress is no good. It doesn't fit. It's too big.

Customer 6

Customer: Sorry ... How much is this T-shirt?
Shop assistant: It's £20.

Customer 7

Customer: Excuse me. Have you got any umbrellas?
Shop assistant: No. I'm afraid we haven't, sorry. You could try a supermarket.
Customer: Is there a supermarket near here?
Shop assistant: Yes, it's about a five-minute walk along this street. It's on the left.

Customer 8

Shop assistant: That's £36.98.
Customer: Can I pay by gift card?
Shop assistant: Yes, that's fine. Shall I put the receipt in the bag?
Customer: Thank you.

WHEN YOU ARE ...	... YOU USE THESE PHRASES
... looking for things	a _____ b _____ c _____ d _____ e _____
... trying things on	f _____ g _____ h _____
... paying for things	i _____ j _____

SPEAKING AND PRONUNCIATION 1

1 10.08 **Listen and repeat. Note the stress, for example,** *Have you got any T-shirts?* **Mark /ə/. Remember, we often use /ə/ for** *there* /θə/, *a* /ə/, *can* /kən/, *have* /həv/, *are* /ə/ **and** *for* /fə/.

Note where one word links to the next word, for example try this on? Practise saying the phrases.

2 Correct the mistakes. You can listen again to the audio for Exercise 1 (10.08**) to help you. Then practise saying the sentences.**
   a I looking a dress.
   b Is a bank near here?
   c Have you some trousers?
   d Is there smaller?
   e Have you got this on different colour?
   f I can try this?
   g Where the fitting rooms?
   h The shirt not fit.
   i How much this?
   j I can pay dollars?
   k Can I pay with card?

3 What do you say?
   a You can't find the men's clothes.
   b You want to pay in cash but you need to get some money from the bank first.
   c You found a nice jacket but it is very small.
   d You found a lovely coat but it is too big.
   e You found a blue jumper but you want it in black.
   f You want to see if the T-shirt fits.
   g You want to know the price of the shoes.
   h You want to pay in euros.
   i You want to pay with a credit card.

VOCABULARY 6: CUSTOMER SERVICES

> **LANGUAGE TIP**
> You bought something but there is a problem. You take it back to the shop and talk to Customer Services. What can you get? You can usually get a *replacement*, a *refund*, a *credit note* or an *exchange*.

1 **Match the phrases to the descriptions.**

> get a replacement   get a credit note
> get a refund   get an exchange

a The shop gives you the money you paid.
b The shop gives you a new item, the same as the one you bought, but the new one has no problems.
c The shop gives you the same item but, for example, in a smaller size.
d The shop doesn't give you the money you paid, but you can have something else in the shop, for the same price.

Conversation 2: Taking things back to the shop

1 10.09 **Listen to four short conversations. Four customers are taking things back to a shop. The shop assistant asks them all for something. What is it?**

Customer 1

Customer: Good morning. I bought this hairdryer yesterday but it isn't working.
Shop assistant: Oh, I am sorry about that. Have you got the receipt?
Customer: Yes, here you are.
Shop assistant: Would you like a refund or a replacement?
Customer: I'd like a replacement, please.
Shop assistant: Have you got the card you paid with?
Customer: Yes, here you are.

Customer 2

Customer: Good morning. I bought this but it doesn't fit. Can I exchange it for a smaller one?
Shop assistant: Have you got the receipt?
Customer: Yes.
Shop assistant: And the card you paid with?
Customer: Yes, here you are.
Shop assistant: Thank you. That's fine.

10 Shopping and money   221

Customer 3

Customer: Good morning. I bought this dress but it's damaged. I'd like a refund, please.
Shop assistant: Oh yes, I see. That's no good. Have you got the receipt?
Customer: Yes, here you are.
Shop assistant: That's fine. I'm sorry about that.
Customer: That's OK. Thank you.

Customer 4

Customer: Good morning. I bought this last week but I don't want it now. Can I get a refund?
Shop assistant: Is there anything wrong with it?
Customer: No, I just changed my mind.
Shop assistant: I'm afraid we only give refunds if the item is faulty or damaged. We can do an exchange or give you a credit note.
Customer: Oh. OK. A credit note is fine. Thank you.
Shop assistant: But I'll need the receipt.
Customer: No problem – here it is.

2 10.09 **Listen again, and read the conversations. For each customer, choose the correct words from the options below and write the correct sentence.**

There **is/isn't** a problem and she gets **a refund/a credit note/a replacement/an exchange**.

Example: Customer 1: *There is a problem and she gets a replacement.*

3 10.09 **Why did the customers take their items back? Listen again and write a sentence for each customer.**

Example: Customer 1: *It isn't working.*

Customer 2: _____
Customer 3: _____
Customer 4: _____

4 Fill in the gaps in part B of the table. The sentences in part A and part B have the same meaning.

A	B
a I want a new one because this one is damaged.	I'd _____ a _____, please Can I get a replacement, please?
b I want you to return the money I paid.	I'd like a refund, please. Can I _____ a _____, please?
c I'd prefer a different size/colour.	I'd _____ to exchange it for a bigger/smaller/red one, please. _____ I _____ it for a bigger/smaller/red one, please?
d I wanted it before, but now I don't want it.	I just _____ my _____.

5 Look at the table in Exercise 4. Which phrases are polite? The ones in Part A or the ones in Part B?

SPEAKING AND PRONUNCIATION 2

1 10.10 Listen and repeat. Note the stress, for example, *I bought this but it isn't working*. Mark /ə/. Remember, we often use /ə/ for *but* /bət/, *doesn't* /dəznt/, *a* /ə/, *can* /kən/ and *for* /fə/. Note where one word links to the next word, for example *but it isn't working*.

2 Look at the pictures. Describe the problem and say what you want.

Example: a I bought this yesterday but it's not working. I'd like a replacement, please.

a bought yesterday/not working/new one

b bought last week/damaged/money back

c bought on Monday/not fit/different one

d bought last weekend/not want/money back

e bought them yesterday/not fit/different pair

3 **Look at the questions. Choose the correct answers from the box. Use one of the answers twice.**

> Yes, here you are.
>
> I'd like a refund, please.
>
> A credit note is fine, thanks.
>
> No, I just changed my mind.

a Is there anything wrong with it?
b Have you got the receipt?
c Have you got the card you paid with?
d Would you like a refund or a replacement?
e We can do an exchange or give you a credit note. Which would you prefer?

 4 10.11 **Practise the answers to Exercise 3 until you can say them without looking. Now imagine you are talking to a shop assistant. Listen and respond.**

Reading and writing

READING 1: A SOCIAL MEDIA POST

 1 **Paulina is on holiday in London. Read her social media post. Is Paulina's holiday good?**

Paulina Bartosz

Well here I am in London. The weather is fantastic and I love it here. We arrived on Thursday and I spent all day Friday, all day Saturday and all day yesterday shopping!!
On Friday I went to Portobello Market. It is a wonderful place, with lots of stalls outside on Portobello Road. There are a lot of second-hand market stalls and antiques and so many people walking about. Some things are very expensive but some things are really cheap. I bought a bag with a picture of a London bus and a couple of really nice T-shirts. On Saturday we went to Oxford Street. The street is very long and really busy but it is great fun and there are so many things to look at and buy. There is every clothes shop you can think of on Oxford Street. I looked at a lot of different things but I didn't spend too much money. There are also a lot of souvenir shops. I love all those things with pictures of the British flag and all the famous landmarks and I bought a few things to give to my family. I also went to a couple of the large department stores on Oxford Street. Selfridges is amazing. It is so big it is possible to spend a whole day there. It's got a lot of clothes and health and beauty things, the most expensive watches and jewellery, anything you can think of really. I spent a long time in the technology department looking at all the photography equipment. I didn't have enough money to buy a new camera but I bought a really nice new case for my phone. It's my souvenir from London!
I bought quite a few things to bring back as presents. I bought a lovely tin of biscuits for my mum and some make-up for my sister – it was cheaper in the supermarket than in Selfridges. And I bought my dad a book so he can practise his English!

16 June at 21:25

 2 Read the post again. Are the sentences a–m true or false? Choose T or F.

  a She spent two days shopping.   T/F
  b Everything at Portobello Market is very cheap.   T/F
  c She bought a bag and two T-shirts at Portobello Market.   T/F

d	It takes a long time to walk along Oxford Street.	T/F
e	Oxford Street isn't very interesting.	T/F
f	There are a lot of fashion shops on Oxford Street.	T/F
g	There aren't many souvenir shops on Oxford Street.	T/F
h	She spent a lot of money on Oxford Street.	T/F
i	Selfridges is on Oxford Street.	T/F
j	Selfridges sells a lot of different things.	T/F
k	She didn't buy anything in Selfridges.	T/F
l	She bought things for her family in the supermarket.	T/F
m	She bought four presents in the supermarket.	T/F

READING 2: TAKING THINGS BACK TO SHOPS

 1 Read the information. What does it give advice about? Choose the two correct answers.

a Returning something if you decide you don't want it.
b Returning something you bought online.
c Returning something because it isn't working.

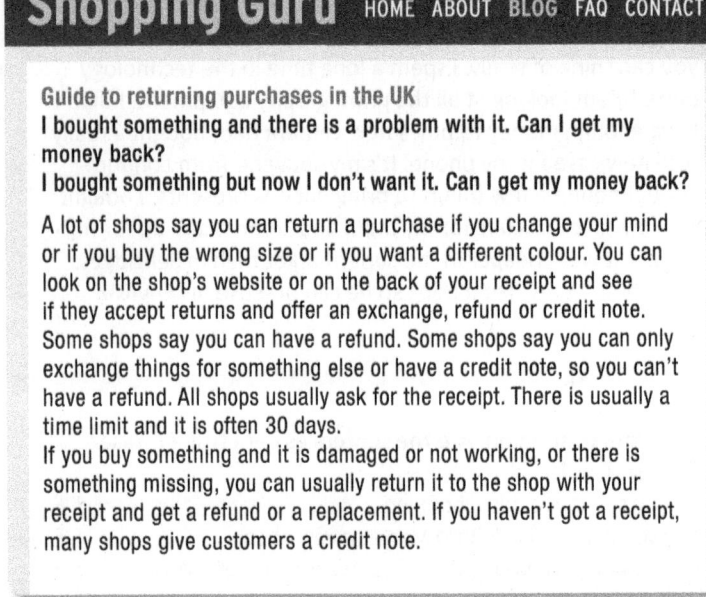

2 Read the advice again and fill in the gaps. Choose the correct phrase from the box.

> can usually   can sometimes   can't usually

a If you buy something and change your mind you _____ get a refund.
b If you change your mind and you haven't got a receipt, you _____ get a refund.
c If you change your mind but you used the item you _____ get a refund.
d If you change your mind after two months you _____ get a refund.
e If you buy something and want a different colour you _____ get an exchange.
f If you buy something and it doesn't work, you _____ get a refund.
g If you buy something and it is damaged, you _____ get a refund.

3 Read this information from a shop called Better Buys. Answer Yes or No to questions a–c.

AT BETTER BUYS WE WANT YOU TO BE HAPPY WITH EVERYTHING YOU BUY

- Are you unhappy with your purchase?
- Did you change your mind?
- Is the item in its original condition?
- Have you got your receipt?

If you are not 100% satisfied you can have a replacement or your money back.

- Is there a problem with your purchase?
- Have you got your receipt?

If you buy something and it is faulty you can have a replacement or your money back.

a You bought a handbag and it was damaged. You haven't got your receipt. Can you get a refund?
b You bought some earrings yesterday but now you don't like them. You have got your receipt. Can you get a refund?
c You bought a mobile phone case but it is too small for your phone! You have got the receipt. Can you get a replacement?

WRITING: COMPLAINING TO A SHOP

 1 Tom bought a camera from a shop but it was faulty. Read the email he sent to the shop. Did he get a replacement?

✉ **New message**

From: tom.mitcham@canadamail.com
Subject: Faulty Neonsurepix XL6870 compact digital camera
Date: 16 March
To: thegeneralmanager@camerasforyou.co.uk

Dear Sir/Madam,

On **15 March** I bought a **Neonsurepix XL6870 compact digital camera** and a Sundak memory card from your shop, **Cameras For You**, at **23 High Street, Dunwich**. I enclose a copy of the receipt. When I tried to **use the camera, it didn't work. The camera did not recognize the memory card**. I took the camera back to your shop the same day and asked for a replacement. The shop assistant told me he didn't have any more of the same **cameras** and so I asked for a refund. The assistant told me you don't give refunds, only a replacement or a credit note. I'm not happy about this! The **camera** was **faulty** when I bought it and I'd like a replacement or a refund. Please let me know by email when I can collect a replacement or get a refund.

I look forward to hearing from you.

Best regards,
Tom Mitcham

2 Using Tom's email in Exercise 1 to help you, write an email about problem A. Change the words in bold text. Then write an email about problem B. Can you do it without looking at Tom's email?

the item	A	B
the date	3 September	4 August
the shop	Phone Centre	BG's Homestore
the address	2, Main Street, Littleton	91, High Street, Newtown
the problem	it didn't work	it was damaged

✉ New message − ↗ ×

10 Shopping and money

Test yourself

1 **Look at the sentences about buying things from a website. Are the sentences true or false?**
   a You can buy a basketball in the Health & Beauty section.
   b You can buy a birthday card in the Flowers & Gifts section.
   c You can buy video games in the Entertainment & Books section.
   d You can buy headphones in the Technology section.
   e You can buy a packet of biscuits in the Clothing section.
   f You can buy a ring in the Jewellery & Watches section.
   g You can buy a towel in the Home & Garden section.
   h You can buy painkillers in the Sport & Leisure section.
   i You can buy a box of chocolates in the Food & Wine section.
   j You can buy a coat in the Baby & Child section.

2 **Do we use the words when we shop online, when we shop in the supermarket or both? Put the words in the correct place in the table.**

aisle   shelf   checkout   barcode   receipt
pay cash   pay with coins   get change
carrier bag   click on the section you want
add to your basket   add to your trolley
pay for shopping with a gift card
pay by debit card   pay by credit card
use a purse   use a wallet   fill in your card number

IN THE SUPERMARKET	ONLINE	BOTH

3 Choose the correct response to each question or sentence a–j.

a I'm looking for a swimming costume.
b Can I try this on?
c This doesn't fit.
d Have you got this in a size 12?
e How much is this T-shirt?
f Can I pay by card?
g I bought this radio but it isn't working.
h Is there anything wrong with it?
i I can't give you a refund a receipt.
j Can I exchange this for a colour?

1 OK, a credit note is fine.
2 Try a bigger size.
3 Yes, of course you can.
4 It's £40.
5 Have you got a receipt?
6 Yes, the fitting rooms are over there.
7 No, I just changed my mind.
8 Would you like a refund or a replacement?
9 Our sports department is without on the fifth floor.
10 I'm afraid that's the different smallest size we've got.

4 Books usually cost £10 each. Look at the special offers. Are the amounts correct? Correct the wrong amounts.

Example: **a** *Not correct. The correct amount is £10.*

SPECIAL OFFERS	HOW MUCH ARE THREE BOOKS?
a Buy two get one free	£20
b Three for two on books	twenty quid
c 50% off when you buy two or more	a tenner
d Save 1/3 on books	£15
e Half price books (maximum two per customer)	£15

SELF CHECK

I CAN ...

○ ... manage simple business in shops.
○ ... manage shopping online.
○ ... manage returning products to shops.

Review 2

This Review tests the main vocabulary and language from Units 6–10. Each task has a number of points. Do all the tasks. When you finish, check your answers. How many points can you get? There is a table at the end of the test. It tells you your score.

 1 **Read the examples. Write five more phrases to describe good weather and five more phrases to describe bad weather.**

Good weather: *It's a lovely day!*

Bad weather: *What terrible weather!*

                                                    Points: _____/10

2 **Add three more words to each group.**

Example: newsagent, shopping centre, clothes shop, chemist, supermarket, souvenir shop

  a red, blue, green, _____ _____ _____
  b bus, train, ferry, _____ _____ _____
  c a single room, _____ _____ _____
  d full board, _____ _____ _____
  e a jacket, a shirt, _____ _____ _____

                                                    Points: _____/15

3 **There is a mistake with the prepositions in each sentence. Correct the mistakes.**

Example: I am flying for Italy.   I am flying **to** Italy.

  a The train arrives to London this evening.
  b We are travelling to Italy in train.
  c I am going by foot.
  d She is visiting to London next year.
  e What time do you usually get to home?
  f Where's my passport? I left it in the table.
  g The taxi rank is at the left in front of the cinema.
  h The bus stop isn't far. It's about two minutes of here.
  i Can I pay for the tickets by cash?
  j I paid with credit card.

                                                    Points: _____/10

4 Read the sentences. Fill in the gaps with the correct form of the adjective.

Example: It is usually *colder* (cold) in the north than in the south.

a A B+B is usually _____ (cheap) than a hotel but a youth hostel is usually the _____ (cheap).
b A café is usually _____ (expensive) than a takeaway but a restaurant is usually the _____ (expensive).
c In the UK, it is usually _____ (hot) in the summer than in the winter. The weather in the winter is usually _____ (bad) than the weather in the summer.
d One of the _____ (good) places to go sightseeing is London but a lot of cities are _____ (beautiful) than London.
e The _____ (quick) way to travel is by plane but it is sometimes _____ (easy) to travel by train than by plane.

Points: _____/10

5 Look at the sentences. Choose the correct word.

Example: The film was very ~~interested~~/**interesting**.

a The journey took twelve hours. It was really **tired/tiring**.
b There was nothing to do on the journey. I was very **bored/boring**.
c The hotel was old and the rooms were dirty. We were really **disappointed/disappointing**.
d I'm going on holiday tomorrow! I'm really **excited/exciting**.
e We stayed in a fantastic hotel. It was **amazed/amazing**.

Points: _____/5

6 Complete the words. Then choose the correct word, travelling or hotels.

Example: return ticket travelling/~~hotels~~

a v _ _ _ n _ _ _ s travelling/hotels
b pas _ _ _ _ t travelling/hotels
c co _ _ _ _ t _ _ le travelling/hotels
d rec _ _ _ _ _ _ n travelling/hotels
e b _ _ _ _ ing c_ _ d travelling/hotels
f ha_ _ lu _ _ _ ge travelling/hotels
g del _ _ _ d travelling/hotels
h cen _ _ _ l travelling/hotels
i _ n _ _ i _ _ travelling/hotels
j sec _ _ _ _ y travelling/hotels

Points: _____/10

7 Make the sentences negative.

Example: I speak Spanish. I don't speak Spanish.

a You can smoke here. You _____
b We were in London. We _____
c She went to France. She _____
d I was tired. I _____
e It's very interesting. It _____

Points: _____ /5

8 Read about Isabella and Mike's weekend. Then write about it. Use the past simple form of the verbs and change the highlighted words. Start:

Her weekend was brilliant. She went to the beach with Paul and they had a great time ...

My weekend _____ (be) brilliant. I _____ (go) to the seaside with Paul and **we** _____ (have) a great time.

We _____ (stay) in a small hotel with a view of the sea and when **we** _____ (arrive) the weather _____ (be) lovely. On Saturday morning, **we** _____ (spend) a little time shopping at a local market. I _____ (buy) some souvenirs and then **we** _____ (walk) down to the sea and _____ (find) a lovely little café. **We** _____ (eat) lunch outside and _____ (go) for a walk on the beach. It _____ (be) beautiful. I _____ (take) a lot of photos and **we** _____ (visit) a castle just outside the town. The tourist office _____ (say) it was the oldest castle in the area. On Sunday **we** _____ (get) up late. After a fantastic breakfast, **we** _____ (hire) two bikes and _____ (go) cycling. It was lovely but after about an hour it _____ (start) raining so **we** _____ (not go) very far. The views _____ (be) amazing!

Points: _____ /30

9 Write the verbs in the past simple.

Example: like liked

a feel
b fly
c forget
d get
e give
f know
g leave
h lose
i make
j see
k ask
l enjoy
m try
n travel
o use
p enrol
q want
r work
s look
t do

Points: _____ /20

10 Look at the problems. How do you complain? Use the word in brackets and write sentences.

Example: You are in a hotel room. The lights don't turn on (working).

Excuse me. I'm afraid the lights aren't working.

a You are in a hotel room. You can't connect to the hotel Wi-Fi. (working)
b You are in a hotel room. You've got sheets but no pillows. (there)
c You are in a restaurant. The rice is very salty and you can't eat it. (too)
d You are in a restaurant. The soup is cold and you want it to be hot. (enough)
e You are in a restaurant. They put wine on your bill. You didn't have any wine. (mistake)

Points: _____ /5

11 Read the answers. Use the words in brackets and write the questions.

Example: Perhaps the steak. (like) What would you like?

a It's about 250 kilometres. (far)
b It's £23 return. (ticket)
c At half past ten. (train, leave)
d Three and a half hours. (take)
e Probably by train. (best, there)
f Take the first left and it's on the right. (train station)
g Sorry. We are fully booked. (vacancies)
h Yes, the price is for full board. (dinner)
i Ten o'clock. (check-out)
j It's hot and sunny. (weather)

k He was at home. (where, yesterday)
l I bought a T-shirt and a couple of books. (what)
m £4.99. (much, this T-shirt)
n We only accept cash I'm afraid. (credit card)
o No, I'm afraid that's the smallest size we've got. (size)

Points: _____ /15

12 Choose the correct container. Use each word once.

> can   piece   glass   portion
> packet   cup

Example: a glass of water/wine

a a _____ of crisps/biscuits
b a _____ of toast/bread
c a _____ of coke/beer
d a _____ of rice/vegetables
e a _____ of coffee/tea

Points: _____ /5

13 Make the sentences more polite.

Example: I want to exchange it for a bigger one.
I'd like to exchange it for a bigger one.

a Where is The Rex Hotel?
b I want to make a reservation.
c The TV isn't working.
d Please book theatre tickets for me.
e We want a table for two.
f I want a steak.
g I want a refund.
h Give me the bill.
i The bill is not correct.
j Help me, please.

Points: _____ /10

14 Are the foods countable or uncountable? Choose C (countable) or U (uncountable) and complete the phrase with *some* ...

Example: orange C/U~~ *some oranges*

a biscuit C/U some _____
b cheese C/U some _____
c egg C/U some _____

d tomato C/U some _____
e burger C/U some _____
f butter C/U some _____
g meat C/U some _____
h broccoli C/U some _____
i bread C/U some _____
j fruit C/U some _____

Points: _____ /20

15 Look at the sentences from conversations in a tourist office, a restaurant and a clothes shop. Find the mistakes. Write the sentences correctly.

Example: You should to visit the Art Gallery.
You should visit the Art Gallery.

a It's well worth to go on a guided tour.
b I'd recommend to hire a car.
c How many pasta would you like?
d I don't want much vegetables.
e Can I have a rice?
f Can I to try this on?
g I'm looking for some pair of jeans.
h Have you got this in different colour?
i It not fit.
j I can have replacement?

Points: _____ /10

Check your answers in the Answer key. How many points did you get?

Look at the table. Is your score excellent, very good, quite good or not too bad? Is it a good idea to do some more practice?

140–180	Excellent – congratulations! You are ready to move on to a higher level.
100–139	Very good. You understand a lot of English and can use a lot of vocabulary and language points from Units 6–10. Note the things that are difficult and practise them again.
60–99	Quite good. You understand some English and can remember some of the vocabulary and language points from Units 6–10. It is a good idea to look at the difficult points and practise them again.
59 or less	Not too bad! English can be difficult to learn. It is a good idea to read Units 6–10 again and repeat some of the exercises for more practice. When you feel more confident, do the test again.

Answer key

KEY POINTS ABOUT ENGLISH PRONUNCIATION

1 a yes **b** yes **c** yes **d** no **e** no **f** no
3 a what **b** name **c** give **d** friendly **e** hospital
4 a 2 **b** 1 **c** 3
5 a <u>Lon</u>don **b** Aus<u>tra</u>lia
6 a Good <u>morn</u>ing. **b** How are <u>you</u>? **c** My name's <u>Cin</u>dy.
7 a I <u>live</u> in <u>Rome</u>. **b** I <u>come</u> from <u>Spain</u>. **c** I <u>don't know</u>.
8 a no **b** yes **c** no **d** no **e** yes **f** no
9

Does she <u>speak English</u>?	<u>Yes</u>, she <u>does</u>.
Can you <u>swim</u>?	I can <u>speak French</u>.
<u>Yes</u> I <u>can</u>.	She can <u>speak Arabic</u>.
I'd <u>love to</u>.	I'm <u>going</u> to <u>France</u>.
There are <u>two chairs</u>.	<u>How</u> are <u>you</u>?
Are there any <u>more</u>?	<u>Yes</u>, there <u>are</u>.

10 The words 'name' and 'is' sound like one word. The last sound in 'name' (/m/) links to the first sound in 'is' (/ɪz/)
11 a I live_in China. **b** Get started_in_English!
12 Person A
13

	FRIENDLY, POLITE, INTERESTED ☺	NOT FRIENDLY, RUDE, NOT INTERESTED ☹
a Hello	X	
b Good morning		X
c How are you?	X	
d Thank you		X
e Sorry	X	
f Excuse me	X	
g OK		X

UNIT 1 HELLO! WHERE ARE YOU FROM?

US and UK cities
1 and 2 a London, **b** Manchester, **c** Glasgow, **d** Belfast, **e** Birmingham, **f** Washington D.C., **g** New York, **h** Los Angeles, **i** New Orleans, **j** San Francisco

Vocabulary 1: Greetings
1 and 2 'Hello': (informal) Hi, Hi there, Hello; (formal) Good morning, Good afternoon, Good evening.
'Goodbye': (informal) Bye, Bye bye, Goodbye, See you later, See you tomorrow; (formal) Good night

Vocabulary 2: Countries
1 a Japan, **b** Canada, **c** Russia, **d** Brazil, **e** France, **f** Indonesia, **g** Australia, **h** The United States, **i** Korea, **j** Germany, **k** Egypt, **l** Spain, **m** India, **n** South Africa, **o** The UK, **p** China
2 a United Kingdom **b** Scotland **c** England **d** Wales **e** Northern Ireland
3 Japan, France, Korea, Spain, Canada, Indonesia, Germany, India, Russia, Australia, Portugal, South Africa, Brazil, The United States, Egypt, China, England, Scotland, Wales, Northern Ireland, The United Kingdom

Conversation 1: *What's your name? Where are you from?*
1 Tom
2 and 3 My name's Tom. I'm from England. My name's Anita. I'm from India.
5 and 6 What's your name? Where are you from?

Vocabulary 3: Nationalities
1

COUNTRY	NATIONALITY
India	Indian
Germany	German
France	French
The United States	American
Spain	Spanish
Brazil	Brazilian
Egypt	Egyptian
Indonesia	Indonesian
England/the UK	English
Wales/the UK	Welsh

Answer key

Russia	Russian
South Africa	South African
Canada	Canadian
Japan	Japanese
Korea	Korean
Australia	Australian
China	Chinese
Portugal	Portuguese
Ireland/the UK	Irish
Scotland/the UK	Scottish
The UK	British

2 <u>In</u>dian, <u>Ger</u>man, French, Am<u>e</u>rican, <u>Spa</u>nish, Bra<u>zil</u>ian, <u>E</u>gyptian, Indo<u>ne</u>sian, <u>Eng</u>lish, Welsh, <u>Rus</u>sian, South <u>Afr</u>ican, Ca<u>na</u>dian, Japa<u>nese</u>, Ko<u>rea</u>n, Aus<u>tra</u>lian, Chi<u>nese</u>, Portu<u>guese</u>, <u>Ir</u>ish, <u>Scot</u>tish, <u>Bri</u>tish

Conversation 2: *I'm* + nationality
Tom: I'm English; **Anita** I'm Indian.

2
<u>My</u> name's <u>Tom</u>. I'm from <u>England</u>. I'm <u>English</u>.
<u>My</u> name's <u>Anita</u>. I'm from <u>India</u>. I'm <u>Indian</u>.

3

Sarah	South Africa	South African
Yuki	Japan	Japanese
Natasha	Russia	Russian.

b My name's Nelson. I'm from Brazil. I'm Brazilian.
c My name's Sarah. I'm from South Africa. I'm South African.
d My name's Yuki. I'm from Japan. I'm Japanese.
e My name's Natasha. I'm from Russia. I'm Russian.

5
Ali:	Hello!
Anita:	Hi.
Ali:	My name's Ali. What's your name?
Anita:	My name's Anita. Where are you from?
Ali:	I'm from France. I'm French. And you?
Anita:	I'm from India. I'm Indian.
Nelson:	Hello!
Sarah:	Hi.

Nelson:	My name's Nelson. What's your name?	
Sarah:	My name's Sarah. Where are you from?	
Nelson:	I'm from Brazil I'm Brazilian. And you?	
Sarah:	I'm from South Africa. I'm South African.	

6

Yuki:	Hello!
Natasha:	Hi.
Yuki:	My name's Yuki. What's your name?
Natasha:	My name's Natasha. Where are you from?
Yuki:	I'm from Japan. I'm Japanese. And you?
Natasha:	I'm from Russia. I'm Russian.

Vocabulary 4: Languages
1 and 2

COUNTRY	LANGUAGE	NATIONALITY
Spain	Spanish	Spanish
Germany	German	German
Brazil	Portuguese	Brazilian
England	English	English
The United States	English	American
China	Chinese	Chinese
France	French	French
Egypt	Arabic	Egyptian
Russia	Russian	Russian
Japan	Japanese	Japanese
Korea	Korean	Korean
India	Hindi, Bengali	Indian

3 ese, (i)an

4 Top 10 languages: 1 English; 2 Chinese; 3 Hindi; 4 Spanish; 5 Arabic; 6 French; 7 Bengali; 8 Portuguese; 9 Russian; 10 Urdu

5 Top 10 Internet languages: 1 English; 2 Chinese; 3 Spanish; 4 Arabic; 5 Indonesian/Malaysian; 6 Portuguese; 7 French; 8 Japanese; 9 Russian; 10 German

Conversation 3: *Where do you live? Do you speak English?*
1 a Canada, **b** France, **c** English, **d** a little French, **e** French
2 Sally: I live in Canada. I speak English. I don't speak French.
Mike: I live in France. I speak a little French.

3 and 4 a I <u>live</u> in <u>Canada</u>. **b** I <u>speak English</u>. **c** I <u>speak</u> a little <u>French</u>. **d** I don't speak <u>Chinese.</u>
5 a I live in India. I speak Bengali. **b** I live in Egypt. I speak Arabic. **c** I live in Hong Kong. I speak Chinese.
6 a I speak Spanish. I speak a little Arabic. I don't speak English. **b** I speak Russian. I speak a little Portuguese. I don't speak Bengali. **c** I speak German. I speak a little English. I don't speak Korean.
7 and 8 <u>Where</u> do you <u>live</u>? Do you <u>speak French?</u>

Conversation 4: Polite phrases
1 First picture, Conversation 2. Second picture, Conversation 1.
2 a excuse me **b** sorry **c** sorry **d** excuse me
3 d, a, b, c, e
4 please
5 a please **b** please **c** please **d** thank you **e** thank you
6 Ex<u>cuse</u> me, <u>Sorry</u>, Please, <u>Thank</u> you, I don't under<u>stand</u>, Can you speak more <u>slowly</u>, please?

Listening: Meeting people
1a
2

Claudia	German	England	English
Rama	Indonesian	Canada	English French Indonesian

3

	FATIMA	SOFIA
I'm from Russia.		√
I'm from Pakistan.	√	
I live in Dubai.	√	
I live in London.		√
I speak Russian.	√	√
I speak English.		√
I speak Arabic.	√	

Pronunciation 1: Greeting people and sounding friendly
1 a 😊, b ☹, c ☹, d 😊, e 😊

Pronunciation 2: Letters of the alphabet, spelling
2

/ei/	/i:/	/e/	/ai/	/eu/	/u:/	/a:/
A, H J, K	B, C D, E G, P T, V	F, L M, N S, X, Z	I, Y	O	Q, U W	R

3 a America, **b** New York, **c** United Kingdom, **d** Quebec, **e** European, **f** Italian, **g** Australia, **h** New Zealand, **i** Jamaica, **j** Spanish

Pronunciation 3: Saying email and web addresses
2 a www **b** . **c** @ **d** .com **e** / **f** .org **g** .co.uk **h** -
4 www.tripadvisor.co.uk
www.visitbritain.com
www.washington.org
enquiries@visitlondon.com

Reading and writing: Personal forms
1 a children, **b** date of birth, **c** married, **d** address, **e** single
2 Female: Mrs, Miss, Ms; Male: Mr
3 All correct (✓)

Reading: A visa application form
1d

Test yourself
1

	INFORMAL	FORMAL
Hello	Hi Hi there Hello	Good morning Good afternoon Good evening
Good bye	Bye bye Bye See you later See you tomorrow	Good night Goodbye

2

Live in ...	Speak ...	Nationality
England	English	English
France	French	French
The United States	English	American
Saudi Arabia	Arabic	Saudi (Arabian)
Germany	German	German
China	Chinese	Chinese
Spain	Spanish	Spanish

3

a What's your name?	My name's (your name).
b Where are you from?	I'm from (your country). I'm (your nationality).
c Where do you live?	I live in (your city/country).
d Do you speak English?	No, I don't. Yes, I do./a little. I speak (your first language). I speak a little (language). I don't speak (language).

UNIT 2: FAMILY AND FRIENDS, JOBS AND HOME

Family life and homes in the UK
1 b **2** a **3** c **4** a **5** a

Vocabulary 1: Family, plural nouns
1

		and
grandfather	grandmother	grandparents
father	mother	parents
son	daughter	children
brother	sister	
husband	wife	

2 Hamish (grandfather), Prudence (grandmother), Jean (mother), Bryan (father), Julian (brother), Ruby (sister), Michael (husband), Paul (son), Ellie (daughter)

3 b father **c** children **d** grandmother **e** grandfather

4 and 5

1 +s	2 y → i +es	3 fe → v + es	IRREGULAR PLURALS
girl – **girls** son – sons daughter – daughters brother – brothers sister – sisters boy – boys	family – **families** baby – babies	wife – **wives** life – lives	child – **children** man – **men** woman – **women** person – **people**

6 grandmother, grandfather, grandparents, mother, father, parents, sister, brother, husband, wife, son, daughter, children, men, women, people, girls, boys, families, babies, lives

Vocabulary 2: Jobs and workplaces

1 a4 **b**2 **c**6 **d**5 **e**1 and 7 **f**3

2 a1 **b**2 **c**4 **d**6 **e**7 **f**3 **g**5

3 I'm a nurse. I work in a hospital. I'm a businesswoman. I work in an office. I'm a factory worker. I work in a factory. I'm a teacher. I work in a school. I'm a doctor. I work in a hospital. I'm a computer programmer. I work at home. I'm a shop assistant. I work in a shop.

Conversation 1: *Have got; a, an and any*

1 Bob b, David c

2 We've got three children. I've got a sister and a brother. My sister hasn't got any children. They've got two children. David's got a very good job.

3

+	–	?
I/you/we/they have got	I/you/we/they haven't got	Have I/you/we/they got?
He/she/it has got	He/she/it hasn't got	Has he/she/it got?

4 and 5

A	AN	ANY
with singular nouns	with singular nouns that begin with a, e, i, o, u	with plural or uncountable nouns in a question or a negative sentence
house job car garden house job	iPod umbrella iPhone	brothers or sisters children free time questions friends grandparents

6

Mary: Tell me about your family.

Joanna: Well, I am married and we've got three children, two girls and a boy. I've got two sisters and a brother. My brother is married but he hasn't got any children.

Mary: What about your sisters?

Joanna: My older sister hasn't got any children. She isn't married. She's got a very good job. She's an engineer. My other sister is married and they've got two children, a boy and a girl.

My, his, her, etc.
1 b His **c** Her **d** Their **e** Our

Conversation 2: Questions and answers about *he* or *she*

1 a, b

2

		Nationality	Lives in	Speaks
Amélie	wife	French	Canada	English (+ French)
Louise	sister	American	Brazil	Spanish (+ English)

3

QUESTIONS	ANSWERS
What's her name?	Her name's Amélie.
Where is she from?	She's from France. She's French.

Where does she live?	She lives in Brazil.
Does she speak English?	No, she doesn't. Yes, she does.
What about Spanish and Portuguese?	She speaks Spanish but she doesn't speak Portuguese.

4 She works in an office. She is/'s a businesswoman.

Vocabulary 3: Describing your home
1 a3 **b**6 **c**1 **d**2 **e**7 **f**4 **g**5

2 a de<u>ta</u>ched <u>house</u>, a <u>terr</u>aced <u>house</u>, a <u>se</u>mi-de<u>ta</u>ched <u>house</u>, a flat, a <u>vill</u>age, a town, a <u>ci</u>ty

3 I <u>live</u> in <u>France</u>. I <u>live</u> in the <u>north</u> of <u>Eng</u>land. I <u>live</u> in the <u>south</u> of <u>France</u>. I <u>live</u> in the <u>east</u> of Ja<u>pan</u>. I <u>live</u> in the <u>west</u> of <u>Ger</u>many. I <u>live</u> in a <u>town</u> near <u>Lon</u>don. I <u>live</u> in a <u>vill</u>age <u>ten miles</u> from <u>Man</u>chester.

Conversation 3: *Where do you live? What's it like?*
1 a

Vocabulary 4: Describing people and places
1 Places: modern; Places and people: beautiful, important, noisy, interesting; People: hard-working, funny, young

2

small	big
new (places) young (people)	old
quiet	noisy
funny	serious
boring	interesting

3 boring

5 b quite small **c** quite big **d** very big/really big

6 <u>ty</u>pical, big, small, new, <u>mo</u>dern, <u>love</u>ly, nice, <u>frien</u>dly, <u>bor</u>ing, old, <u>qui</u>et, great, im<u>por</u>tant, <u>noi</u>sy, <u>beau</u>tiful, young, <u>se</u>rious, kind, <u>fun</u>ny, hard-<u>work</u>ing, <u>ve</u>ry <u>small</u>, <u>quite</u> <u>small</u>, <u>quite</u> <u>big</u>, <u>ve</u>ry <u>big</u>, <u>real</u>ly <u>big</u>

Adjectives with *to be*
1 is/'s, are

2

	+	–	?
I	I am (I'm)	I'm not	Am I?
you we they	you are (you're) we are (we're) they are (they're)	you aren't we aren't they aren't	Are you? Are we? Are they?
he she it	he is (he's) she is (she's) it is (it's)	he isn't she isn't it isn't	Is he? Is she? Is it?

3 b Is it very big? **c** Is she funny? **d** They're / They are nice and friendly. **e** I'm / I am hard-working.
4 Where do you live? What's it like?

Using *there is, there are*; articles
1 Yes
2 There are a lot of places to visit. There is a really good market in the town. There aren't any nightclubs. There isn't any Wi-Fi or mobile reception at the house.
3 a a gym, a nightclub, a post office **b** mobile reception **c** banks, people
4 b There is 5G coverage. **c** There is a pub./There are some pubs.
d There isn't a cinema. **e** There isn't any 3G coverage. **f** There are some banks.
g There are some hotels./There is a hotel. **h** There are a lot of supermarkets.
i There is mobile reception. **j** There isn't a post office. **k** There aren't any shops.
5 a T **b** F **c** T
6 In the town, there is a hotel and there are some pubs. There isn't a cinema but there are a lot of internet cafés. There's a market and there are some supermarkets.
7 In the city there are a lot of hotels and a lot of pubs. There are some cinemas, a lot of internet cafès and a lot of banks.

Listening: Describing family and where you live
1 Michael c, Christina b
2 b M **c** L **d** C

Pronunciation: Weak forms and linking – prepositions and articles
1 There's a <u>ca</u>fé. There <u>isn</u>'t a <u>shop</u>. There <u>isn</u>'t any <u>Wi</u>-Fi. There <u>aren</u>'t any <u>tour</u>ists. <u>Is</u> there a ho<u>tel</u>? <u>Are</u> there any <u>shops</u>? <u>I've</u> got a <u>cat</u>. <u>He's</u> got a <u>car</u>. She <u>has</u>n't got an um<u>bre</u>lla. We <u>have</u>n't got a <u>gar</u>den. Have you <u>got</u> an <u>iPho</u>ne?

Speaking: Describing family and where you live
1

Christina:	Is this your family, Michael?
Michael:	Yes. It's not a very good photo but this is my wife, Helen, and our son, Harry. We've got three children. This is a good photo, my wife with Harry and next to Harry is his brother, Paul and his sister, Anna.
Christina:	Is this where you live?
Michael:	Yes. It's a small detached house in a very beautiful village in the south of England. It's about 50 miles from London. It's very quiet and there isn't a lot to do, but we like it. There is a shop and a pub but there aren't any restaurants or cafés and there isn't a bank or a post office. What about you, Christina? Where do you live?

Reading 1: Personal details
1 a He's from The United States. **b** (Her name's) Amélie Lafayette. **c** She's from France. /She's French. **d** Yes, they've/they have got a daughter. Her name is Marie. **e** He lives (in Montreal) in Canada.

Reading 2: Describing your home
1 b
2 a, b, c, d, e, g, k, m

Writing 1: A description of where you live
1 There is a big living room with a sofa and a TV. There are two bedrooms, one with a single bed and one with a double bed. There's a bathroom with a shower but there isn't a bath. In the kitchen, there is an oven and a fridge but there isn't a microwave. There is Wi-Fi in the flat but there isn't a phone. There isn't a garden.

Test yourself
1 b husband **c** son **d** sister
2 b women **c** children **d** brothers **e** lives **f** babies **g** people **h** families
3 a I am a nurse. I work in a hospital. **b** I am a teacher. I work in a school. **c** I am a computer programmer. I work at home. **d** My sister is a businesswoman.

She works in an office. **e** My grandmother hasn't got a job. She doesn't work.
4 b Her name is Susana. **c** She lives in Spain. **d** She speaks Spanish. **e** She doesn't speak French. **f** She's from Australia. **g** She's Australian. **h** She works in a hospital. **i** She's a nurse. **j** She's very kind. **k** She's got two children. **l** She hasn't got a car.
5 b Where is he from? **c** What's his name? **d** Does he speak English? **e** Does he live in a city? **f** What's it like? **g** Has he got any children? **h** Are there any hotels in his town?
6 b It's quite small. **c** It's very boring. **d** The people are really friendly. **e** There are some beautiful old houses. **f** There's a lovely pub. **g** There aren't any shops. **h** There isn't a café. **i** There isn't any Wi-Fi in the pub.

7

PLACES	PEOPLE AND PLACES	PEOPLE
noisy, modern, new, big, typical, small	Any three of: beautiful, lovely, nice, boring, great, old, interesting, friendly, noisy, quiet, important	Any three of: serious, kind, funny, young, hard-working

UNIT 3: NUMBERS, TIMES AND DATES

Festivals, celebrations and important dates
1 and 2

A	B	C
Festival	**2026**	**2027**
Chinese New Year	17 February	6 February
Ramadan	17 February–18 March	7 February–8 March
Passover	1–9 April	21–29 April
Easter	5 April	28 March
Eid al-Udha	26 May	16 May
Jewish New Year (Rosh Hashana)	11–13 September	1–3 October
Diwali	8 November	29 October
Christmas	25 December	25 December

3 a 1876, **b** 1973, **c** 1943, **d** 1927, **e** 1901, **f** 1903, **g** 1885, **h** 1817

Vocabulary 1: Numbers
1 1 one, 3 three, 4 four, 5 five, 6 six, 7 seven, 9 nine, 11 eleven, 12 twelve, 13 thirteen, 15 fifteen, 16 sixteen, 17 seventeen, 18 eighteen, 19 nineteen
2 b 32, **c** 48, **d** 56, **e** 64, **f** 75, **g** 89, **h** 97, **i** 100
3 b 200, **c** 2200, **d** 220, **e** 2000, **f** 202 **g** 2,022
4 One thousand and twenty and two; One thousand and two hundred. The word *and* is pronounced /ənd/.
6 5, 11, 16, 60, 20, 33, 71, 95, 100, 206, 350, 2000, 2010, 3053, 4900

Vocabulary 2: Days, months, seasons
1 Sunday, Monday, Tuesday, Wednesday, Thursday, Friday, Saturday
2 January, February, March, April, May, June, July, August, September, October, November, December
3 a spring, **b** summer, **c** autumn (US fall), **d** winter
4 a winter, **b** summer, **c** autumn
5 Mon<u>day</u>, <u>Tues</u>day, <u>Wed</u>nesday, <u>Thurs</u>day, <u>Fri</u>day, <u>Sat</u>urday, <u>Sun</u>day, <u>Jan</u>uary, <u>Feb</u>ruary, March, <u>Ap</u>ril, May, June, Ju<u>ly</u>, <u>Au</u>gust, Sep<u>tem</u>ber, Oc<u>to</u>ber, No<u>vem</u>ber, Dec<u>em</u>ber, spring, <u>sum</u>mer, <u>au</u>tumn, <u>win</u>ter

Vocabulary 3: Dates
1 3/1 the third of January, 25/11 the twenty-fifth of November, 4/4 the fourth of April, 8/10 the eighth of October
2 1st first, 3rd third, 4th fourth, 5th fifth, 7th seventh, 8th eighth, 12th twelfth, 20th twentieth, 22nd twenty-second, 25th twenty-fifth, 31st thirty-first. Different ending: ones with **first, second, third**
3 first, <u>sec</u>ond, third, fourth, fifth, sixth, <u>sev</u>enth, eighth, ninth, tenth, e<u>lev</u>enth, twelfth, <u>thir</u>teenth, <u>four</u>teenth, <u>fif</u>teenth, <u>six</u>teenth, <u>sev</u>enteenth, <u>eigh</u>teenth, <u>nine</u>teenth, <u>twen</u>tieth, twenty-<u>first</u>, twenty-<u>sec</u>ond, twenty-<u>third</u>, twenty-<u>fourth</u>, twenty-<u>fifth</u>, twenty-<u>sixth</u>, twenty-<u>sev</u>enth, twenty-<u>eighth</u>, twenty-<u>ninth</u>, <u>thir</u>tieth, thirty-<u>first</u>
5 7/11, 12/4, 3/9, 5/6, 25/12, 1/1, 3/5, 31/7, 4/8, 21/4, 30/3, 22/9, 8/12, 2/10, 20/3
6 a the first of January, **b** the twenty-third of November, **c** the fourth of October, **d** the fifteenth of April, **e** the twenty-second of March **f** the thirty-first of July
7 23rd November b, 1st January a, 31st July f, 4th October c, 22nd March e

8 b 1789 **c** 2015 **d** 1830 **e** 1066 **f** 1642 **g** 2013 **h** 1974
9 b 1900 **c** 1702 **d** 2000 **e** 2001 **f** 2009

Conversation 1: Using numbers in questions and answers
1 b
2 b 05/04/1993 **c** 19, **d** WB14 7JR, **e** 01723 453123, **f** 07396 213431
3 b When were you born? **c** What's your address? **d** What's your postcode? **e** What's your phone number? **f** What's your mobile number?
4 a When were you born? **b** When was your daughter born? **c** I was born in 1989. **d** He was born in 1972. **e** She was born in the first year of the 21st century, in 2000!
5 a 3 (1989), **b** 1 (1881), **c** 3 (2003), **d** 2 (19th C), **e** 2 (16th C), **f** 2 (20th C)

Phone numbers
1 For 0 we usually say *oh* not *zero*. For 55 we say *double five*.
3

453123	four five three one two three
01925	oh one nine two five
213431	two one three four three one
07322	oh seven three double two
664011	double six four oh double one

The time
1 Excuse me. Could you tell me what time it is, please?
2 a It's midday, **b** It's one o'clock, **c** It's eleven o'clock, **d** It's midnight. **e** It's four o'clock, **f** It's six o'clock
3 a It's ten past six, **b** It's twenty past six, **c** It's twenty-five past six, **d** It's twenty to seven, **e** It's five to seven
4 a It's six fifteen. **b** It's half past six. **c** It's quarter to seven.
5 it's <u>one</u> o'<u>clock</u>, it's <u>six</u> o'<u>clock</u>, it's <u>mid</u>night, it's el<u>ev</u>en o'<u>clock</u>, it's mid<u>day</u>, it's <u>quar</u>ter to <u>six</u>, it's <u>six</u> fifteen, it's <u>half</u> past <u>six</u>, it's <u>six thir</u>ty, it's <u>quar</u>ter to <u>seven</u>, it's <u>six</u> forty-<u>five</u>, it's <u>ten</u> past <u>six</u>, it's <u>twenty</u> past <u>six</u>, it's <u>six twenty</u>, it's <u>twenty</u>-five to <u>seven</u>, it's <u>six</u> thirty-<u>five</u>, it's <u>ten</u> to <u>seven</u>, it's <u>six fifty</u>

6 b

7

6 a.m.	9 a.m.	2 p.m.	4.30 p.m.	7.45 p.m.	9 p.m.	11 p.m.	2 a.m.
06.00	09.00	14.00	16.30	19.45	21.00	23.00	02.00

Conversation 2: *What time ...?*

1 a, c, d

2 a It opens at 9.30, **b** It closes at 6 p.m., **c** It starts at 11 o'clock, **d** It finishes at 12.15, **e** 2.

3 and 4

the museum, the bank, the park, the post office, the art gallery, the shop	What time does it open?	**a** What time does it close?
the tour of the city, the football match, the tour of London, the film, the TV programme, the English class, the concert	**b** What time does it start?	What time does it finish?

5 b How long does it last? It lasts one hour. **c** How long does it last? It lasts three hours. **d** How long does it last? It lasts five hours.

Prepositions of time

1 a False. He was born in 1978. **b** False. He was born in the twentieth century. **e** False. His daughter was born in April. **f** False. His daughter was born in spring.

2 a F b T c T d F e F f F g F

3 and 4

IN	ON	AT
the morning, the afternoon, months, the evening, seasons, years, centuries January, autumn, 2012, 1999, March, spring, the 20th century	dates, days Monday, 21 July, Friday, 10/11/14	festivals, night, the weekend, time dinnertime, Christmas, 8 o'clock, Easter, 7.30, lunchtime

5 b in, **c** in, **d** in, **e** on, **f** in, **g** at, **h** on, **i** at, **j** at, **k** at, **l** in, **m** at

Pronunciation: Weak forms of *does*, *was*, *were*, *of*, *at*, and
1 The underlined words are all stressed and we say them with a strong voice. The highlighted words are not stressed and we say them with a weak voice. They all have the sound /ə/ does /dəz/, were /wə/, was /wəz/, of /əv/, at /ət/, and /ənd/

Listening 1: A phone conversation about meeting
1 no
2 a 07795 340431 **b** 07452 456 799 **c** 020 8563 4536. Date next Tuesday is 3(rd) April or 03/04.

Listening 2: UK and US festivals and celebrations
1 a Hallowe'en **b** Thanksgiving **c** Mother's Day **d** Christmas **e** US Independence Day **f** Easter

2 Thanksgiving, US Independence Day.

Speaking 1: Enrolling for a course
Receptionist: Hello, can I help you?
Student: Good morning. Can I enrol for the English conversation class?
Receptionist: Yes, of course. You just need to complete the enrolment form. We can do that now if you like. What's your name?
Student: **a** Maria Costa.
Receptionist: And your date of birth? What's your date of birth?
Student: **b** The seventh of November 1992.
Receptionist: And where do you live?
Student: **c** 4, Cross Street, Millchester.
Receptionist: And what's your postcode?
Student: **d** SK38 5RR.
Receptionist: Fine. And what's your phone number?
Student: **e** 0161 458 6950.
Receptionist: Just two more questions ... have you got an email address?
Student: **f** mariacosta567@gmail.sp.
Receptionist: And where are you from, what's your nationality?
Student: **g** Spanish.
Receptionist: Great. So if I could just take payment, that is all done and you can start on Monday.
Student: Lovely. Thank you very much.
Receptionist: See you Monday.

Speaking 2: In a tourist office

1

Advisor: Good morning. Can I help you?
Tourist: Yes please. I'd like some information about the City Art Gallery.
a What time does it open?
Advisor: Ten o'clock in the morning.
Tourist: **b** And what time does it close?
Advisor: Seven thirty in the evening.
Tourist: Thank you. And there is a concert today in the Royal Albert Hall.
c What time does it start?
Advisor: Six o'clock.
Tourist: **d** Great, and how long does it last?
Advisor: About two hours.
Tourist: **e** What time does it finish?
Advisor: About eight thirty. There's an interval of about 30 minutes.
Tourist: Thank you.

Reading: Tourist posters

1 b yes, **c** yes, **d** no **e** yes
2 b yes, **c** yes, **d** yes
3 b 12.20 p.m. **c** Saturday **d** 11.30 p.m. **e** 08712 231 231 **f** 1st January or 1/1 or New Year's Day **g** 7:30 p.m. **h** 01852 566430 **i** 7 p.m. **j** 3 p.m. **k** No. **l** 1 p.m. **m** No **n** Yes **o** 3 p.m. **p** 10 a.m. **q** 4 p.m.

Writing 2: Greeting cards

1 a Happy Birthday! **b** Happy Anniversary! **c** Merry Christmas! **d** Happy Diwali! **e** Happy Mother's Day! **f** Happy Thanksgiving! **g** Happy New Year! **h** Congratulations!

Test yourself

1

Days of the week	Months of the year	Seasons	Parts of the day
Tuesday, Monday, Wednesday, Thursday, Friday, Sunday	January, March, December, April, August, October	summer, autumn, spring, winter	morning, afternoon, night, evening

2 Five hundred, Five hundred and five, Five hundred and fifty, Five hundred and fifty-five, Five thousand, Five thousand and five, Five thousand and fifty, Five thousand and fifty-five, Five thousand five hundred, Five thousand five hundred and fifty
3 b in **c** in **d** in **e** at **f** on **g** at **h** at
4

4 a.m.	four in the morning
five o'clock in the afternoon	5 p.m.
half past four	four thirty
five twenty	twenty past five
four o'clock in the afternoon	16.00
ten to five	four fifty
4.15	quarter past four

5 4/1, 19/4, 12/6, 31/10, 2/12
6 a does **b** last **c** were **d** 's

UNIT 4: EVERYDAY LIFE, SPORTS AND FREE TIME

Popular sports in the UK and the US

1

THE UK	THE US
swimming	American football
running	baseball
cycling	basketball
football	ice hockey

3 Answers and Audioscript 04.01 b Over 50% of young people (16–25 years old) play sport once a week. **c** About 50% of people don't play any sport. **d** 46% of English people watch football on television. **e** 25% of people in the UK watch the Wimbledon final. **f** 90% of the UK population watched some of the 2012 Olympics on television.

Vocabulary 1: Sports
1 foo<u>t</u>ball, <u>cri</u>cket, <u>jog</u>ging, <u>bas</u>ketball, <u>hock</u>ey, <u>swim</u>ming, <u>ten</u>nis, <u>vol</u>leyball, <u>base</u>ball, <u>rug</u>by, golf, <u>cyc</u>ling
2 b American football

3

play	football, cricket, basketball, hockey, tennis, volleyball, baseball, rugby, golf
go	cycling, jogging, swimming

Vocabulary 2: Other leisure activities
1 a watch TV/television **b** listen to music **c** read **d** go to the cinema **e** go to a museum/an art gallery **f** go out with friends **g** go shopping **h** go on the internet **i** play computer games **j** go on social media

2 watch T<u>V</u>, watch tele<u>vi</u>sion, go <u>out</u> with <u>friends</u>, <u>lis</u>ten to <u>mu</u>sic, <u>go</u> <u>shop</u>ping, <u>go</u> on the <u>in</u>ternet, go on <u>so</u>cial <u>me</u>dia, read, play com<u>pu</u>ter games , <u>go</u> to the <u>ci</u>nema, g<u>o</u> to a mu<u>se</u>um, g<u>o</u> to an <u>art</u> gallery

Conversation 1: *like/love/hate* + verb +*ing*

1 Sandra

2

	🎬	🍽️	🚶	🎮	📺
Tom	♡	♡		✖	♡
Sandra		♡			♡

	📖	💻	🎧	🖼️	f#
Tom	♡	♡	♡	✖	✖
Sandra	✖	♡	✖	♡	♡

3

♡♡♡	**e** I love going on Facebook™.
♡♡	**d** I like going on the internet.
♡	**a** I quite like reading.
✖	**c** I don't like using social media.
✖✖	**b** I hate playing computer games.

4 b I love watching TV. **c** I like going out with friends. **d** I like going on the internet. **e** I quite like listening to music. **f** I don't like going to museums or art galleries. **g** I hate playing computer games. **h** I love going out with friends and family. **i** I like watching television. **j** I quite like going to museums and art galleries. **k** I don't like reading. **l** I don't like listening to music.

Vocabulary 3: Everyday verbs and nouns

2

get up early	06.30	go to bed early	20.30
get up late	10:00	go to bed late	01.30

3 and 4

do	have	get	go
the <u>house</u>work the <u>clean</u>ing the <u>shopp</u>ing the <u>wash</u>ing the washing <u>up</u>	a <u>shower</u> <u>break</u>fast <u>lunch</u> <u>dinn</u>er	<u>up</u> <u>dressed</u> <u>home</u> up <u>early</u> up <u>late</u>	to <u>work</u> <u>out</u> to <u>bed</u> to bed <u>early</u> to bed <u>late</u> online

Vocabulary 4: *How often?*
1 c I go out for lunch twice a month
2 once (one time); twice (two times)
3

<u>al</u>ways	✓	✓	✓	✓
<u>u</u>sually	✓	✓	✓	✗
<u>some</u>times	✓	✓	✗	✗
<u>nev</u>er	✗	✗	✗	✗

4 We say 'once /ə/ month'.
5 a and **c** are correct.
6 b twice a month **c** always **d** usually **e** never **f** sometimes

Conversation 2: Present simple third person (*he* or *she*)
1 Yes
2 a F **b** T **c** T **d** F **e** F **f** F

3 and 4

I You We They	**He** **She** **verb + s**	I You We They	**He** **She** **verb + es** **(if the verb ends in ss, x, ch, sh or o)**	I You We They	**He** **She** **+ irregular verb**
play	**a** plays	watch	**f** watches	have	**j** has
listen	**b** listens	finish	**g** finishes		
live	**c** lives	do	**h** does		
cook	**d** cooks	go	**i** goes		
get	**e** gets				

5

I/You/We/They	He/She	I/You/We/They	He/She
use	uses	say	says
live	lives	choose	chooses
speak	speaks	know	knows
read	reads	decide	decides
write	writes	see	sees
look	looks	start	starts
practise	practises	give	gives
put	puts	help	helps

6 a Do I ...? / Do you ...? **b** I don't ... / You don't ... **c** Does he ...? / Does she ...? **d** He doesn't ... / She doesn't ... **e** Does he go on Facebook™? He doesn't go on Facebook™.

7 a He doesn't watch television. **b** He doesn't listen to music. **c** Does he use the computer? **d** Does he go to work early?

8 She **gets up** early and **goes** to the gym at seven o'clock. She **has** a shower and breakfast and then she **goes** to work. She **starts** work at nine o'clock and **finishes** at five thirty. She usually **has** lunch in a café near work. She **doesn't like** staying in the office for lunch. She **does** the shopping before she **goes** home. She **gets** home at about seven o'clock and **cooks** dinner. In the evening, she usually **watches** television or **uses** the computer. She **likes** going on the internet. She **doesn't go** to bed late but she often **reads** before she **goes** to sleep.

Can/Can't
1 b drive **c** speak French **d** use a computer **e** ride a bike **f** cook **g** sing **h** swim **i** use Microsoft Excel
2 a
3 a F **b** T **c** T
4 a I can do it. **b** I can't do it.
5 a He can cook. **b** He can speak French. **c** I can't speak French. **d** He can't ride a bike. **e** Can you play the piano?
6

I You He/She/It **can + verb** We They	I You He/She/It **can't + verb** We They	I you **Can** he/she/it **+ verb?** we they
I can swim. He can cook. He can speak French.	I can't speak French. He can't ride a bike.	Can you play the piano?

Listening: A journalist asks people about their everyday life
1 Person 1
2 Person 1 a F **b** F **c** F **d** T **e** F **f** T **Person 2 g** T **h** T **i** F **j** T **k** F **l** T
3 a five o'clock **b** eleven thirty **c** Friday, Saturday **d** doesn't like **e** loves using

Pronunciation 1: Third person singular verb endings

There are three ways of pronouncing the final 's', /s/, /z/ and /iz/.

2

/S/	/Z/	/IZ/
visits takes gets starts	plays goes reads stays listens	watches finishes uses

Answer key 261

Pronunciation 2: *Can* and *can't*

1 I can speak French but I can't speak Spanish. Can you? Yes, I can, and I can speak Japanese. Can you speak Japanese? No, I can't.

2

affirmative	I can speak French	/kən/
question	Can you?	/kən/
negative	I can't speak Spanish	/kɑːnt/
short answer negative	No, I can't	/kɑːnt/
short answer affirmative	Yes, I can	/kæn/

Pronunciation 3: Questions in the present simple

1 Where does he work? What time does he start? When do you go? What do you cook?

2

QUESTION WORD	DO/DOES	SUBJECT	MAIN VERB
When What	do /də/	you	go? cook?
Where What time	does /dəz/	he/she	work? start?

Reading 1: A free time questionnaire
1 yes
2 a T **b** F **c** T **d** F **e** T **f** F

Reading 2: A personal profile
1 a Tracy **b** Susan **c** Margaret

2

	MARGARET	SUSAN	TRACY
♡	going out with friends, visiting family, going to museums and art galleries, going to the cinema, watching sports, listening to music, going on the internet	going to the theatre and the cinema, watching television, going out with friends to restaurants, listening to jazz music	animals, going on the internet, playing computer games, playing the guitar and listening to music
✗	playing sports, using Facebook™	cooking, using the computer, going on the internet	watching television
(can)	use a computer speak English	speak German, English and Japanese play tennis swim	speak English
(can't)	play the piano	speak French	play the guitar very well speak French

3 Tracy

Test yourself

1 a football **b** cricket **c** jogging **d** basketball **e** hockey **f** swimming **g** tennis **h** volleyball **i** baseball **j** rugby **k** golf **l** cycling

2

DO	HAVE	GET	GO
the washing	breakfast	home	jogging
the washing up	a shower	up	to work
the housework	lunch	dressed	out
the cleaning	dinner	up early	to bed
the shopping		up late	to bed early
			to bed late

3 a I have breakfast at eight o'clock. **b** I go to English classes once a week. **c** I am never late. **d** I love learning English. **e** I don't like doing homework. **f** I can't speak English very well. **g** My teacher helps me a lot. **h** My girlfriend speaks English very well.

4 a She goes to the gym every day. **b** He has breakfast at eight o'clock. **c** He doesn't work in the evening. **d** I play tennis twice a week. **e** I like going to the cinema. **f** He doesn't like cooking dinner. **g** He loves watching TV. **h** She doesn't like going on Facebook™. **i** I can play the piano. **j** He can't play the guitar.

5 a He loves going out with friends **b** He quite likes going to the cinema **c** He doesn't like using social media **d** He hates doing the housework **e** He always gets up early in the summer **f** He doesn't have breakfast at home **g** He has lunch at work **h** He sometimes goes to bed after midnight **i** He goes to the gym twice a week **j** He is never late for work **k** He goes out for lunch on Sunday **l** He doesn't go to the gym at the weekend **m** He can speak Portuguese **n** He can't use a computer very well **o** He usually finishes work late **p** He cooks dinner every night **q** He starts work at seven o'clock in the morning **r** He watches television every evening **6 a** cook **b** cooking **c** cook **d** cook **e** cook **f** cook **g** cooks **h** cooking **i** cook **j** cook **k** cook **l** cooking **m** cook **n** cooks **o** cook

UNIT 5: GOING OUT

Popular places for going out
1 b, c, a
2 a F **b** F **c** F **d** T **e** F **f** F

Vocabulary 1: Asking how people are and responding
1 c, e, b, d, a
2 b ☺ **c** ☺☺☺ **d** ☺ **e** ☺☺☺

f ☺☺

3 <u>How</u> are <u>you</u>? I'm <u>very</u> <u>well</u>. I'm <u>fine</u>. I'm <u>good</u>, <u>thanks</u>. I'm O<u>K</u>. I'm <u>not bad</u>. <u>So</u>-<u>so</u>.

Vocabulary 2: Social activities
1 a go to a concert **b** go to an art gallery **c** go to someone's house for a meal **d** go to a restaurant or a café **e** go to the cinema **f** go to the theatre **g** go to the pub

2 a go to a restaurant or a café **b** go to someone's house for a meal **c** go to the cinema **d** go to the pub

3 <u>go</u> to a <u>concert</u>, <u>go</u> to an <u>art</u> gallery, <u>go</u> to someone's <u>house</u> for a <u>meal</u>, go <u>round</u> for <u>dinner</u> or <u>lunch</u>, <u>go</u> to a <u>restaurant</u>, <u>go</u> to a <u>café</u>, go <u>out</u> for a <u>meal</u>, go <u>out</u> for <u>dinner</u>, go <u>out</u> for <u>lunch</u>, go <u>out</u> for something to <u>eat</u>, <u>go</u> to the

cinema, go and see a film, go to the theatre, go to the pub, go out for a drink
4 b He likes going out for dinner. **c** She likes going to the theatre. **d** I like going to the pub. **e** I like going to a restaurant. **f** They like going out for a meal.

Vocabulary 3: Time phrases
1 b tomorrow **c** Wednesday **d** Thursday **e** the day before yesterday
f Saturday **g** Sunday
2 a next **b** last **c** this
3 a 1st September **b** 8th September **c** 5th September **d** 29th August
e 10th September **f** 4th September
4 to<u>day</u>, <u>yes</u>terday, the <u>day</u> before <u>yes</u>terday, to<u>mor</u>row, the <u>day</u> after to<u>mor</u>row, <u>last week</u>, <u>this week</u>, <u>next week</u>, last <u>Tues</u>day, this <u>Thurs</u>day, next <u>Wednes</u>day

Conversation 1: Making, accepting and declining an invitation
1 a Saturday **b** go to the pub **c** go for a coffee, now
2 b to **c** go **d** Do **e** fancy **f** going **g** Do **h** to **i** go
3 a to do **b** doing **c** to do
4 *Would you like to do something?* is the most polite; the other two are quite informal.
5 Would you <u>like</u> to go to the <u>cin</u>ema? Do you <u>fancy</u> going to the <u>cin</u>ema? Do you <u>want</u> to go to the <u>cin</u>ema?
6 a Do you fancy going *or* Do you want to go **b** Do you fancy going out *or* Do you want to go out **c** Do you want to go
7 a Would you like to go **b** Would you like to go out **c** Would you like to go
8 Saying *yes*: Yes, that would be great. Yes, I'd love to. Saying *no*: I'm really sorry, I can't. I'm afraid I can't. I can't do (Friday etc.). (Thursday etc.) is no good.
9 <u>Yes</u>, <u>that</u> would be <u>great</u>. <u>Yes</u>, I'd <u>love</u> to. I'm <u>really</u> <u>sorry</u>, I <u>can't</u>. I'm a<u>fraid</u> I <u>can't</u>. I <u>can't</u> do <u>Fri</u>day. I <u>can't</u> do <u>next week</u>. I <u>can't</u> do <u>eight thir</u>ty. <u>Thurs</u>day is no <u>good</u>. <u>23 Ju</u>ly is no <u>good</u>. The <u>eve</u>ning is no <u>good.</u>

Vocabulary 4: Using *It's too* + adjective
1 a nice **b** quiet **c** lovely **d** beautiful **e** great **f** new **g** typical **h** noisy **i** big
2 a expensive **b** good **c** cheap **d** bad
3 It's too big.
4 b too expensive **c** too noisy **d** too small
5 bad, good, cheap, ex<u>pen</u>sive, It's <u>too big</u>. It's <u>too noi</u>sy. It's <u>too</u> ex<u>pen</u>sive. It's <u>too small</u>.

Conversation 2: Making suggestions and arrangements
1 a No **b** Yes
2 b How about **c** Let's **d** Why don't we + verb? **e** How about + verb + ing or noun? **f** Let's + verb
3 That's a great/nice/lovely idea. That sounds great/nice/lovely.
4 <u>How</u> about <u>out</u> for a <u>meal</u>? <u>How</u> about a <u>drink</u>? <u>Why</u> don't we go to the <u>cin</u>ema? <u>Let's</u> watch T<u>V. No</u>, it's too <u>noisy. No</u>, it's too ex<u>pen</u>sive. <u>No</u>, I'm not <u>hun</u>gry. <u>That's</u> a good i<u>dea. That</u> sounds <u>lovely</u>.
5 a Let's go out for lunch. **b** Why don't we meet at the train station? **c** That sounds great. Let's meet at two o'clock. **d** Why don't we go out for a drink? **e** How about meeting in The King's Head at seven tomorrow?
6 a How about going out for lunch? **b** Let's meet at the Manchester Deli at one o'clock. **c** Why don't we go and see a film? **d** How about meeting in front of the cinema at six o'clock?

Conversation 3: Talking about preferences
1 a café
2 a T **b** F **c** F **d** T
3 a I'd prefer to, I'd rather **b** I'd prefer to **c** I'd rather
4 prefer to have, rather have
5 c They'd prefer to go in the evening.
6 I'd pre<u>fer</u> to have a <u>sand</u>wich. She'd pre<u>fer</u> to go to the <u>cin</u>ema. We'd pre<u>fer</u> to meet to<u>mor</u>row. I'd <u>rath</u>er go to a <u>ca</u>fé. He'd <u>rath</u>er stay at <u>home</u>. They'd <u>rath</u>er go to the <u>cin</u>ema.
7 a A sandwich is OK but I'd prefer to have a meal. **b** A glass of water is OK but I'd rather have/I'd prefer to have a glass of wine. **c** A restaurant is OK but I'd rather go/I'd prefer to go to the pub. **d** A cup of coffee is OK but I'd rather have/I'd prefer to have a cup of tea. **e** The TV is OK but I'd rather go/I'd prefer to go to the cinema.

Conversation 4: Using the present continuous for plans
1 going out to the cinema
2 a Friday **b** Saturday **c** Sunday **d** because
3 a is coming, are going **b** 'm going
4 a is **b** coming **c** are **d** going **e** am/'m **f** going **g** he **h** she **i** you **j** they
5 all true
6 My <u>mum</u> is <u>com</u>ing to <u>Lon</u>don on <u>Fri</u>day. We are /ə/ <u>go</u>ing out for <u>lunch</u> on <u>Fri</u>day. I am /əm/ <u>go</u>ing to a <u>con</u>cert on <u>Thurs</u>day. She is <u>work</u>ing at <u>home</u> on <u>Tues</u>day. We are /ə/<u>go</u>ing to the <u>cin</u>ema at the <u>week</u>end. I'm <u>see</u>ing him this <u>even</u>ing.

7 Wed – coffee with Sarah, Thurs – lunch with Suzy, Sun – cinema with Sam, because they are not planned/arranged, it is just an idea or a suggestion.
8 a On Monday I am going to the dentist. **b** On Tuesday I am working at home. **c** On Tuesday I am having lunch with mum. **d** On Friday Mum and I are going to London for the day. **e** On Saturday I am meeting Paula at the Manchester Deli. **f** On Saturday evening we are going to the cinema. **g** On Sunday I am having lunch with mum and dad at one o'clock. **h** On Sunday afternoon Paul is playing football at two o'clock.
9 a On Monday, she is going to the dentist at ten o'clock and she is having lunch with Jackie at two o'clock. **b** On Wednesday, Jackie and Linda are going to the cinema. **c** On Thursday she is going to the doctor at eleven o'clock. **d** On Saturday morning she is playing tennis at eleven o'clock. **e** On Sunday she is having lunch with her mum and dad at one o'clock.
10 a Are you doing anything on Friday? **b** Is Friday/Saturday/Sunday any good? **c** Are you free on Friday/Saturday/Sunday? **d** How about Friday/Saturday/Sunday?
11 Are you <u>do</u>ing anything on <u>Fri</u>day? Is <u>Sat</u>urday any <u>good</u>? <u>How</u> about <u>Sun</u>day? Are you <u>free</u> on <u>Sun</u>day?

Listening 1: Planning to meet
1 a Go to a café and go to the cinema. **b** At the café at six.
2 a F **b** T **c** F **d** F **e** T **f** F **g** T **h** F **i** F **j** F

Listening 2: Plans and arrangements
1 a Go to a café and go to an art gallery **b** At the gallery at twelve
2 a good **b** Tuesday **c** Tuesday **d** on Wednesday **e** is **f** Simon **g** Simon **h** Simon

Reading: A party invitation
1a wedding **b** New Year **c** birthday
2 a T **b** T **c** F **d** F **e** T **f** T **g** F

Writing: Email invitations: Making and changing plans
1 a first email – Linda, second email – Paula **b** go for a coffee **c** 11 a.m. on Friday
2 Linda's email: I'm good, Thursday is no good, I'd rather go to, It's really nice./It's great./It's really good. Let's meet at 11 on Friday./ How about meeting at 11 on Friday? How about 11 on Friday? **Paula's email:** Would you like/Do you want/How about, Are you doing anything on Thursday or Friday?/How about Thursday or Friday?/ Is Thursday or Friday any good?

How about/Let's meet at/Why don't we meet at, I'd prefer to go, How about 11?/Are you free at 11?/Are you doing anything at 11?

Test yourself
1 I'm very well, I'm fine, I'm good, thanks, I'm OK, I'm not bad, So-so.
2 b go to a pub, go out for a drink **c** go to a concert **d** go to the theatre **e** go to an art gallery **f** go to someone's house for a meal, go round for a meal/dinner/lunch/coffee **g** go to a restaurant/café, go for coffee/out for a meal/dinner/lunch/something to eat
3 a Would you like to go out for a meal? Yes, I'd love to. **b** Do you fancy going for a coffee? I'm really sorry, I can't. **c** Do you want to go to the cinema? Yes, that would be great. **d** Do you fancy a meal? I'm afraid I can't. **e** Would you like a cup of tea? I'd rather have a cup of coffee. **f** Do you fancy a sandwich? I'd prefer to have a meal. **g** How about meeting on Friday? I can't do Friday. **h** Let's meet at six o'clock. Six o'clock is no good. **i** Why don't we meet at the train station? That's a great/good idea. **j** How about a café? That sounds great. **k** Let's meet in The Queen's Head. No, it's too noisy. **l** How about The Red Lion? No, it's too expensive. **m** Are you free on Tuesday? I'm sorry, I can't do Tuesday. I'm meeting my dad. **n** Are you doing anything at the weekend? My brother is visiting us. **o** How about Monday? We are going out for dinner.
4 a tomorrow **b** Sat 16th **c** Wed 13th **d** the day before yesterday **e** last Monday **f** Sat 16th **g** next Saturday **h** Tues 12th **i** Fri 15th **j** next Friday

REVIEW 1
1 So-so, good, not bad, very well, OK
2 a Tuesday, Thursday **b** yesterday, the day after tomorrow **c** July
3 b I live in England. **c** I live in a detached house. **d** It's too noisy. **e** I am really tired. **f** He works in a factory.
4 a The first of February nineteen fifty-six **b** The twenty-second of December two thousand and two **c** The fifth of January nineteen ninety-nine **d** The thirtieth of October two thousand and ten **e** The fourteenth of August two thousand and sixteen
5 (a) in **(b)** at **(c)** in **(d)** in **(e)** on **(f)** on **(g)** at **(h)** in **(i)** at **(j)** on

6 a **b** **c** **d** **e**

7 a babies **b** boys, girls **c** children **d** families **e** cities **f** people **g** countries **h** men, women

8 a www.londonlife/shopping.org.uk **b** info@visitamerica.com **c** www.englishhelp/grammar/presenttenses.co.uk

9 a W W W dot U-K-T-O-U-R-I-S-T dot org slash A-D-V-I-C-E **b** M-A-R-E-K-O dot Y-U-M-I three five seven at yahoo (Y-A-H-O-O) dot com

10 a What time does it start? **b** How long does it last? **c** When were you born? **d** How old are you? **e** When's your birthday? **f** What's your telephone number? **g** What's your postcode? **h** What's your address? **i** What's your name? **j** Where are you from? **k** Where do you live? **l** What's his name? **m** Where does he live? **n** Does he speak English? **o** Has he got any children?

11 a They don't live in New York. **b** I don't like listening to music. **c** He doesn't get up early. **d** She doesn't speak Japanese. **e** There aren't a lot of people. **f** He isn't from New Zealand. **g** It isn't very beautiful. **h** He can't speak French. **I** He hasn't got a car. **j** I haven't got a lot of free time.

12 a quite **b** really **c** too **d** There is **e** there are **f** there isn't a **g** there aren't any **h** there are a lot of **i** there isn't a **j** there isn't any

13 a fancy going **b** to go **c** a good idea **d** about **e** is no **f** I am **g** How about meeting/Are you free **h** prefer to **i** to go **j** rather **k** meet **l** is/sounds **m** too **n** don't we meet **o** perfect/great/good/OK

14 a He is **b** He works **c** He loves **d** He's got **e** he can **f** He loves his **g** he hasn't got **h** he can't **i** He goes **j** plays **k** goes **l** He cooks **m** he doesn't like **n** he goes **o** he goes **p** he has **q** he goes **r** He stays **s** he doesn't **t** he's

15 a He can speak English. **b** I can't speak Japanese. **c** He is friendly. **d** They are hard-working. **e** This is my family. I have got three children. **f** This is Anna's family. She has got two sisters. **g** She doesn't like going to the cinema. **h** She loves watching TV. **i** On Sunday I am having lunch with mum and dad. **j** On Sunday Paul is playing football at 2 o'clock.

UNIT 6: TRANSPORT AND DIRECTIONS

Travelling around the UK by public transport
1 a (plane), **g** (coach), **h** (train)
2 a Y **b** Y **c** N **d** Y **e** Y

Vocabulary 1: Travel and places
1 a plane, **b** ferry, **c** taxi, **d** car **e** bicycle **f** bus **g** coach **h** train **i** underground (tube) **j** foot
2 a airport – plane, **b** station – train, **c** taxi rank – taxi, **d** bus stop – bus, **e** coach station – coach
3 on foot

4 train, <u>under</u>ground (in London), tube, bus, plane, coach, <u>ta</u>xi, <u>mi</u>ni cab, car, <u>fer</u>ry, <u>bi</u>cycle, bike, by <u>train</u>, by <u>car</u>, on <u>foot</u>, <u>air</u>port, <u>sta</u>tion, <u>ta</u>xi rank, <u>bus</u> stop, <u>coach</u> station, <u>fer</u>ry port

Vocabulary 2: Public transport
1 a book, single, return **b** hand luggage, hold luggage **c** check-in, security, gate **d** boarding card, **e** passport **f** delayed **g** cancelled **h** platform
2 de<u>layed</u>, <u>can</u>celled, <u>plat</u>form, <u>check</u>-in, se<u>cu</u>rity, gate, <u>book</u> a <u>tick</u>et, <u>hold</u> luggage, <u>hand</u> luggage, <u>suit</u>case, <u>sin</u>gle ticket, re<u>turn</u> ticket, <u>pass</u>port, <u>board</u>ing card, ar<u>rive</u>

Vocabulary 3: Prepositions of place and movement
2 a under **b** next to **c** behind **d** in **e** in front of **f** on **g** above
3 in, on, <u>next</u> to, in <u>front</u> of, be<u>hind</u>, a<u>bove</u>, under
4 a in **b** next to **c** behind **d** in front of **e** on, above **f** under
5 a No (arrives in Liverpool) **b** Yes, yes **c** No (leave Manchester) **d** Yes **e** No (going home) **f** Yes **g** Yes **h** No (visiting London)
6 a in **b** to **c** – **d** to **e** to **f** to **g** –

Pronunciation 1: Sentence stress, /ə/ for *a* and *an* and linking
1 a Can‿I have‿a /ə/ re<u>turn</u> ticket, pl<u>ease</u>? **b** I'd <u>like</u> to book‿a /ə/<u>flight</u>. **c** The <u>flight</u>‿is <u>can</u>celled. **d** The <u>train</u>‿is de<u>layed</u>. **e** Which <u>plat</u>form‿<u>is</u>‿it? **f** How <u>much</u> is‿a /ə/ <u>first</u> class <u>tick</u>et? **g** It's‿a<u>bove</u> the <u>seat</u>. **h** I've got‿a /ə/ <u>sin</u>gle <u>tick</u>et. **i** <u>Quick</u>! The <u>flight</u>‿is <u>board</u>ing! **j** The train‿ar<u>rives</u>‿in <u>Lon</u>don‿at <u>ten</u>‿o'clock.

Pronunciation 2: The word *to*
1 a /tə/ **b** /tuː/
2 /tə/ to London, to Manchester, to New York, to San Francisco, to Dallas; /tuː/ to East London, to England, to America, to Oxford, to Edinburgh

Conversation 1: Questions about travel
1 a Edinburgh (Scotland) **b** (about) 400 miles
2 a eight hours, very expensive **b** by coach, very cheap **c** by train, about five hours **d** by plane, can be very cheap if you book in advance
3 a How far is it? **b** How much is a ticket? **c** What time does it leave? **d** What time does it arrive? **e** How long does it take? **f** What's the best way to get there?
4 How <u>far</u>‿is‿it? How <u>much</u>‿<u>is</u>‿a <u>tick</u>et? What <u>time</u> does‿it <u>leave</u>? What <u>time</u> does‿it‿ar<u>rive</u>? How <u>long</u> does‿it <u>take</u>? <u>What's</u> the best way to <u>get</u> there?
5 a How much is a ticket? **b** How long does it take? **c** What's the best way to get there? **d** How far is it? **e** How long does it take? **f** What time does it leave? **g** What time does it arrive? **h** How much is a ticket?

Conversation 2: Using *can/can't* for permission
1 a in a train **b** No
2 and 3

A	B
You can't	smoke
You can't	use a phone
You can't	sit in a reserved seat
You can't	put bags on the floor
You can't	travel without a ticket

4 a You can't park here. **b** You can't drink alcohol here. **c** You can't take photographs here. **d** You can't smoke here. **e** You can't use a mobile (phone) here. **f** You can't run here. **g** You can't eat or drink here. **h** You can't swim here.
5 a Can **b** Can **c** can **d** Can
6 a Can I park here? **b** Can I use this ticket? **c** Can I smoke here? **d** Can I pay cash? **e** Can I pay by card?

Asking for and giving directions
1 b
2 C
3 Tourist 1 the post office D, the shopping centre B; **Tourist 2** the taxi rank F, the bus station E; **Tourist 3** the Station Hotel A
4 b the Station Hotel **c** the post office **d** the bus station
5 Could you tell me where the taxi rank is? Take the first left, take the second right. Go along the road for about 100 metres. It's on your right. It's about five minutes from here. Could you tell me where the bus station is? It's not far. It's on the left in front of the taxi rank.
6 a Go, for about, take, second right, right, next to **b** Take, first, the second right, Go along, for, It's, the, about, minutes from here

Listening 1: Airport announcements
1 No
2 a F **b** F **c** T **d** T **e** F **f** T **g** T **h** F

Listening 2: Public transport in London
1 bus and underground (tube)
2 a bus **b** underground **c** tube **d** tube **e** can't **f** bus **g** can **h** can't **i** ticket **j** bus **k** travel card **l** can **m** bus **n** tube

Reading 1: A web page about Heathrow Airport
1 a, b, c, e, f, h
3 a T **b** T **c** T **d** T **e** T **f** F **g** F **h** T **i** F **j** T

Writing: Directions in an email
1 b
2 a no **b** train **c** 30 minutes **d** yes **e** about £20 **f** yes **g** on foot **h** no **i** yes
j four o'clock **k** five o'clock **l** about an hour

Test yourself
1 Planes: check-in, hold luggage, security, boarding card, airport, passport, hand luggage; **Planes and trains**: a single ticket, a return ticket, delayed, cancelled; **Trains**: underground, station, platform

2

3 a tell me where, is **b** Take the **c** on the **d** along, for **e** is it **f** not far **g** from **h** much is a **i** time does **j** does, take **k** way **l** in **m** to **n** go
4 a You can't smoke here. **b** You can't sit here. **c** Can I pay by card?
d You can take a drink into the theatre.

UNIT 7: HOTELS AND ACCOMMODATION

Types of accommodation
1 b youth hostel **c** budget hotel **d** full English breakfast **e** B+B
f continental breakfast
2 £ youth hostel, ££ B+B or budget hotel, £££ expensive hotel; no meals = room only, one meal = bed and breakfast, two meals = half board, three meals = full board.

Vocabulary 1: Services and facilities
b 5 **c** 3 **d** 4 **e** 6 **f** 1 **g** 7 **h** 2

Vocabulary 2: Describing accommodation
1 Positive: hotel and rooms: clean, comfortable, excellent value, central, great; staff: helpful, great; **Negative**: hotel and rooms: basic
2 a expensive **b** dirty **c** noisy **d** unfriendly **e** rude **f** awful
3 clean, <u>com</u>fortable, <u>ex</u>cellent <u>va</u>lue, <u>hel</u>pful, <u>cen</u>tral, great, a<u>ma</u>zing, good, <u>bri</u>lliant, fan<u>tas</u>tic, <u>ex</u>cellent, <u>com</u>fy, <u>qui</u>et, <u>aw</u>ful, ex<u>pen</u>sive, <u>dir</u>ty, <u>ba</u>sic, <u>noi</u>sy, rude, po<u>lite</u>, <u>frien</u>dly, un<u>frien</u>dly

Vocabulary 3: Describing rooms
1 a a cot **b** a double room **c** an en suite room **d** a room with a view **e** a single room **f** a family room **g** a twin-bedded room
2 a <u>single</u> room, a <u>double</u> room, a <u>twin</u>-bedded room, a <u>fam</u>ily room, a cot, an en <u>suite</u> room, a <u>room</u> with a <u>view</u>

Vocabulary 4: Booking accommodation
1 When you make a booking: b, c, d, g, h, j, k, l, m; **When you arrive at the hotel:** e, f, i,
3 b Do I need to /tə/ <u>pay</u> a /ə/ de<u>pos</u>it? **c** What <u>time</u> is <u>check</u>-out?
d Does /dəz/ the <u>price</u> include <u>break</u>fast? **e** <u>Where</u> is <u>break</u>fast served?
f I've got a /ə/ reservation. **g** From /frəm/ <u>Mon</u>day <u>10th</u> of /əv/ July to /tə/ <u>Wednes</u>day <u>12th</u> of /əv/ Ju<u>ly</u>. **h** For /fə/ <u>three nights</u>. **i** I'd like to /tə/ <u>make</u> a /ə/ reser<u>va</u>tion. **j** I'd like to /tə/ <u>book</u> a /ə/ <u>twin</u>-bedded <u>room</u>.

Conversation 1: Complaining about problems
1 Things not working: air-conditioning, TV, hairdryer, lights, radio, heating, internet, lift/elevator; **things missing:** clean sheets, clean towels, toilet paper, hairdryer, pillows
2 yes
3 Things not working: shower, lights; **things missing:** soap, hairdryer, clean towels
4 a isn't **b** aren't, noun **c** there isn't a **d** there isn't any, uncountable **e** there aren't any, plural
5 a I'm afraid **b** straight away, immediately

Conversation 2: Making requests
1 b theatre, tickets **c** tour **d** car **e** directions **f** airport **g** luggage **h** taxi
2 a hotel
3 d, g, h
4 a–d Could you
5 Could you <u>help</u> me? Could you arrange <u>car</u> hire? Could you look after my <u>luggage</u>? Could you call me a <u>taxi</u>?

Listening 1: Making a booking and arriving with a booking
1 2
2 a F **b** T **c** F **d** T **e** F **f** F
3 a family **b** 4 **c** Thursday **d** 3rd September **e** 10

Answer key   273

Listening 2: Complaining about the room
1 4
2 Missing: clean towels and toilet paper; Not working: television, lights
3 a send some up **b** sort it out **c** The hotel offers Mr Lopes and his family a free meal.

Speaking 2: Complaining about the room
1 and 2 a Mr Lopes **Hello**? I'm **calling from room** 408. I'm **afraid** the television **isn't working. Could** someone sort it out?
b Mr Lopes   **Hello**? It's **room** 408 **again**. I'm **afraid there aren't any** clean towels. **Could you** send some up?
c Mr Lopes   **Hello**? I'm **calling from room 408 again. I'm afraid** the lights **aren't working. Could someone sort** it out?
d Mr Lopes   **Hello**? It's **408 again. I'm afraid there isn't any** toilet paper. **Could you send** some up?
e Mr Lopes   **Yes**; Yes, **thank you**. Everything **is fine**; That **would be** lovely, thank **you very much**. What **time is** dinner?
3 and 4 a Hello? I'm calling from room 34. I'm afraid the air-conditioning isn't working. Could someone sort it out? **b** Hello? It's room 34. I'm afraid there aren't any pillows. Could you send some up? **c** Hello? I'm calling from room 34. I'm afraid the internet isn't working. Could someone sort it out? **d** Hello? It's room 34 again. I'm afraid there isn't any shampoo. Could you send some up? **e** Hello? I'm calling from room 34. I'm afraid the television isn't working. Could someone sort it out?

Reading: Booking.com
1 a F **b** T **c** T **d** T

Reading: Descriptions and reviews
2

	HOTEL IRIS	THE VICTORIA HOTEL
free internet	no	yes
free parking	no	yes
laundry service	yes	yes
restaurant	yes	yes
expensive	no	yes
recommended	yes	yes

3 a F **b** T **c** T **d** T **e** F **f** T **g** F **h** T **i** T **j** T

Writing 1: An email booking

1 a a family room **b** No (bed and breakfast) **c** 4 **d** 7 **e** Monday 10 July
2 (sample answer)

> Dear Sir/Madam
> I would like to book **full board** in a **double** room at the Victoria Hotel. The booking is for **five** nights, from **Saturday 3 September** to **Wednesday 7 September** for **two** people. Could you tell me if I need to send **a deposit**?
> **I look forward to hearing from you.**
> Best regards
> [your name]

Writing 2: A hotel registration form

Name	*Jose Lopes*	Nationality	Spanish
Address	Rua de la Frontera 29, Vila Real, 4306-435 9 Valegio, Spain		
City or town	Vila Real	Car registration number	HO 23 42 81 P
Date of arrival	*Monday 10 July*	Date of departure	*Monday 17 July*
Method of payment	Credit card ☒	Cheque ☐	Cash ☐
Room rate	Full board ☐	Bed and breakfast ☒	Room only ☐
Signature	*Jose Lopes*	Room number	408

Test yourself

1 a clean **b** cheap / excellent value **c** noisy **d** awful **e** rude **f** unfriendly
2 a 2 **b** 1 **c** 5 **d** 4 **e** 3
3 a 5 **b** 4 **c** 6 **d** 3 **e** 7 **f** 1 **g** 2
4 a I**'ve got** a reservation. **b Have** you **got** a room with a sea view?
c Does the price **include** breakfast? **d** What time **is** dinner? **e** There **isn't any** soap. **f There aren't any** towels. **g** The lights **aren't working**. **h** The Wi-Fi **isn't working**. **i Could you** call me a taxi?

UNIT 8: SIGHTSEEING AND THE WEATHER

Coming to the UK on holiday
2 and 3

MUSEUM OR ART GALLERY	CHURCH OR CATHEDRAL	MONUMENT, CASTLE OR PALACE	CITY, COUNTRY OR REGION	OTHER ATTRACTION
British Museum Madame Tussaud's Museum of Modern Art, New York	St Paul's Cathedral	Buckingham Palace the Tower of London the Houses of Parliament Windsor Castle Stonehenge The Statue of Liberty	London the Cotswolds Scotland Wales the south-west of England New York City	River Thames Big Ben the London Eye The Empire State Building The Grand Canyon Yellowstone National Park The White House Niagara Falls

4 a is a good idea **b** should **c** a great place to **d** well worth **e** recommend visiting

Vocabulary 1: The weather
1 It's freezing, it's cold, it's chilly, it's warm, it's hot, it's boiling
2 a It's sunny. **b** It's cloudy. **c** It's windy. **d** It's showery. **e** It's snowing. **f** It's stormy. **g** It's raining.
3 and 4

What a lovely day! It's really sunny. It's a really nice day. It's a beautiful day. It's warm. It's hot. It's boiling. It's sunny.	It's really wet. It's quite windy. It's pouring with rain. What terrible weather! What miserable weather! It's cloudy. It's windy. It's showery. It's stormy. It's raining.	It's very cold. It's absolutely freezing! It's freezing. It's cold. It's chilly. It's snowing.

5
What a lovely day! It's a beautiful day, it's really sunny, it's hot, it's boiling, it's warm, it's really wet, it's quite windy, it's pouring with rain, what terrible weather! What miserable weather! It's raining, it's showery, it's cloudy, it's stormy, it's very cold, it's absolutely freezing, it's snowing, it's chilly

Vocabulary 2: Comparing
2 a hotter **b** hottest
3 a er **b** est
4

ADJECTIVE	COMPARATIVE	SUPERLATIVE
cold	colder	the coldest
warm	warmer	warmest
nice	nicer	nicest
hot	hotter	hottest
wet	wetter	wettest
sunny	sunnier	sunniest
dry	drier	driest
beautiful	more beautiful	the most beautiful
miserable	more miserable	the most miserable

5 a It is usually hotter in July than in January. **b** The weather in summer is usually more beautiful than the weather in winter. **c** It is wetter in spring than in summer. **d** January is the coldest month. **e** August is the hottest month. **f** The best month for dry weather is July.

Conversation 1: Past simple
1 Yes
2 a They had a good holiday. **b** They travelled by plane. **c** The did a lot of things. **d** They weren't bored. **e** The food was quite cheap. **f** They ate in restaurants. **g** They didn't hire a car. **h** It rained once.
3 b got **c** went **d** had **e** was **f** flew **g** stayed **h** gave **i** did **j** were **k** met **l** saw **m** visited **n** took **o** found **p** ate **q** used **r** bought **s** wanted **t** rained **u** left **v** felt **w** tried **x** enrolled
Regular verbs: stayed, visited, wanted, rained, tried, enrolled.
We make the past tense of regular verbs by adding -ed. If there is a single vowel and a single consonant, we double the consonant. If the verb ends in -e we just add -d.
4 a asked **b** worked **c** arrived **d** looked **e** enjoyed **f** started

5 b lose c spend d know e tell f make
6 a Were b weren't c Was
7 a When did you come home? b Where did you go? c What did you do? d Who did you meet? e What did you see? f How many photos did you take? g Where did you eat? h What did you buy? i When did you leave? j How much did you spend?
8 a We came home yesterday. b We went to New York. c We did a lot of things. d We met some nice people. e We saw some monuments. f I took a lot of photos. g We ate in little restaurants. h We bought a lot of clothes. i We left yesterday. j I spent a lot of money.
9 We **came** back yesterday. We **got** a cheap flight and we **went** to Portugal. We **had** a brilliant time. We **flew** to Lisbon and we **stayed** in a lovely hotel in the centre of the city. We **didn't know** Lisbon so we **went** to the Tourist Information Centre. They **gave** us some good ideas about different things to do. We **did** so much in just one week. We **met** some really nice people, we **went** to the seaside, we **saw** some amazing buildings and monuments and we **visited** a couple of museums. I **took** a lot of photos. We **found** some lovely little restaurants in the old part of the city and we **ate** out nearly every night. We **didn't hire** a car. We **used** the local transport and it **was** fine. I **didn't spend** too much money but we **bought** a lot of souvenirs. I **wanted** to buy more but we **didn't have** room in our suitcase! The weather **was** really good for the whole week apart from one day when it **rained** a bit. When we **left** it was a lovely day and I **felt** so sad saying goodbye to Lisbon. I **didn't want** to go home! I **tried** to learn some Portuguese and yesterday I **enrolled** on a Portuguese course!
10 a What was it like? b What did you do? c Where did you go? d Was the food nice? e Did you hire a car? f Did you spend a lot of money? g Was the weather good?
11 stay, visit, want, enjoy, rain

-ed and -ing adjective endings
1

-ed	-ing
amazed	amazing
bored	boring
tired	tiring
interested	interesting
disappointed	disappointing

worried	worrying
excited	exciting
frightened	frightening

2 a bored **b** exciting

3 I'm a<u>ma</u>zed, I'm <u>bo</u>red, I'm <u>ti</u>red, I'm <u>in</u>terested, I'm disa<u>ppoin</u>ted, I'm ex<u>ci</u>ted, I'm <u>frigh</u>tened, it's a<u>ma</u>zing, it's <u>bo</u>ring, it's <u>ti</u>ring, it's <u>in</u>teresting, it's disa<u>ppoin</u>ting, it's ex<u>ci</u>ting, it's <u>frigh</u>tening

4 a, b, c, e are correct

5 a tiring, tired **b** amazing **c** boring

Pronunciation 1: -ed verb endings
2

/t/	/d/	/id/
talked	loved	needed
liked	played	waited
asked	enjoyed	
watched	used	
helped	studied	
	rained	

Pronunciation 2: Irregular past simple verbs
1 came, got, went, had, flew, gave, did, met, saw, took, found, ate, bought, left, felt, forgot, lost, spent, knew, told, made

Listening 1: A conversation about the weather
1 a ☺ **b** ☺ **c** ☹ **d** ☹ **e** ☹ **f** ☺

2

TODAY	WHEN ANNA WAS IN PORTUGAL	WHEN ANNA'S FRIENDS WERE IN PORTUGAL	WHEN ANNA WAS IN DUBAI	LAST WEEK	NEXT WEEK
~~windy~~	~~boiling~~ hot sunny	~~cloudy~~	~~really sunny~~ absolutely boiling	~~windy~~ ~~chilly~~ ~~cloudy~~ cold wet	~~sunny~~ warm

Listening 2: A conversation about a holiday
1 Yes
2 a one week **b** The Statue of Liberty, The Brooklyn Bridge, The Metropolitan Museum of Art, Museum of Modern Art, Times Square, The Empire State Building, Central Park **c** 4 hours **d** No **e** No

Speaking: Talking about a holiday
1 and 2
a Have you <u>got</u> any recommen<u>da</u>tions? **b** Are there any guided <u>tours</u> of the <u>city</u>? **c** Would you recommend eating in the ho<u>tel</u> or going <u>out</u>? **d** Is hiring a <u>car</u> a good id<u>ea</u>? **e** What's the <u>wea</u>ther <u>like</u>? **f** Have you got any <u>oth</u>er <u>tips</u>?
4 You should <u>vis</u>it the Mu<u>se</u>um of Modern <u>Art</u>. I'd <u>rec</u>ommend going to <u>Cen</u>tral <u>Park</u>. <u>Go</u>ing on a guided <u>tour</u> is a <u>great</u> way to see the <u>main</u> <u>sights</u>. It's <u>well</u> worth <u>vis</u>iting the <u>Empire</u> <u>State</u> <u>Build</u>ing. <u>Most</u> nights we went <u>out</u>. I think that's the <u>best</u> idea.

Reading: A tourist information leaflet
1 a National Gallery and Hyde Park **b** National Gallery and Portobello Market **c** Portobello Market and Oxford Street **d** Portobello Market and Hyde Park
2 a F **b** F **c** T **d** F **e** F

Writing: Describing a holiday
1 Yes **2** This is to tell you about our visit to Scotland. We **spent** three days in the Highlands and it **was** absolutely beautiful. We **stayed** in a small guest house and **spent** most of the time walking. I **wanted** to see Ben Nevis, the **tallest** mountain in Scotland, but it **was** cloudy and it **rained** for the first two days. Then on our last day the weather **was better**, the rain **stopped** and we **saw** Ben Nevis. I **didn't climb** to the top but we **walked** for about three hours! I **was** really tired! We **met** some lovely people and they **told** us about a little pub in the village so we **went** there for dinner on our last evening and **had** a fantastic time. I really **enjoyed** it.
Edinburgh **was** also lovely but it **was busier** than the mountains (and **more expensive**!). We **spent** two days there. I **forgot** my driving licence so we **didn't hire** a car but **travelled** by bus. In fact, using public transport **was** probably **easier** than driving. I **lost** my bag on the second day and I **was** really worried but someone **found** it in the hotel bar and **took** it to the hotel reception. We also **visited** Edinburgh Castle and I **took** a lot of photos and I **got** some great pictures. Someone **told** me the view from Edinburgh Castle **was** well worth seeing and he **was** right. It **was** amazing.

Test yourself

1 Good weather: What a lovely day! It's really sunny. It's a beautiful day. It's hot. It's boiling. It's warm. Bad weather: It's really wet. It's quite windy. It's pouring with rain. What terrible weather! What miserable weather! It's raining. It's showery. It's cloudy. It's stormy. It's very cold. It's absolutely freezing. It's snowing. It's chilly.

2 a went **b** had **c** enjoyed **d** was, were **e** wanted **f** got **g** did **h** came **i** arrived **j** took

3 a Did you go to Scotland last year? **b** I didn't see him yesterday. **c** They weren't here last week. **d** Were you on holiday last week? **e** I was / We were in New York. **f** I took a lot of photos. **g** Did you lose your passport? **h** I forgot my money. **i** He didn't buy any souvenirs. **j** I spent a lot of money. **k** We really enjoyed it. **l** I tried to learn Spanish.

4 a hotter **b** colder **c** better, the best **d** worse **e** more expensive

5 a visiting **b** visit **c** doing **d** Travelling **e** tired **f** boring **g** disappointing **h** excited

UNIT 9: RESTAURANTS AND FOOD

Food in the UK
1 a 3 **b** 1 **c** 2
2 a roast beef **b** a cheese sandwich **c** fish and chips **d** a Chinese meal **e** a cream tea **f** a packet of crisps

Vocabulary 1: Types of food
1 b apple **c** orange **d** strawberry **e** tomato **f** carrot **g** cabbage **h** salad **i** egg **j** cheese **k** yoghurt **l** butter **m** chicken **n** beef **o** lamb **p** fish **q** bread **r** rice **s** pasta **t** potato **u** sugar **v** biscuit **w** cake **x** chocolate
2 1 Fruit 2 Vegetables 3 Dairy foods 4 Meat and fish 5 Carbohydrates 6 Sugary foods
3 fruit, ba<u>na</u>na, <u>app</u>le, <u>or</u>ange, <u>straw</u>berry, <u>veg</u>etables, to<u>ma</u>to, <u>car</u>rot, <u>cab</u>bage, <u>sal</u>ad, <u>dair</u>y foods, egg, cheese, <u>yogh</u>urt, <u>but</u>ter, meat, fish, <u>chic</u>ken, beef, lamb, carbo<u>hy</u>drates, bread, rice, <u>pas</u>ta, po<u>ta</u>to, <u>sug</u>ary foods, <u>sug</u>ar, <u>bis</u>cuit, cake, <u>choc</u>olate
4 The following foods are *usually* uncountable: g cabbage, **h** salad, **j** cheese, **k** yoghurt, **l** butter, **m** chicken, **n** beef, **o** lamb, **p** fish, **q** bread, **r** rice, **s** pasta, **u** sugar, **w** cake, **x** chocolate, fruit, meat, vegetables, dairy foods, carbohydrates, sugary foods
5 b apples **c** oranges **d** strawberries **e** tomatoes **f** carrots **i** eggs **t** potatoes **v** biscuits

If a word ends in *y*, we change the **y** to **i** and add **es**.
If a word ends in *o*, we add **es**.
6 a an **b** plural **c** some **d** some, some

7

A PACKET OF ...	A PIECE OF ...	A SMALL/BIG PORTION OF ...
crisps biscuits sugar	cake chocolate apple cheese orange chicken fish fruit meat bread	rice pasta potatoes fish chicken beef meat lamb salad vegetables carrots cabbage

Vocabulary 2: Drinks
1, 2, 3

	a Do we usually drink it hot?	b Is it an alcoholic drink?	c Is it good for you?	d Bottle	e Can	f Cup	g Glass	h Pint (UK)/ litre
milk	no	no	yes	yes	no	no	yes	yes
coffee	yes	no	no	no	no	yes	no	no
tea	yes	no	no	no	no	yes	no	no
orange juice	no	no	yes	yes	no	no	yes	yes
coke	no	no	no	yes	yes	no	yes	yes
water	no	no	yes	yes	no	no	yes	yes
beer	no	yes	no	yes	yes	no	yes	yes
wine	no	yes	no	yes	no	no	yes	yes

Pronunciation: Containers and quantities
1 <u>pack</u>et, piece, <u>por</u>tion, glass, <u>bot</u>tle, cup, can, pint, <u>li</u>tre, milk, <u>coff</u>ee, tea, <u>or</u>ange juice, coke, <u>wa</u>ter, beer, wine

We pronounce *a* /ə/ and *of* /əv/. We stress the container and the food or drink.

a /ə/ <u>packet</u> of /əv/ <u>bis</u>cuits
a /ə/ <u>glass</u> of /əv/ <u>milk</u>
a /ə/ <u>piece</u> of /əv/ <u>cake</u>
a /ə/ <u>cup</u> of /əv/ <u>tea</u>

Conversation 1: Countable and uncountable nouns + *much/many*
1 orange juice, a cup of coffee, some yoghurt, some strawberries, an egg, some (two pieces of) toast, chicken, (a small portion of brown) rice, salad, (three) biscuits
2 a much **b** many **c** much **d** much **e** many
3 a many **b** many **c** much **d** many **e** much **f** many
4 with uncountable nouns: much; **with plural, countable nouns:** many
5 a I'd like some salad but not too **much**, please. **d** I'm on a diet. I can't have too **many** potatoes. **e** The restaurant was very good but there weren't **many** people there. **g** We haven't got **much** time. Is the restaurant near here? **h** I don't want **many** carrots, thank you. Just some cabbage. **k** I didn't eat **many** biscuits, really!

Conversation 2: Phrases to use in a restaurant
1 g, e, a, f, h, c, b, d. The waiter says: Good evening. Certainly. Come this way. Here's the menu and the wine list. Someone will be with you shortly to take your order. Can I get you any drinks while you look at the menu? Are you ready to order? What would you like? Certainly. Good choice. Would you like any side orders or salads? I'm so sorry. I'll sort it out immediately. I'm so sorry. I'll see to it straight away. Here you are. I'm sorry about the mistake. No, people can leave a tip if they think the service was good.
2 a Yes **b** a burger, fish/salmon, a green salad and some extra chips
3 a What are you having? What do you fancy? **b** I fancy … I'm having …
c How about (a burger); Why don't you (have a burger) **d** I'd prefer to have; I'd rather have … **e** good, lovely, delicious; great, nice, amazing, fantastic, excellent, awful, expensive, cheap
4
  a We'd like a table for two, please.
  b What are you having?
  c Can I have + (the food). I'd like + (the food).
  d How was + (the food)?
  e Excuse me … I'm sorry but … + (the problem).
  f Can I have the bill, please?
  g Is service included?
  h I'm sorry but I think there is a mistake with the bill.
  i I'm so sorry.
  j That's OK. Never mind.

5
- **a** The table is too near the kitchen. The table is too near the toilets.
- **b** This/It is too salty. This/It is too sweet.
- **c** This/It is not hot enough.

6 We'd like a/ə/ table for /fə/ two please. This table is too near the kitchen. What do /də/ you fancy? What would /wəd/ you like? What are /ə/ you having? I fancy the salmon. I'd like the salmon. Can /cən/ I have the steak? How about steak and /ən/ chips? Why don't you have steak and /ən/ chips? I'd prefer to /tə/ have fish. I'd rather have fish. How was /wəz/ your /jə/ salmon? Excuse me, I'm sorry but ... This is too salty. This is too sweet. It isn't hot enough. My glass is dirty. The food is lovely. The chips are /ə/ really good. Can /cən/ I have the bill please? Is service included? I'm sorry but I think there is a /ə/ mistake with the bill. I'm so sorry. That's OK. Never mind.

Listening 1: In a café
1 They want a snack.
2 a F **b** T **c** F **d** F **e** T **f** F **g** F

Listening 2: In a restaurant
1 No
2 a They usually have a takeaway. **b** Two glasses of champagne, chicken pasta, salmon with vegetables, a green salad and some extra chips. **c** The food is cold (not hot enough) and they didn't bring the salad. Jenny's glass is dirty. **d** Nothing. **e** At home.

Speaking: In a restaurant
3 a Excuse me, I'm sorry but the table is too near the toilets and my glass is dirty. **b** Excuse me, I'm sorry but the salad is too salty and the soup isn't hot enough. **c** Excuse me, I'm sorry but we ordered white wine. This is red wine. **d** Excuse me, I'm sorry but we ordered some bread. We haven't got it yet. **e** Excuse me, I'm sorry but I think there is a mistake with the bill. You charged us for two burgers. We only had one.

Reading 1: Restaurant descriptions and reviews
1 b The King's Head **c** The Red Lion **d** City Deli
2 a City Deli **b** Coffee Time **c** The King's Head **d** The Red Lion

3

	THE RED LION	KING'S HEAD	COFFEE TIME	THE CITY DELI
Where is it?	in the city centre	ten-minute walk from the city centre, by the river	a ten-minute bus ride from the city centre, near the college	in the city centre in the main shopping area
What kind of food is there?	traditional British meals	sandwiches, bar snacks	cakes, biscuits sandwiches, hot snacks	European food, either eat-in or takeaway, snacks and sandwiches or a meal
What's the food like?	good quality/ traditional	delicious	good, home-made	great, European
When is it open?	Tuesday–Sunday	every day	Mon–Sat until 7 p.m.	Monday–Saturday 11 a.m.–late
What's it like?	fantastic, busy, excellent and quick service, very friendly staff	small, traditional, country-style, quiet	friendly, busy	fantastic, modern, not very friendly
Is it cheap or expensive?	not cheap	reasonably-priced (not very expensive)	very cheap	expensive

4 a The Red Lion **b** King's Head **c** The City Deli **d** The City Deli **e** King's Head **f** The City Deli **g** Coffee Time **h** The Red Lion

Reading 2: A restaurant website
2 a T **b** T **c** T **d** F **e** F **f** T **g** F **h** F

3 a soup, mushroom omelette, green salad, garlic bread, all of the desserts

Test yourself

1

FRUIT AND VEGETABLES	SNACKS	DRINKS	CARBOHYDRATES	MEALS
salad, tomatoes, an apple, a banana	a cheese sandwich, chocolate, a biscuit, a packet of crisps (an apple, a banana)	milk, beer, tea, water	bread, rice, pasta, potatoes	a hamburger, roast beef, fried chicken, fish and chips

2 a, b, f, g, h, j, l

3 a I'd like a table for five, please. **b** Can I have steak and chips?/I'd like steak and chips. **c** How is your fish? **d** Excuse me, I'm sorry but this isn't hot enough. **e** Can I have the bill, please? **f** Is service included? **g** I'm sorry but I think there is a mistake with the bill. **h** That's OK. Never mind. **i** How many millilitres are there in a pint? **j** How much is an Americano?

4 a My soup is not hot enough. **b** This portion is too small. **c** The service isn't quick enough. **d** The restaurant is too expensive.

5 a I don't want many potatoes. **b** They can't have much rice. **c** There wasn't much wine. **d** He hasn't got many biscuits. **e** I ate too much pasta.

UNIT 10: SHOPPING AND MONEY

Shops and shopping in the UK

1 a chemist **b** supermarket **c** shopping centre **d** newsagent **e** market **f** department store

2

	IS IT CHEAP?	CAN YOU BUY FOOD AND DRINK?	CAN YOU BUY CLOTHES?	CAN YOU BUY HEALTH AND BEAUTY PRODUCTS?
shopping centre	no	yes	yes	yes
department store	no	sometimes	yes	yes
market	yes	yes	sometimes	no
supermarket	sometimes	yes	sometimes	sometimes
chemist	no	no	no	yes
newsagent	no	yes	no	no

3 a clothes **b** Amazon **c** convenient and cheap **d** delivery cost

Vocabulary 1: Clothes and colours
1 and 2 a a <u>pair</u> of <u>black jeans</u> **b** some <u>gold rings</u> **c** a <u>brown skirt</u> **d** a <u>pink jacket</u> **e** a <u>purple shirt</u> **f** a <u>green dress</u> **g** a <u>blue</u> <u>T</u>-shirt **h** a <u>blue</u> and <u>yellow jumper</u> **i** a <u>pair</u> of <u>red shoes</u> **j** a <u>pair</u> of <u>white trousers</u> **k** a <u>grey coat</u> **l** a <u>silver bag</u>
3 before the noun

Vocabulary 2: Shopping online
1 a health and beauty **b** clothing **c** technology **d** sport and leisure **e** jewellery and watches **f** flowers and gifts **g** food and wine **h** baby and child **i** home and garden **j** entertainment and books
2 a some green soap **b** a pair of red trousers **c** a black laptop **d** a blue football **e** a gold ring **f** some yellow flowers **g** some red wine **h** a pair of white shoes **i** some pink towels **j** a green and red book

Vocabulary 3: In the supermarket
1 a basket **b** trolley **c** aisle **d** shelf **e** checkout **f** barcode **g** carrier bag **h** pay for **i** change **j** receipt

Vocabulary 4: Money
1 a purse **b** get some money out/use an ATM **c** credit card **d** cash **e** gift card **f** coins **g** wallet **h** debit card
2 cash, coins, <u>cred</u>it card, <u>deb</u>it card, <u>gift</u> card, purse, <u>wall</u>et, <u>get</u> some <u>mon</u>ey out, <u>use</u> an ATM

Vocabulary 5: Special offers
1 a £24 **b** £27 **c** £24 **d** £28.80 **e** £18 **f** £24 **g** £27 **h** £24
2 e

Listening 1: Buying souvenirs
1 souvenir shops, supermarkets, clothes shops, department stores, museum shops
2 a souvenir shop **b** supermarket **c** supermarket **d** supermarket or clothes shop **e** department store

Listening 2: English money
1 a Incorrect. There are £5, £10, £20 and £50 notes. **b** Incorrect. There are 1p, 2p, **5p**, 10p, 20p, 50p, £1 and £2 coins. **c** Incorrect. £1 coins are gold in colour. (Two pound coins are gold and silver in colour.) **d** Incorrect. A *fiver* is the same as £5. **e** Incorrect. A *tenner* is the same as £10. **f** Correct.

Audioscript 10.05
a Forty-one quid b forty-one p c four hundred and twenty-eight pounds d twenty-eight p e four quid f a tenner g ten p h ten pounds and twenty-eight p i forty-two p j four pounds twenty-eight k four pounds ten p l twenty-eight quid
2 **a** £41 **b** 41p **c** £428 **d** 28p **e** £4 **f** £10 **g** 10p **h** £10.28 **i** 42p **j** £4.28 **k** £4.10 **l** £28

Audioscript 10.06
a a fiver b Six quid c Seven quid d a tenner e Seven p f Sixty-one p g Seven pounds fifty h Six pounds sixty
3 **a** less **b** less **c** more **d** more **e** less **f** less **g** more **h** more
4 **a** £5 **b** £6 **c** £7 **d** £10 **e** 7p **f** 61p **g** £7.50 **h** £6.60

Conversation 1: Buying clothes
1 **a** 8 **b** 2 **c** 5 **d** 3 **e** 4 **f** 6 **g** 1 **h** 7
2 **a–e** I'm looking for some red trousers (some sports shoes/a jumper). Is there a supermarket (chemist/market) near here? Have you got any umbrellas (sports shoes/belts)? Have you got this in a bigger (smaller) size? Have you got this in a different colour (in red/in black)? **f–h** Where are the fitting rooms? Can I try this on? It doesn't fit. **i, j** How much is this? Can I pay by gift card?

Speaking and pronunciation 1
1 I'm loo<u>k</u>ing for a /fər ə/ <u>dress</u>. Is there a /ðərə/ <u>chem</u>ist's near <u>here</u>? Have /həv/ you <u>got</u> any <u>T</u>-shirts? Have /həv/ you got this in a /ə/ <u>smaller size</u>? Have /həv/ you got this in a /ə/ <u>bigger size</u>? Have /həv/ you got this in a /ə/ <u>different colour</u>? Can I /kən/ <u>try</u> this <u>on</u>?
<u>Where</u> are the /əðə/<u>fitting</u> rooms? It <u>doesn't fit</u>. How <u>much</u> is <u>this</u>? Can I /kən/ <u>pay</u> in <u>dollars</u>? Can I /kən/ <u>pay</u> in <u>euros</u>? Can I /kən/ <u>pay</u> in <u>cash</u>? Can I /kən/ <u>pay</u> by <u>card</u>?

2 **a** I'm looking for a dress. **b** Is there a bank near here? **c** Have you got any trousers? **d** Have you got this in a smaller size? **e** Have you got this in a different colour. **f** Can I try this on? **g** Where are the fitting rooms? **h** The shirt doesn't fit. **i** How much is this? **j** Can I pay in dollars? **k** Can I pay by card?
3 **a** Where are the men's clothes?/I'm looking for the men's clothes. **b** Is there an ATM near here? **c** Have you got this jacket in a bigger size? **d** Have you got this coat in a smaller size? **e** Have you got this jumper in black? **f** Can I try this on? **g** How much are the shoes? **h** Can I pay in euros? **i** Can I pay by credit card?

Vocabulary 6: Customer services
1 a get a refund **b** get a replacement **c** get an exchange **d** get a credit note

Conversation 2: Taking things back to the shop
1 the receipt
2 Customer 2 There is a problem and she gets an exchange. **Customer 3** There is a problem and she gets a refund. **Customer 4** There isn't a problem and she gets a credit note.
3 Customer 2 It doesn't fit./It's too big. **Customer 3** It's damaged. **Customer 4** She (just) changed her mind.
4 a I'd like a replacement, please. **b** Can I get a refund, please? **c** I'd like to exchange it for a bigger/smaller/red one, please. Can I exchange it for a bigger/smaller/red one, please? **d** I just changed my mind.
5 Part B

Speaking and pronunciation 2
1 I bought <u>this</u> but <u>it</u> isn't /bət/ <u>work</u>ing. I bought <u>this</u> but <u>it</u>'s /bət/ <u>dam</u>aged. I bought <u>this</u> but <u>it</u> /bət/doesn't/dəznt/<u>fit</u>. I bought <u>this</u> but <u>I</u> / bət/don't <u>want</u> <u>it</u> now. I <u>chan</u>ged my <u>mind</u>. I'd <u>like</u> a /ə/ re<u>place</u>ment. I'd <u>like</u> a /ə/ re<u>fund</u>. I'd like to ex<u>change</u> this for a /fər ə/ <u>big</u>ger one. I'd like to ex<u>change</u> this for a /fər ə/ <u>smal</u>ler one. I'd like to ex<u>change</u> this for a /fər ə/ <u>black</u> one. Can <u>I</u> /kən/ get a /ə/ re<u>place</u>ment? Can <u>I</u> /kən/ get a /ə/ re<u>fund</u>? Can <u>I</u> /kən/ ex<u>change</u> this for a /fər ə/ <u>big</u>ger one? Can <u>I</u> /kən/ ex<u>change</u> this for a /fər ə/ <u>smal</u>ler one? Can <u>I</u> /kən/ ex<u>change</u> this for a /fər ə/ <u>black</u> one?
2 b I bought this last week but it's damaged. I'd like a refund, please./Can I get a refund, please? **c** I bought this on Monday but it's too big/it doesn't fit. I'd like an exchange, please./Can I get an exchange, please?/Can I exchange it for a smaller one, please? **d** I bought this last weekend but I don't want it now. I changed my mind. I'd like a refund, please./Can I get a refund, please? **e** I bought these yesterday but they're too small/they don't fit. I'd like an exchange, please./Can I get an exchange, please?/Can I exchange them for a bigger pair, please?
3 a No, I just changed my mind. **b** Yes, here you are. **c** Yes, here you are. **d** I'd like a refund, please. **e** A credit note is fine, thanks.

Audioscript 10.11 and answers to Exercise 4
Is there anything wrong with it?
No, I just changed my mind.
Have you got the receipt?
Yes, here you are.

Have you got the card you paid with?
Yes, here you are. *Would you like a refund or a replacement?*
I'd like a refund, please.
We can do an exchange or give you a credit note. Which would you prefer?
A credit note is fine, thanks.

Reading 1: A social media post
1 yes
2 a F **b** F **c** T **d** T **e** F **f** T **g** F **h** F **i** T **j** T **k** F **l** T **m** F

Reading 2: Taking things back to shops
1 a, c
2 a can usually **b** can't usually **c** can't usually **d** can sometimes **e** can usually **f** can usually **g** can usually
3 a No **b** Yes **c** Yes

Writing: Complaining to a shop
1 No

Test yourself
1 a F **b** T **c** T **d** T **e** F **f** T **g** T **h** F **i** T **j** T
2

IN THE SUPERMARKET	ONLINE	BOTH
aisle	click on the section you want	checkout
shelf	fill in your card number	receipt
barcode		add to your basket
pay cash		pay for shopping with a gift card
pay with coins		pay by debit card
get change		pay by credit card
carrier bag		
add to your trolley		
use a purse		
use a wallet		

3 a 9 Our Sports department is on the fifth floor. **b 6** Yes, the fitting rooms are over there. **c 2** Try a bigger size. **d 10** I'm afraid that's the smallest size we've got. **e 4** It's £40. **f 3** Yes, of course you can. **g 8** Would you like a refund or a replacement? **h 7** No, I just changed my mind. **i 1** OK, a credit note is fine. **j 5** Have you got a receipt?
4 a Correct. **b** Correct. **c** Not correct. The correct amount is £15. **d** Not correct. The correct amount is £15. **e** Correct.

Review 2

1 Good weather: any five of: It's warm, It's hot, It's a (really) nice day, What a nice/lovely day, It's a nice/lovely/beautiful day, isn't it?
Bad weather: any five of: It's chilly, It's cold, It's (absolutely/really) freezing, It's cloudy, It's stormy, It's windy, It's snowing, What terrible/miserable weather, It's terrible/miserable/awful weather, isn't it?

2 a any three of: gold, white, silver, black, grey, pink, purple, brown, yellow, orange
b any three of: underground (in London, 'tube'), plane, coach, taxi (or mini cab), car, bicycle (bike), foot
c any three of: a double room, a twin-bedded room, a family room, an en suite room, a room with a view
d room only, half board, bed and breakfast
e any three of: a pair of trousers/shoes/jeans, a bag, a coat, a ring, a dress, a skirt, a T-shirt, a jumper

3 a The train arrives in London this evening. **b** We are travelling to Italy by train. **c** I am going on foot. **d** She is visiting London next year. **e** What time do you usually get home? **f** Where's my passport? I left it on the table. **g** The taxi rank is on the left in front of the cinema. **h** The bus stop isn't far. It's about two minutes from here. **i** Can I pay for the tickets in cash? **j** I paid by credit card.

4 a cheaper, cheapest **b** more expensive, most expensive **c** hotter, worse **d** best, more beautiful **e** quickest, easier.

5 a tiring **b** bored **c** disappointed **d** excited **e** amazing

6 a vacancies, hotels **b** passport, travelling **c** comfortable, hotels **d** reception, hotels **e** boarding card, travelling **f** hand luggage, travelling **g** wdelayed, travelling **h** central, hotels **i** en suite, hotels **j** security, travelling

7 a You can't smoke here. **b** We weren't in London. **c** She didn't go to France. **d** I wasn't tired. **e** It isn't very interesting.

8 They stayed in a small hotel with a view of the sea and when **they arrived** the weather **was** lovely. On Saturday morning, **they spent** a little time shopping at a local market. **She bought** some souvenirs and then **they walked** down to the sea and **found** a lovely little café. **They ate** lunch outside and **went** for a walk on the beach. It **was** beautiful. **She took** a lot of photos and **they visited** a castle just outside the town. The tourist office **said** it was the oldest castle in the area. On Sunday **they got** up late. After a fantastic breakfast, **they hired** two bikes and **went** cycling. It was lovely but after about an hour it **started** raining so **they didn't go** very far. The views **were** amazing!

9 a felt **b** flew **c** forgot **d** got **e** gave **f** knew **g** left **h** lost **i** made **j** saw **k** asked **l** enjoyed **m** tried **n** travelled **o** used **p** enrolled **q** wanted **r** worked **s** looked **t** did

10 a Excuse me. I'm afraid the Wi-Fi isn't working. **b** Excuse me. I'm afraid there aren't any pillows. **c** Excuse me. I'm afraid the rice is too salty. **d** Excuse me. I'm afraid the soup isn't hot enough. **e** Excuse me. I think there's a mistake with the bill. We didn't have any wine.

11 a How far is it? **b** How much is a (return) ticket? **c** What time does the train leave? **d** How long does it take? **e** What's the best way to get there? **f** Where is the train station? **g** Have you got any vacancies? **h** Does the price include dinner? **i** What time is checkout? **j** What's the weather like? **k** Where was he yesterday? **l** What did you buy? **m** How much is this T-shirt? **n** Can I pay by credit card? **o** Have you got this in a smaller size

12 a packet **b** piece **c** can **d** portion **e** cup

13 a Could you tell me where The Rex Hotel is? **b** I'd like to make a reservation, (please). **c** I'm afraid the TV isn't working. **d** Could you book theatre tickets for me, (please)? **e** We'd like a table for two, (please)./Could we have a table for two, (please)? **f** I'd like a steak. **g** Can I have a refund, (please)? **h** Can I have the bill, please? **i** (Excuse me/ I'm sorry but) I think there is a mistake with the bill. **j** Can you help me, please?

14 a C, biscuits **b** U, cheese **c** C, eggs **d** C, tomatoes **e** C, burgers **f** U, butter **g** U, meat **h** U, broccoli **i** U, bread, **j** U, fruit

15 a It's well worth going on a guided tour. **b** I'd recommend hiring a car. **c** How much pasta would you like? **d** I don't want many vegetables. **e** Can I have some rice/a portion of rice? **f** Can I try this on? **g** I'm looking for a pair of jeans./I'm looking for some jeans. **h** Have you got this in a different colour? **i** It doesn't fit. **j** Can I have a replacement?

Can-do statements

UNIT	CEFR LEVEL	ACTFL LEVEL	CAN-DO STATEMENTS
UNIT 1	A1 / A2	Novice High / Intermediate Low	I can introduce myself and ask and answer questions about personal details. (A1) I can recognize and produce simple phrases and sentences to describe where I live. (A1) I can use basic greeting and leave-taking expressions. (A1) I can fill in forms of personal details (A2)
UNIT 2	A1 / A2	Novice High / Intermediate Low	I can introduce myself and ask and answer questions about personal details. (A1) I can recognize and produce simple phrases and sentences to describe where I live and people I know. (A1) I can use phrases and sentences to describe my family, other people, where I live and my job. (A2)
UNIT 3	A1	Novice High	I can talk about numbers and time. (A1) I can ask and answer questions and fill in forms about personal details. (A1)
UNIT 4	A2 / A2	Novice High / Intermediate Low	I can ask and answer questions about personal details. (A1) I can understand the general idea of a simpler informational material and short simple descriptions. (A1) I can use a series of phrases and sentences to describe daily routines. (A2) I can explain what I like or dislike. (A2)
UNIT 5	A2 / A2	Novice High / Intermediate Low	I can indicate time by such phrases as next week. (A1) I can understand the general idea of simpler informational material. (A1) I can find specific, predictable information in simple everyday material. (A2) I can describe plans, arrangements. (A2) I can make arrangements to meet, decide where to go and what to do. (A2) I can explain what I like or dislike. (A2)

Can-do statements

UNIT	CEFR LEVEL	ACTFL LEVEL	CAN-DO STATEMENTS
UNIT 6	A2 / A2	Novice High / Intermediate Low	I can follow short, simple directions. (A1) I can understand the main point in announcements. (A2) I can find specific, predictable information in simple everyday material. (A2) I can understand everyday signs and notices. (A2) I can ask about things and make simple transactions. (A2)
UNIT 7	A2 / A2	Novice High / Intermediate Low	I can understand very short, simple texts. (A1) I can understand the general idea of simpler informational material and descriptions. (A1) I can ask people for things. (A1) I can find specific, predictable information in simple everyday material. (A2) I can understand everyday signs and notices. (A2) I can give my opinion on practical problems and ask for things. (A2)
UNIT 8	A2	Intermediate Low	I can describe past experiences and personal experiences. (A2) I can make suggestions. (A2) I can exchange information and give an opinion. (A2) I can use simple descriptive language to compare objects. (A2)
UNIT 9	A1 / A2	Novice High / Intermediate Low	I can understand the general idea of simpler informational material and short simple descriptions. (A1) I can find specific, predictable information in simple everyday material. (A2) I can understand sentences and frequently used expressions related to areas of most immediate relevance. (A2) I can order a meal. (A2)
UNIT 10	A1 / A2	Novice High / Intermediate Low	I can talk about numbers, quantities, cost. (A1) I can locate specific information in lists and isolate the information required. (A2) I can ask about things and make simple transactions. (A2) I can give and understand information about quantities, numbers, prices. (A2) I can make simple purchases. (A2)

Notes

RAISING READERS
Books Build Bright Futures

Dear Reader,

We'd love your attention for one more page to tell you about the crisis in children's reading, and what we can all do.

Studies have shown that reading for fun is the **single biggest predictor of a child's future life chances** – more than family circumstance, parents' educational background or income. It improves academic results, mental health, wealth, communication skills, ambition and happiness.[1]

The number of children reading for fun is in rapid decline. Young people have a lot of competition for their time. In 2024, 1 in 10 children and young people in the UK aged 5 to 18 did not own a single book at home.[2]

Hachette works extensively with schools, libraries and literacy charities, but here are some ways we can all raise more readers:

- Reading to children for just 10 minutes a day makes a difference
- Don't give up if children aren't regular readers – there will be books for them!
- Visit bookshops and libraries to get recommendations
- Encourage them to listen to audiobooks
- Support school libraries
- Give books as gifts

There's a lot more information about how to encourage children to read on our website: **www.RaisingReaders.co.uk**

Thank you for reading.

---

[1] OECD, '21st-Century Readers: Developing Literacy Skills in a Digital World', 2021, https://www.oecd.org/en/publications/21st-century-readers_a83d84cb-en.html

[2] National Literacy Trust, 'Book Ownership in 2024', November 2024, https://literacytrust.org.uk/research-services/research-reports/book-ownership-in-2024